THE
HAPPINESS
HOOKUP

A Unique Handbook for Happiness
In This Crazy World

MICHELLE HAYWOOD

© Michelle Haywood 2021

ISBN: 978-1-09836-961-3

Library of Congress cataloging in publication data
The Happiness Hookup/Michelle Haywood
TXu002196957 | 2020

CONTENTS

CAN I SAY SOMETHING, FIRST? IX

CHAPTER ONE: THE HAPPINESS ZONE IS THIS WAY 1

HITS OF HAPPY CAN'T COMPARE TO LIFE IN THE HAPPINESS ZONE 1

HAPPINESS WILL GO NUTS WHEN IT SEES YOU 2

SO, LET ME BREAK IT TO YOU LIKE THIS … YOU'RE A BUBBLE 2

BUBBLE(OLOGY) 4

CHAPTER TWO: ONLY LIGHT MINDS PROPEL TO THE
HAPPINESS ZONE 15

LET'S UNDERSTAND HOW YOUR MIND HAS BEEN WORKING UP TO NOW ... 15

SNATCH THE CONTROLS FROM YOUR AUTO-DEFENSE SYSTEM: "YUREEGO" ... 21

DO OUR BRAIN-DRIVEN THOUGHTS *REALLY* GOVERN OUR LIVES? ... 26

GOT SENSE? 33

EMBRACE YOUR NEW BUOYANT STATE OF MIND 34

"I'M 'BOUT TO RETRAIN THIS BRAIN!" 34

"I AM PERFECT" 41

"I'M IMMUNE TO NEGATIVITY" 46

"I CAN'T LOSE" 50

"GRATITUDE'S MY ATTITUDE" 51

"NOW, IS WHAT'S UP!" 52

"ON ERYTHING I LOVE ME" 52

SEE DENSE BUBBLES IN A BRIGHTER LIGHT 56

SOME JUST NEED A NEW "LEASH" ON LIFE 56

BAGGAGE HANDLERS AND OTHER CLOSE EN*CLOWN*TERS 58

ASSHOLES ARE PEOPLE TOO 63

BE A REAL SOLDIER, TAKE IT ON THE CHIN 64

USE BUOYANT PERSPECTIVES AND "HELIUM-EFFECT" PRACTICES ... 65

CONSTANT CHANGE IS THE NATURE OF THE UNIVERSE 65

KNOW THAT NO ONE CAN BURST YOUR BUBBLE 66

LIFE IS BUT A DREAM 66

THE ANT CONTEMPLATES GOD 68

POINT #1: DON'T OVERTHINK SHIT. TAP YOUR INSTINCT.............................68

POINT #2: BE HUMBLED. THERE'S A BIGGER PICTURE IN PLAY. JUST DO YOUR WORK.............................69

WORDS TO LIVE BY.............................70

WHEN LIFE'S A BLUR YOU CAN'T FOCUS ON WHAT COUNTS.............................70

IT IS WRITTEN. QUE SERA SERA.............................71

THE ONLY THING TO TAKE PERSONAL IS "PERSONAL TIME".............................72

NOT GETTING YOUR WAY? WELL, THAT'S OK.............................73

THE ART OF CONVERSATION: TRYING TO PROVE YOU'RE RIGHT IS *WRONG* (FOR LACK OF A BETTER WORD).............................74

DON'T CLAIM THAT BAGGAGE! LOSE "IT" OR BE THE "*LOSER*".............................80

JEALOUSY: JUST. ENVIOUS. AND. LOUSY.............................82

DON'T HATE, ELEVATE.............................87

BE UNAPOLOGETICALLY YOU.............................88

JUDGMENT IS WAAAY OUT OF YOUR JURISDICTION.............................90

HONESTY AND OPENNESS.............................91

TAKE TWO CHILL PILLS.............................92

DEEP BREATHING.............................95

KNOW WHO TO MESS WITH.............................96

SHIT JUST GOT REAL, NOW WHAT?.............................97

WHEN IT RAINS IT POURS, HUH?.............................106

FEELING STUCK OR TRAPPED?.............................108

WORRIED? DON'T.............................109

FORGIVE AND LET THAT SHIT GO.............................111

THAT'S NOT FAIR!.............................113

GRIEF.............................113

IN CASE OF DEPRESSION OR ANXIETY.............................122

TAKE LIFE'S CHALLENGES HEAD ON: LEARN.............................126

GO FOR IT.............................127

FOLLOW YOUR HEART.............................130

EAT POPCORN AND WATCH THE MOVIE 🎥🍿.............................132

CHAPTER THREE: YOUR BUBBLE IS YOUR TEMPLE.............................137

YOU'RE ALL THE WAY LIVE.............................142

TAKE "CHARGE" OF THAT ELECTRIC BUBBLE TEMPLE OF YOURS 142

FUEL UP WITH LIVE PLANT ENERGY 143

YOUR NAV SYSTEM 148

FAST FOR 12-HOURS DAILY 151

WATER IS AMAAAZING! DRINK THAT LIQUID LIFE 151

FILL UP WITH NATURE'S BUBBLE FUEL: OXYGEN 153

SLEEP TIGHT 154

POSTURE FOR ENERGY FLOW 155

PHYSICAL MOTION & PRODUCTIVITY: THE WIND BENEATH YOUR BUBBLE 156

SUNSHINE BRIGHTENS YOUR LIFE *AND THE CORNERS OF YOUR MIND* ☀ 156

DON'T SUGARCOAT WHEN YOU *KNOW* THAT IT'S TOXIC 157

CHAPTER FOUR: FULLY ACCEPT AND EMBRACE YOUR SOUL JOURNEY 161

GOD IS 162

IT'S OVER YOUR HEAD, 'CAUSE REALITY'S *DEEEEP* 166

THE GOD PARTICLE 168

ENERGY 169

DARK MATTER & SPACE/TIME 170

UNIVERSAL FORCES (STRONG, GRAVITATIONAL, ELECTROMAGNETIC, OH, MY!) 171

STRING THEORY 172

THE MANDELBROT SET 173

CYMATICS 174

QUANTUM ENTANGLEMENT 175

10 DIMENSIONS? PARALLEL UNIVERSES/THE MULTIVERSE? 🐢 176

SOUL BASICS 177

LOVE 177

MANY LIVES 182

KARMA HAS MAD PATIENCE 186

FEED YOUR GOOD WOLF 188

DON'T BURN BRIDGES – IT'S A SOUL JOURNEY THING 189

YOU GOTTA STAY IN YOUR LANE 190

RELIGION: CULTURAL INTERPRETATIONS OF A UNIVERSAL TRUTH 191

CHAKRA MEDITATION 196

DAILY PRAYER **206**

CHAPTER FIVE: DON'T LOOK, HAPPINESS IS EYEING YOUR BUBBLE **207**

YOU'RE ALL HOOKED UP **207**

GO ALL THE WAY UP **208**

PUT 5 ON IT **208**

LAST BUT NOT LEAST **209**

CAN I SAY SOMETHING, FIRST?

I called it a crazy world, yes. It's a wonderful world, but we face so much crises today, it's mind-boggling. There are so many who are struggling and unhappy. Yet, I believe the biggest issue facing humanity is the fact that so few of us have peace of mind and Happiness. So few of us are true to our nature. So few of us see others and the world as a part of ourselves. And so few of us know what to do to change it.

For me, this book is all about family, those connected to me by blood and/or spirit. It was written as a message to my millennial children, and a tribute to three little birds (Daddy, Aunt Joan and Grandma) from whom I've received love and guidance throughout my life, and always will. In the midst of writing it, I thought of a few people who might be lifted by some of these ideas. Then, I thought of more and more family and friends to share it with. As I completed my first draft the stresses that came with managing Path to Greatness, while losing several very close loved ones back to back, began to lift. Simultaneously, many other unfortunate turn of events added to my worries. However, now I was seeing things much more clearly. I started to feel that I could handle the very obvious fact that more of my loved ones were approaching heaven's door. And this was all in the midst of very strange times. Every day as I wrote, global warming made headlines. Either huge glaciers were melting and breaking off or a category 4 hurricane was barreling to the coast, or the Amazon rain forest was ablaze as the President skipped the Global Warming meeting at the G7 Summit. Or Coronavirus halted and threatened American life and lives around the globe. Still, I was eating popcorn and watching this movie called *My Life* and landing on happy feet. I could clearly FEEL another level of energy physically, mentally and spiritually in the midst of writing. I knew, then, that I would share this with all of my friends and family, and probably some strangers too. I want everyone to feel as happy as I do *now*, still deep in the midst of life's challenges.

There's no rulebook for parenting, and no rules were followed here. Believe me. This was written in my natural language, expletives and all. Keep in mind that you're eavesdropping on a long conversation from mother to children. This is an 'ear hustle' on your part, so take nothing personally. This message encompasses a large part of my personal worldview for them to have in lasting and available form. My worldview was born out of a mix of love, creativity, popular science, common sense, ancient wisdom and a fierce determination for Happiness. I've tried to put it all together in a form that's easier to relate to, process and retain. I love where it ended up because I'm placing more effort into managing the energy of 'MY bubble' and it's working like a charm for me. All it takes is one new change of perspective or behavior to change your life. If you are open to changing your mind, I hope you find ideas, here, that connect for you. If you already know that you absolutely can't change your mind, put this down until you know you can. When you *do* decide to read it, keep this in mind: **It's up to each of us to decide the standards by which we live. Those standards should refresh and continuously elevate if we want our lives to be elevated.** You won't just keep rising up if your standards don't. At the end of the day, this is simply a collection of 'thought standards' designed to lift and inspire. I hope with all my heart that *someone* will be lifted.

But this is for **you**, Jet and Sky. I want you guys to discover that you can exist in a personal space of Happiness, even in the roughest of storms. This book was created for you. I wrote this in the year I learned to truly LIV [that's 54 in Roman numerals ;-)]. I'm proud of myself for finding the "free time" to write it. Now, you guys need to find the "free time" to actually read it! It contains the personal thoughts, beliefs and philosophies that have worked for me throughout my life. I wanted you to have my thoughts and voice recorded in a way that will be with you always. Whenever you need it. I call it a hookup because I'm trying to hook *you guys up* with Happiness while also throwing you a hook to grab onto to continually rise up throughout the course of your lives. You're supposed to have fun with this thing called life. Life was meant to be rich with experiences and education, not "perfect." Never forget that. Understand that through it all, and above all else, it's *your role to love up on yourself and create your life*. Your life is and has been for some time fully in your hands. I believe knowing the things I've compiled for you here will allow you to set yourself on the path to a genuinely fun, fruitful and very happy life.

There's nothing new under the sun and there's nothing *truly* new here. Almost every single thing here you've heard from me before. I discovered a new way of sharing that same information in an interesting format that might help it to stick. More details on almost everything here can be found from simply looking for it on the Internet. While my guidance and perspectives will be a good kick-start, you each should keep up with what's *really* going on, especially with scientific laws, advances and discoveries. They hold clues to the nature of life. Understanding the nature of life can really help you to process things. If you want to know more on something I've referenced here, you know what to do. Look it up and learn, but always assume that humanity does not have all the answers. Follow your instincts and hold tight to the thoughts, beliefs and philosophies that lift you.

You're both grown now. I love the confident individuals you've become. I know you're in the process of finding your way. I want you to know that I'm in full acceptance of your soul journeys, wherever they take you. I can't help but pray, however, that you rise to a level of boundless Happiness. I also pray that you constantly learn, love and teach through your example. I love you unconditionally, whether that's right or wrong. I will always be here for you, as a loving mother, to guide and share in your lives. But I'm finally lettin' go of *official* parenting. I know, right! Hard to believe, but you guys are getting spaaace. It's time for you to take the reins and enjoy the full freedom to create and live your lives. This book marks that transition for each of us. Know that not just now but fifty years from now when I shed this body and am just a bubble of love energy, I'll **always** be there for you. I'll be around. That's cash you can take to the bank.

This Happiness Hookup is an updated and expanded version of the earlier book(let) I wrote for you guys years ago, "Flow." While I changed the name from *Flow* to *The Happiness Hookup*, my definition of Flow still stands and applies more than ever. Hold on to it. And flow with Happiness once you get hooked up.

> **flow** – n./a state of being, in synch with God energy such that it channels through you, enabling health, Happiness, prosperity and an almost effortless fulfillment of desires.

Flow began with "God Is" as Chapter One. You know the drill, so I saved this and other very familiar messages for Chapter Four. I want to reiterate that my reference to God, throughout the book, refers to the Universal, conscious, creative force present in every particle in the Universe. God, here, has no gender, no human-like needs, and no rules except the Golden One. We're not automatically connected to God's unifying and powerful force, nor are we automatically filled with the pure love that is at the heart of God. You see proof of this every day. You can feel when you or anyone else is truly connected. Prayer and meditation are tools to do it, but we each connect in the way that works for us. You know I'm one who likes to connect dots. I love for my beliefs to connect with accepted science, but I always keep in mind that science is evolving too. Lack of scientific proof doesn't mean something is not very real. God is one example. If you're one who requires scientific proof rather than spiritual guidance, that's perfect. Because over the last decade there have been mind-blowing scientific discoveries. The discoveries are mind blowing for those who didn't believe what spiritual leaders have been trying to tell us for centuries. There exists scientific proof of a governing, conscious force over all things; proof of our connectedness to each other and all things; proof of our ability to use our minds to communicate over vast distances; scientific proof exists that we can use our minds to manifest our desires. I'm not shitting you. Investigate.

We're all adults now, and we know that life comes AT you. What? When you find yourself caught up in something that doesn't feel good, use this guide to remind yourself how to get that good feeling back. Flip directly to a particular message. Read. Reflect. Relax. Restore yourself to a state of Flow and Happiness. Once you already know this stuff, even then, we still need reminders as we course through this thing called life. Shit gets real when you least expect it. Out of the blue you can get a twister when you've weathered storms throughout your life like a pro. None of us can handle twisters without getting blown around and having to rebuild. It's a human thing. We all need reminders, instructions for our maintenance and rebuilding efforts. When shit gets real, fuel up with the knowledge on how to navigate through it (actually, fuel up **before** shit gets real, if possible). I added lots of quotes, visuals and bold headings for you to associate with my written messages. Once you've read the book, you'll be easily reminded of *everything*, simply by scrolling through to look at the **contents, bold headings, quotes and visuals.**

Your names are clues for the heights planned for you from the very start. I not only want Happiness for you guys, I want you to be a force for change in this world. I want you guys to think differently, live differently. Of course, service to humanity is one of the things I want you both to continue. While we've been consistently giving through the toughest of times for our family, I've come to understand that people must be in the right space to have the capacity for service to others. Our world needs more of both. We need people in the right space, happy and flowing. **We need more people to come together to serve humanity!** We are all one, however coined that may sound right now. So, as you guys are where *you* need to be, doing what *you* need to do, the world has already changed.

Before we delve into the book, I want to share this poem I wrote when you guys were little. Now, as I read it, I envision us as bubbles 'mingled in flight.' No matter what changes in our lives or in this crazy world, this message applies eternally.

MATERNAL BLISS

I pour into you,
Like mother's milk.
Replenishing myself for your fill,
'Til you soar gracefully.
In destiny's light,
Our spirits mingled in flight.

CHAPTER ONE

THE HAPPINESS ZONE IS THIS WAY

HITS OF HAPPY CAN'T COMPARE TO LIFE IN THE HAPPINESS ZONE

There are two kinds of happy. There's the kind that is fleeting. The happy you feel when you get something you want. It's like a little hit of happy; then, you're back to normal looking for the next hit. You got a raise, and a hit of happy with it. Somebody gave you a compliment, and you get another hit of happy. Your team wins the game, another hit. But even if you win the one hundred million dollar lottery, the hit only lasts but for so long *(studies tell us one year at best)* and you're back to normal. Normal is "all good," but it's not what we'd call happy. Normal can be "surviving," "making it" or "hanging in there," it's usually not what we'd call *bad*. It's not what we call life in The Happiness Zone, either. Periodic 'hits of happy' and 'hanging in there' is what we've come to believe is ALL we can have. This is how most of us live our lives. That's good! It could be worse, right? The answer is yes. It could be worse at any moment. When you have Happiness, the real thing, it's an altogether different situation.

There is a zone that you can enter, where Happiness is no longer experienced through hits here and there. Once you enter that zone, you live in a constant state of Happiness, with periodic hits of "all good" or "hanging in there." Life happens, but you always return quickly to the state of sustained Happiness. The crazy life situations that challenge you, take on a whole new feel. Strangely, almost nothing can get you down. It's where Happiness lives every day, all the time. Once you enter, no one leaves. Everyone is too busy enjoying the space and enjoying the challenge of seeing how far up their Happiness can go. Those who do drop out of The Zone, come back. They don't stay gone for long. They know how to get there, so they do what they have to do to get back in. I want to hook y'all up with access to The Zone. Sustained Happiness is your birthright! Get ready.

HAPPINESS WILL GO NUTS WHEN IT SEES YOU

Happiness is something to behold. I want you to recognize it as a real live thing. It's flat out sexy! Jeez! Who doesn't love it? Everybody wants it. Some long for it. It's wildly popular, extremely famous, ageless, timeless, highly sought after and hard to hold onto. It feels good to any and everyone who's ever had it. What more can I say? I want my babies hooked up with it. I want Happiness to be yours for life, so I'm initiating a hookup.

Understand that Happiness has been accused of playing hard-to-get, but that's not how Happiness rolls. Happiness is wild and free and gravitates, with the quickness, to those who are truly **open** to a hookup. Happiness is *always* ready and waiting for you.

Happiness is uplifting and fun to be around. Happiness makes you feel amazing! It's beautiful, holistic and natural. And good news! Turns out, Happiness is your soulmate. What? Yes. And its heart is set on being yours so you CAN have Happiness ever after. Sure, you will have to bust a couple of moves to get it, but no worries, just knowing that Happiness truly wants you is clutch.

So, I don't know any better way to break it to you, but without Happiness, you'll be up shit's creek. Real talk. Without Happiness, you're not truly your whole natural self. You're not YOU when you're not hooked up with Happiness ;-). When you ain't got it, please believe that something unnatural is taking place in your mind and/or body. We need to get a handle on that first, to get you hooked up. This thing with relying on hits of Happiness whenever you can get them is lame. So let's get started on how to get you hooked up with your precious soulmate, Happiness.

SO, LET ME BREAK IT TO YOU LIKE THIS ... YOU'RE A BUBBLE

An electric bubble, actually. I know how it sounds, I do. I'm laughing, but all the while it's actually true. Since I can't easily *prove* it to you, let's just **imagine** that you are. That's all you have to do anyway. Just imagine that you are. I'll give you some facts to fuel your imagination and help you to envision and embrace your bubble.

Ancient wisdom first told us that we are fields of vibrating energy; then, Albert Einstein proved it over a hundred years ago. Look it up if you think you can understand his theories. Lots of luck! His proof was mathematical, meaning absolutely **nothing** to everyday folks like us. Physicists and those who understand his math, on the other hand, already know you're an electric bubble. All laughs aside. Now you do too.

You are a field of conscious energy and information with a heart in the center.
We're calling it your bubble.

"THERE HAS BEEN A REVOLUTION IN HOW WE PERCEIVE THE BODY. WHAT APPEARS TO BE AN OBJECT, A THREE-DIMENSIONAL ANATOMICAL STRUCTURE, IS ACTUALLY A PROCESS, A CONSTANT FLOW OF ENERGY AND INFORMATION." - DEEPAK CHOPRA

"Everything is energy and that is all there is to it."

- Albert Einstein

Spiritual leaders have held for centuries that we each have a circular human energy field around us. You are already accepting of the image of an angelic halo, which represents a small human energy bubble around your crown. You never laughed at that, but that's exactly what the halo represents. I'm just saying there's one around your entire body. I promise you that it's not as far out as it sounds. It's not just me who's aware of this, by the way. I always encourage you to believe what your heart tells you. Sleep on the bubble concept (*but don't sleep, if you know what I mean*). Learn more before you decide what you believe. The good thing is, it doesn't really matter whether it's real or whether you believe it or not. All I need from you is a little imagination. The whole point of asking you to identify as this bubble is simply to get you thinking in terms of your **whole self**. I want you to imagine that you are bigger than your body and mind, and I need you thinking in terms of *energy*. Energy is everything, in my book :-). All we need for now, is for you to imagine that you're a bubble full of vibrational energy.

Now, using inspiration from the image above, envision your bubble. Your bubble's not the kind that's featured on the book cover. *Your* bubble is not filled with air. Much like a computer hard-drive, your bubble holds your data. *Your* bubble is filled with your information, coding (kinda like DNA), memories, emotions, your subconscious mind, and everything about you. Imagine that your brain (your personal computer/bio PC/ or AI, as I like to call it) holds **some** data, but imagine that your bubble holds the bulk of it.

Your bubble goes completely through you and extends outside of your body several feet in all directions. Think of those huge, clear bubble balls that you can get inside and roll around to bounce into others as a game. Imagine your bubble as about that size.

As you visualize your bubble, I need you to recognize that you, your essence, is a much bigger picture than you think. You are an absolutely amazing, beautiful, bubble blown into creation by God. Your bubble was meant to **float buoyantly through life**, making observations and learning lessons along the path of your soul journey.

Your bubble is your personal energy field. God, *not me*, put you solely in control of the energy of your bubble. No one ever was or *ever* will be able to manage **your** bubble energy, but you. As you properly build and maintain your life energy you use that energy to bounce, float, and buoyantly rise as you travel along your soul path, with Happiness, of course.

Your bubble energy is like any other energy. It has different wavelengths, different frequencies. The question is, what type of energy is in your bubble? This is what you have to manage to get to Happiness. It's all about the type of energy, and how much of it, that fills your bubble.

BUBBLE(OLOGY)

Time to drop some science to help you understand the gravity of your bubble situation.

Bubbles, by nature, have an uplifting quality. Everyone either loves them or at least nobody hates them. Who ever said, "I hate bubbles!" For most, they evoke whimsy and Happiness, especially to children. I wanted to use bubbles on the cover to inspire the feeling of Happiness. Then, as I continued to write I realized that bubbles actually began to fit perfectly into my theories for attaining Happiness. A bubble was the perfect image for the buoyancy of spirit required for you to attain Happiness. Bubbles also represent the spherical energy field that is believed by ancient mystics to surround you. Bubbles have the ability to float and rise, which is exactly what *you* need to do too. They can't carry baggage. You shouldn't, although you can, but you can learn from the example of the bubble. Their nature is to float, although it's possible for them to drop and sit right on the floor. And the same is true for you. Your nature is to float, but unfortunately, you can do the exact opposite. What I want you to know is that based on the energy of your bubble, whether it's light or heavy energy, the quality of your life, your Happiness, will lift, hover or drop. Like a bubble. I will continuously remind you of this in an effort to rewire your thinking.

Now that I've dropped the "Bubble" bomb, let's look at some science behind it. It's actually proven true that you're an electrically charged field of energy. It's also proven true that you have an electromagnetic field that passes through you and outside of you. I want to get you thinking, just a tad, by sharing some legit science. Then, I'll get back into my own bubble science and how it relates to your Happiness. Here are six basic science facts:

1. **We're literally a bundle of speeding electrons.** That's scientifically proven. We are comprised of atoms, in fact, everything is. If we had the opportunity to see an atom under a microscope, we'd see a lil' mini, tornado-like vortex with even tinier energy vortices inside it. Zoom in closer and we'd see nothing, just a void. Atoms are 99 percent invisible energy, **not** tangible matter. That's just a fact. What's making those itty bitty tornados? Electrons. Electrons are named such because they're electrically charged. Get it? Electron. Duh, right? It's electric! When I said you're an electric bubble, it's so hilarious, but I wasn't kidding.

2. **Electro-physical exchanges control most cellular activity.** That's a truth that modern medicine recognizes today. Electrical energy controls your cells.

3. **The electromagnetic field of our bodies are totally measurable today.** Then, add that scientific experiments have already indicated that information for growth, disease and healing can be transmitted from the human electromagnetic field (I've even heard there are already businesses being developed to take advantage of new technological advances that can tap into the information from the human electromagnetic field for the purposes of healing. What! Sounds crazy, but it's real). There's also been considerable scientific research in search of proof of your bubble and, again, I believe we're on the brink of discovery. The same way that we had to invent the microscope to have proof of atoms, we'll likely need advances in scientific equipment to see and measure this bubble I speak of.

4. **You have an aura that transmits and receives intelligent signals**. I know, right!? German biophysics researcher, Fritz Albert Popp proved the existence of biophotons. Look it up. He proved that all living organisms, including humans had auras that transmitted and received intelligent signals. He also found that plants communicate with each other over long distances. Seriously, though. Laughing or standing in disbelief just puts **you** out of touch with reality, smarty pants. Don't take my word. Research.

5. **Electromagnetic energy, much like radio waves, fill your bubble.** It can be detected three to four feet, with magnetometers, outside the body. Some researchers have detected it ten to twelve feet from the body. It can be detected and measured with sensitive, mainstream medical equipment. Today. Seriously.

6. **Your surface electrical energy can be measured.** It's been known for a long time that we can measure the surface electrical activity of our bodies at the fingertips using a simple voltage meter in

the millivolt setting. You guys wouldn't remember, but back in the day, we could touch the antenna on our TV's and clearly see that there was energy affecting it. The TV screen would clear right up when we touched the antenna. I can remember having to hold antennas in a particular spot with my hand to clearly see a particular scene in a TV show. You laugh, but those were the days.

There's a lot of belief in your bubble, actually. There's a lot of evidence that takes all the laughter out of the equation, too. Until there's clear scientific proof that you're a bubble (look up 'human energy field'), laugh out loud for sure. I laughed, too, when I considered using this concept, but work with me on this one. Many highly spiritual and scientific people already accept this concept as true.

So, if we're just bubbles of energy, how do you explain why we're clearly physical? Well, physicists have been trying to solve that one for a very long time. This is my best way to describe it to you. Remember when we were learning about magnets and how much fun it would be to try to push magnets with the same poles (north, plus north for example) together? You could NOT get those suckers to touch, as if something was there to stop it. We were clearly looking at empty space between the magnets. Nothing was there! So we kept pushing. But something *was* there. A force was there. And a force is what holds matter together. That force is the reason we feel physical even though we're simply energy fields. Everything in this reality we call life, everything, is an energy field. We don't have to understand all the details. We're just here to live our lives, for goodness sake! But understanding that you are an energy field is important for you to get to Happiness.

Now, as amazing as it was that bubbles had the ability to bring Happiness to you as kids, looking at bubbles ain't cuttin' it no more. Still, let's envision beautiful, slowly rising bubbles and connect that image with Happiness. As you do, remember your four year old lightness, freeness and Happiness for just a moment. Now imagine that you are releasing all the baggage that has accumulated from experiences since you were four. Visualize blowing all that old heavy energy into some bubbles and watch them float away. Even better, actually blow some bubbles (we'll get to that). Now hold onto that image of relaxation and Happiness. Tuck it away for later and float with me on some more 'bubble' details.

The energy field around and through you, is "your" field. We **all**, as a matter of fact, **all living things**, have one. **The area of your heart happens to be the center of your energy field.** Your energy field goes out in all directions and forms a globe, of sorts, around the outside of your body. Since it centers on your heart, let's recognize that. Your heart, at the center of your bubble, is generating energy and information for your bubble. This is real talk. Science is the base for 90 percent of the things I tell you in this book. Look into everything I say, but hear me loud and clear when I say that your heart was *always* meant to be the guiding force for your bubble, and your life. I'll share more on the importance of being guided by your heart later.

You're not just any old bubble, by the way. You're a living computer bubble with the ability to store and transmit information within **and** well outside of your bubble. Your bubble holds all the information that makes you, **you**. It holds your programming, your thoughts, everything. Your information's not just in your nugget head. There's much more to you than meets the eye *(As a matter of fact, bubbles have the ability to transmit and receive messages, kinda like 'virtual texting.' So, it's smart to regularly visualize receiving and sending virtual texts of healing love. The powers of visualization are proven and unbelievable. You already know the powers of healing love, so virtual text that love like crazy).*

The problem, with being a bio-computer bubble is that over the course of our lives, most of us have accumulated too much unprocessed data and "computer viruses" *(hard-wired negative thinking)* on top of it. We've taken on a host of bad experiences. You know how your computer or cell phone can be busy processing information and that swirling circle is just a-swirling while you wait? Well, a lot of us have hundreds of swirling circles going on at once. We're continuing to process old shit while filling our minds and bodies with more new shit. Combine that with the fact that we don't even know we're computer bubbles filled with trash and viruses, and voila, we got ourselves a hot mess.

Imagine clearing your bio-computer bubble of all the viruses and all of the trash baggage. Imagine restoring it to the beaming field of pure energy and processing power that you were born with. This is what needs to happen in order for you to be able to connect with Happiness. It takes a little work, but it's easier than you may think. You just gotta clear your cache. Run some virus software, delete old files. Lighten the load on your mind. Lighten and lift your bubble.

Every thought, feeling and belief that you have holds an energy that determines the vibrational frequency of your heart-centered bubble. It's important that you are fully aware of this fact. Worry, frustration and sadness, for example, generate lower frequencies than acceptance, peace and joy. I like to call these lower frequency thoughts and feelings *(such as worry, frustration, sadness, anger)* 'lead' energies, and the higher frequency ones *(like acceptance, gratitude, peace, joy)*, I call 'helium' energies. Lead energy thoughts will lower the vibration of your bubble and weigh down your life! It's simple math. Heavy thoughts equal your heavy dense bubble is on the floor. Remember in science that lead was much farther down the Periodic Table of Elements? Lead carried an atomic weight of 82 and helium was one of the lightest and first listed elements with a weight of just 2. I'm reminding you because you can use that imagery to add up what's going on in your life because of your thoughts and feelings. Always do the math. What's important now, is to recognize that your bubble was not designed to carry the weight of lead energies, not but for fleeting moments of crisis. The problem is that too many of us carry this weight around, day to day, unknowingly. We carry the dense weight of past and present (and sometimes future!) negativity until it becomes second nature to do so. We all need to stop on that.

These low, dense, lead energies can easily stick around if you let them. Lead is not just dense and heavy, it's a poor conductor of energy, as it turns out. That's the **last** thing you need up in your bouncy electric bubble, ESPECIALLY if you want Happiness. Happiness hangs out at a higher frequency. You'll never, ever be within range to even **see** it when you're filled with lead energy.

Just as you can turn your car radio to different radio stations operating on different frequencies, your bubble has the ability to tune into different "stations" based on the frequency of energy you carry. Thoughts and feelings of high energy tune you to the higher frequency stations and everything that's happening there. Simply feeling and thinking good things can bring in some really good shit, as luck would have it. Your energy status, the vibrational energy level of your bubble, is your key to getting onto the stations where Happiness hangs out. The more you think positive thoughts, the more you auto-tune to positive, high-frequency stations. Here, you are immersed in all the spaces where Happiness lives. Once you understand the Bubbleology, Happiness is a no-brainer. It's a no-brainer that a low, dense, lead energy bubble can't access Happiness. When you're dense, you can't tune to the stations of Happiness if you try. Truthfully, we can't *tune* to anything except where our thoughts and feelings auto-tune us. You have to be *very careful* with your thoughts and feelings because you can be rolling with some sad, angry, worried thoughts and accidentally auto-tune yourself to some shady shit. Don't be that bubble.

When you are tuned to a radio station, can you hear what's happening on another station? No. You have to be tuned in to the station you want or you're missing the action. Period. Tuned into frustration and seeking Happiness? It don't work like that. Look at it this way. Think of your thoughts and feelings and your vibrational energy level more like a credit score. You know how the banks and car dealerships look **straight** through you if you ain't got no credit, right? Well, it's kinda like that. If you carry those lead energies, you got zero credit for Happiness. You don't exist to Happiness. And while there's always a crowd on the lower vibe stations, the **live** parties are in the Happiness Zone. I want you on the stations where you can hook up with Happiness. I'm telling you some inside information. This is the place to be and nobody's going to press you to get in. Some would call this a 'secret.' This is a hookup I'm offering. It's up to you what you do with it. Your mind has to be made up that you want it. Then, you have to do what it takes, which is simply to control your thoughts and energy and feelings so you can auto-tune. When it comes to Happiness, I want to emphasize "out of sight, out of mind." *Yeah*, out of sight of Happiness means you're not on Happiness' mind. **True.** But I'm thinking more like, out of the sight of Happiness means out of ***your*** mind.

Speaking of "out of mind," we've come to expect that the outside world, the things that happen in our lives, influence or determine our Happiness. That's some serious problem thinking. Swayed by outside forces, you can count on losing any Happiness you might have. It's like announcing that you're granting the custom designed dream car that you rely on for **everything** to anyone who requests it. The odds are high that you will lose that car. The outside world is not in the business of your Happiness. So, leaving your Happiness to outside forces means, well, you're going to lose it, fo' sho'! Your Happiness is literally, YOUR BUSINESS to manage. You HAVE to run it like a business, guys. Like THE most important business that you have. Let me put it to you this way. You are now the CEO of MyBubble, the tech company formed to deliver the highest possible vibrational frequency to human bubbles. It's a small start-up, relying on your personal success as the human prototype to close the interested investors. Your success in managing your own energy to reach higher frequencies, against all outside forces, is anticipated to create explosive success for MyBubble. Stocks will surge as will your options for almost everything in life. Your energy has been already measured and had been found to fluctuate between the stations of ALL GOOD and SURVIVING, with dips as low as the MISERABLE Station when big disappointments hit. MyBubble is projecting that the company's advanced Bubbleology (bubble science) will help to produce results that put you solidly on the ALL GOOD Station in 60 days. You're entering The Happiness Zone in 90 days by following the bubble science protocol developed by MyBubble scientists. Imagine this 'Happiness Hookup' as a corporate hand-book to walk you through. You have 60 days to reach the first goal. Can you do it to reap the millions in profit that come as you prove the science works? It's ALL in how you think. Figure out what works for you.

Do the math when it comes to your Happiness. As you manage your energy levels moving forward, a lil' bubble math might help. I've referred to helium and lead level energies several times, because every-thing is either an energy that is lifting or weighing you down. We already associate helium with lift, and lead with heaviness, so I'm using these to help you envision the energy value of the things in your life. Conveniently, helium and lead already have scientific numbers assigned to them. Use these to envision the 'virtual weight' of your thought energy.

You'll see on The Rise to Happiness chart that the lift needed to get you into The Happiness Zone has to do with the total amount of helium versus lead energies you carry. Imagine that positive 'helium level'

thoughts, attitudes, environments, beliefs, practices, foods and people, each have an energy value of -2 for you. These actually **remove** weight and lift you. Look at everything as having a *value* in your life. Everything holds a positive or negative value for you. Pick and choose wisely, as the quality of your life depends on it. Now, let's imagine the negative, 'lead level' thoughts, attitudes, environments, etc. as having a value of +82 to your bubble. You don't have to envision the numbers unless it helps, but you can see that allowing your thoughts to drift negative won't add up to Happiness. Every negative thought, belief, or action just adds **weight** causing your bubble to be heavy. They JUST weigh you down. They weigh down your life. If you *do* prefer to look at it from a mathematical perspective, add a lot of helium level -2's to your life. I'm no mathematician, but I know that -2 + (- 2) = a thousand times better than an 82 on your bubble :-) Let those 82's go as fast as they come. You don't need them! They have no value for you. Negative thoughts and feelings are low down and shady. Let them slide.

"Slide, slide, why don't you sliiiide?"
- Slide, by Slave

Make that move, and get good at shaking off all of your negative thoughts.

One of the most wonderful things you'll experience as your bubble rises to the higher frequency stations is that your worldview becomes clearer. Your views about everything become clearer as you rise. The higher your bubble rises, the better able YOU are to see. At higher heights, your understanding of the world and its ups and downs becomes sharper and more complete. Your understanding of others does too. You understand yourself more and you become clearer on what you need to do in life. All of these skills and understandings are yours at the higher levels. Happiness is the icing on the cake.

The work of clearing all the old, negative thought/feeling energy from your life will pay off in ways you can't foresee. You'll be left with the loving soul that was blown into your bubble from the start.

THOUGHT BUBBLE RECAP

 You're a huge bubble full of life energy. Information, programming, thoughts, feelings and everything you consume fill your bubble. Each of these things, combined, determine the energy frequency and weight of your bubble. You are responsible for managing your own energy. Your energy should be at the higher frequencies to connect with Happiness, health and everything you want out of life.

God, the Creative Force, blew your bubble into existence. The air that God used to blow your bubble into existence, that's your soul. It's full of the essence of you and it is eternal. Blown into creation by God, you, your soul, your bubble are one and perfectly created.

The source, kind of like the 'bubble bottle' if you will, is one of those things from the other side that exists, but we never see it, never fully understand it, and that's ok. There are a lot of things like that, by the way. Let it go and just 'B' *(B is for Bubble, of course).*

Every last person, everyone, is a bubble like you. Each bubble contains information. It's not unusual that you can pick up on things from other bubbles. Information passes through space like text messages. Feelings exchange in the same way and will be brought forth as you interact with other bubbles. What you get from each bubble will depend on what's being held in their bubble, what bubble station they're on, and what bubble station *you* are on. The lower, dense stations have awful, distorted reception on top of low level energy *('B' careful, you can catch bad energy as easy as catching a cold).*

Everyone is on a particular bubble station in life. You know what it means when someone says, "we're on the same wavelength," right? Well, that's real. Everything is composed of vibrational energy in the form of wavelengths or waves. Each wavelength holds different features, just like different radio stations or TV channels. You want to be on the right station or channel or wave-length. Pay attention to your station and prepare to rise to the stations you'd like to experience.

Bubble fuel is anything you take into your bubble. Everything entering your bubble space should be for the purpose of nourishing and lifting you. Everything that you experience, read, watch, listen to, eat, drink, and expose yourself to in any way, including the people and environments that interact with your bubble … that's your fuel. It is up to you to put the proper fuel in your bubble. You want helium effect nourishment (like high octane fuel), not toxic lead weight stuff *(that's like pouring leaded-regular with sugar into your tank).*

Your bubble station is important. There are stations in the super low range that you want to avoid at all costs. There are stations at every level. Imagine bubbles floating high, low and in between. Some can be as low as sitting rock solidly dense on the ground with absolutely no buoyancy. Some are in the middle, and some are at Cloud Nine, a heaven on earth kind of elevation. Whatever station you strive for, the experience of increasing BUOYANCY and an ever rising Happiness filled bubble is always the goal.

You don't want to be, and you want to avoid toxic, lead filled bubbles when possible. These belong to people who are held down to a toxic, low level station mostly because of the way they think and the baggage they have held onto throughout life. Most, simply don't know how to let go of the baggage, so **never judge**. They don't know how to process the hard life lessons that occurred on their journey. They don't accept that hard lessons are merely a part of LIFE. They don't know that they were merely supposed to learn from those challenges, or how to lift higher. The accumulated baggage from past experiences are replayed over and over in their minds. They're caught in cycles, **_manufacturing new pain from old memories and missing the beauty all around them in the present moments of life_**. This can be likened to hell on earth. Don't be that bubble, but don't judge either. You can't change their minds, only _they_ can do that. Pray for their ability to lighten themselves someday and rise on **_your_** journey.

Ok, so now that you have all the core information you need about your bubble, we're getting ready to start prepping on how to get your bubble to rise up into The Zone. We know, now, that Happiness can only see the beautiful, floating, bubbles that sparkle in The Happiness Zone. That's the _only_ way that Happiness can see you and connect. Remember that movie where the Predator was looking for Arnold Schwarzenegger, but couldn't see him (thank goodness) because Arnold was covered in mud? Well, it's kind of like that. It's like a virtual mud covers us when our minds and bodies are not in the proper space. Nothing's beaming through the virtual muck and Happiness doesn't know we exist. Mucky mud may have been needed for Predator, but lose the mud for Happiness. It's time to clear all virtual mud from your bubble and start getting good at propelling. Once you understand how to propel your bubble, you don't have to seek out Happiness. Happiness is waiting to embrace a mind and body beaming with buoyancy. The moment Happiness spots the beautiful light spirit of your bubble, it's love at first sight. You'll have Happiness instantly and all you'll have to do to manage that relationship is remain buoyantly in The Zone. Fortunately, this is easy. **Bubbles that enter The Happiness Zone almost never leave**. Even when faced with the worst tragedies, they're adept at processing the situations well and remaining buoyant. Those new to The Zone may fall for a little bit, but they know how to get back. They immediately miss the incredible feeling they've become accustomed to, wanting none of that life on the denser stations. Even rookies get back in The Zone quick.

Which way is The Happiness Zone? I think you got this one, but just in case, it's **up**. Your internal energy has to rise upwards. In order to do so, you must be filled with the lighter, high frequency energy of an unburdened mind; a body flowing with the high vibrational energy of nature; a soul flowing in full acceptance of its journey.

IF THERE WAS A FORMULA FOR HAPPINESS

It would look something like this:

PEACE OF MIND

Lighten up your bubble by reigning in that ego. Slow the rapid pace of thinking thoughts. Sit that mind down for rejuvenating breaks. You will need a mind beaming with peace, humility, acceptance, gratitude, understanding, high-road thinking, calmness, forgiveness and love, starting with the greatest love of all. Chapter Two will guide you through this.

BODY FLOWING WITH NATURE

A body flowing with the natural energy of God's creations will raise your bubble's vibrational frequency and increase its buoyancy. You'll need to stop putting junk in, consume natural plant energy and a few other natural things for your body. Chapter Three will give you all the tips you need to get your body *super* natural.

FULL ACCEPTANCE OF YOUR SOUL JOURNEY

You have to be in Full Acceptance of YOUR SOUL JOURNEY *and everyone else's.* Your brain tells you the way things ought to be, then God shows you how it **is**. Accept what God is showing you. Push for what you want, you were born to create, but accept what *is*. With full acceptance for whatever happens, get into what your heart and soul bubble was created to do. Chapter Four will cover lots of information that will not only help you to become more accepting of the things that happen in your life, but more accepting of others and the world we live in. It will also give you information that helps you to connect the dots that life is too deep to be worried about anything but knocking your own soul journey out of the darn park.

CHAPTER TWO

ONLY LIGHT MINDS PROPEL TO THE HAPPINESS ZONE

Your mind is part of a collective consciousness, evolving both as an individual and as part of the consciousness of humanity. Do your part to elevate your own mind and you'll lift your bubble into The Happiness Zone. You will also lift the consciousness of humanity as a whole. Nice work, if you can get it done. And you can get it done if you try.

LET'S UNDERSTAND HOW YOUR MIND HAS BEEN WORKING UP TO NOW

So, what's been going on? I'll tell you. Your brain has been running the show. Throughout this entire book, when I say mind, I mean brain. The distinction between the mind and the brain has been debated for a long time (centuries, actually). I'm fully aware of it and addressing the mind as brain here. At the end of the day, your brain overrides everything. We'll have to deal with that. It's a well-meaning control freak that needs to sit down sometimes. We're going to address this brain behavior before drifting off into nuances of the "mind." The technical difference is that the brain is an organ and the mind is supposed to be the part of you that can reason or that which holds your consciousness. We're keeping it simple. Since the brain can reason and has some form of consciousness, yet holds the power to govern your life, we're focusing on your brain. We have to check this power over your life, right now. So, in this book mind means brain and vice versa. Once you've mastered the art of having your brain under control, we can look at using new definitions for mind that include higher forms of consciousness.

Your brain is a computer that comes brand spanking new when you are born. It immediately starts to hard-wire itself with every experience and thought that you have. Each one of us has one of these bio-PCs. Our personal computers, our brains, are hard-wired throughout our lives. Imagine software being written by and for your brain, based solely on what *you* experience. That is exactly what happens in your personal computer (PC/brain). I call the brain 'AI' for artificial intelligence, because I believe the heart is our primary, true intelligence. The brain is a useful tool that 'wants to be' and wants us to **think** it is as powerful as the heart. Whether we call it our brain, bio-PC, AI, mind or whatever … that thing needs to learn to sit.

As a newborn baby, each of us had a clear mind and open heart. Then, every moment of every day our brains absorbed every stimuli and experience and began wiring our supercomputers. We each cried because we were hungry. Whether a loving mom immediately nurtured and breastfed us, or someone yelled at us to stop complaining and tossed a bottle of mixture that hit our head, **the response** got wired. You guys always had the first response, by the way. We can surmise that brought some wiring to the table. Perhaps expectations that you would always be cared for whenever you wanted it? Either way whatever happened to us as babies got wired in and determined how we would think the next time. And so on. You rely on this wiring. It's how you think now. **Your brain *automatically* uses the tracks for all those trains of thought that have been laid in the past**. Automatically! Don't miss that part.

Your brain, you soon realized, was a handy learning tool and it became your go-to tool for life. You rely on it for **everything**. It guides you through life. And there's the problem. Just because the brain *can* provide output in the way of processed thoughts, doesn't mean it *should*. Your brain was designed to process and remember for specific purposes of survival. When we rely on it for *every* last thing, that's too much! That's doing the most. I want you to learn to keep your brain in its lane.

It's not that your brain isn't wonderful. Your brain **is** wonderful! It's miraculous and its value to your life is immeasurable. The human brain is the world's most advanced biological computer. It's actually the most advanced computer of any kind. Its capacity to process and hold information is beyond anything humans can wrap their *brains* around, much less build. When used properly, it's an invaluable tool that brings quality and safety to your life. That's when it's used properly, though.

Our brains are for storing and processing information to learn lessons, so we won't repeat the things that cause us damage. Our brain interprets what we pick up with our senses and directs our bodies to respond in ways that keep us sustained and safe. We're supposed to use our brains for things like figuring out the fastest way home; remembering how to brush our teeth every morning; knowing how to determine that the animal staring at us is rabid and how to outmaneuver it to safety. Our brains guide our bodies to carry out the functions necessary for our survival. Brains allow us to exercise our creativity and develop helpful solutions to problems. These are the kinds of thoughts our brains were designed for. Somehow, we all end up using it differently.

We overuse our brains. We use the brain for **everything**. We use it to confidently "know" what people were thinking and what caused the actions of others. We use it to know what others should and shouldn't do. It guides us to adjust our behaviors and our looks in efforts to be impressive to others. Our brains tell us what paths to take in life, who to connect with, which of our life dreams make sense, what to do with our lives and how to maximize each moment. We use it to know, in-advance, how to feel about people and circumstances, before they've presented themselves. Sizing things up based on old facts and experiences is another strong-suit of the brain. While these are some things the brain is quick to engage in, the brain is ill-equipped to understand and process the emctions, actions, and intents of others. The brain doesn't **feel**, it just generates the thoughts that result in feelings. So, as shocking as this may sound, **the brain is not the tool to use to guide us through life**. It becomes the navigation system from hell when used as a life guide. At the same time that it gives you sucky directions and drops you at dead ends, it'll also allow you to feel like shit and leave you there. All the while, you're convinced that its shit never stinks, so you keep using it for life *(pun intended)*.

It may not be a coincidence that brain rhymes with pain. When used to guide your life, that's exactly what it will bring. Your brain is to be used as a learning and memory tool for your life. Let it control your body functions, hold information in memory, and process information so you can learn and be productive. Don't, however, allow brain-thinking to single-handedly chart your destiny.

> **Brain-generated thoughts** have built-in limitations that lock the door to Happiness, but positive control of your thinking can open that door.

When each one of us processes what appear to be the same experiences through our separate computer brains, we each get different results. Each of us is going to focus on something *slightly* different, then, process that through the hard-wired paths of our past experiences. Therefore, everyone's going to have a slightly different image of reality. No problem, right? Nope. Not, unless you need everyone to hold and accept ***your reality***.

IF I COULD ADDRESS THAT RIGHT QUICK, PLEASE DON'T NEED PEOPLE TO HOLD AND ACCEPT YOUR IMAGE OF REALITY. DON'T DO THAT. I DON'T EVEN NEED *you* GUYS TO ACCEPT THIS STUFF, FOR EXAMPLE. THAT'S WHY I'M WRITING IT DOWN, SO THAT I DON'T KEEP TALKING ABOUT IT WHEN YOU DON'T WANT TO HEAR IT. I WANT THE BEST FOR YOU, BUT I ACCEPT YOUR LIFE JOURNEY. I DON'T NEED YOU OR ANYONE TO ACCEPT MY IMAGE OF REALITY. THANK GOODNESS. WHAT IF I DID? THAT WOULD SUCK WHEN PEOPLE DIDN'T ACCEPT IT, RIGHT? DON'T ***need*** OTHERS TO ACCEPT YOU **or** YOUR REALITY. JUST "B."

Another interesting fact about how your brain works is that when you focus on something, it's the nature of the brain to hone in on the negative first, ignoring the rest. It's a survival tool. When focusing on how to run from a bear, we can't notice the Mockingbird chirping in one of the trees we ran past. If we did, we'd stand a greater chance of getting mauled. We tend to ignore as we focus. Because we ignore when we focus, the differences in what we perceive from the exact same experience as others can be mind-blowing. If we recognize the brain for what it is, we can use our brains properly and free ourselves from the limitations that come when we let our brains run our lives. The heart, not the brain, is the tool for running our lives. I keep saying that for a really good reason. I'm trying to get it to hard-wire in your brain ;-) Right now, though, I still want your attention on the limitations of relying on your brain to run your life.

Our brains naturally hold on tight to nervous energy. It's designed that way to keep us focused on the threat at hand. It's to increase our chances of being safe. Holding on to nervous energy increases the chance that we get away from that bear and address threats more readily. Unfortunately, this is an exhausting use of our energy, especially when bears aren't a threat. Holding on to nervous energy generates stress in the body. The nervous energy *(aka **negative** energy)* also increases the chances for false alarms. This leads to alarms for perceived threats blasting off in traffic, in the workplace or anywhere.

Our brains can also have health problems, like a tumor for example, that can directly affect our behaviors. The condition of our brains and the way our brains work have been recognized as the cause of our actions for a long, long time. 'Blame it on my brain,' has spared many criminals. There are lots of court cases where defendants blame issues with their brain for their behaviors. Scientists are learning more about this brain-feelings-behavior relationship as time goes on. What we **do** know now is that the cause of most feelings and almost *every* behavior lies in our brains. It may or may not always be obvious as to how this happens, but the brain **is** the organ that governs our behavior.

With that said, it's imperative that you have control over your mind. When you're feeling down, safely blame your brain. It's either brain health or thought processing at the root of the unhappiness, not circumstances. Yes, it's easy to think positive thoughts when everything's going our way, but that's not the nature of life. Shit happens. You HAVE to adjust your thinking to attain Happiness. If I could change your mind, I would, but God designed it such that each of us is *solely* responsible for changing our own minds. Information and ideas can be presented to you, but *no wise man has the power* to change your thoughts. Only you. That's just an interesting fact of life. You are the only one who has the power to change your mind. Don't stand in your way of Happiness. Step up for yourself. It should be encouraging and challenging, in a good way, that YOU are the one in control. Commit to controlling the way you think because Happiness comes with a *lot* of perks. **A LOT**. Commit to controlling your thoughts and you'll find out soon enough.

It's going to take some work. You'll have to slow that brain down and lay tracks for new trains of thought before you do anything else. I don't know if you've noticed, but your brain is not necessarily your positivity generator. It's biological, but it's still a **computer**. Expect a calculator to be positive if you're expecting positivity to naturally emerge from your brain. Since we'll *need* positivity to exude from you, you'll have to **re-train** that brain. What doesn't come naturally can be trained in. When it comes to re-training that brain, there's good news and bad news. The bad news is that it's going to be tough. The good news is that tough just means practice. Thanks to **neuroplasticity,** all you have to do is: 1) want to change and 2) put work in. Neuroplasticity, as science has discovered, is the amazing ability of the brain to *re-wire*. It is proven by science now! It is totally possible to change your mind! Everyone, no matter how hard-wired their brain is to certain thoughts and feelings and patterns, **can** change their minds around. Changing your mind means automatically changing your life and everything in it. And that's *especially* good news.

To get to Happiness, we'll start by focusing on how to get your mind and body ready. Currently, your mind and body are playing the field, unconvinced that sustained Happiness is available or even "the one" for you. Your mind and body are all over the place and you're paying the price in the form of life outside The Happiness Zone. It may seem necessary or fun to be messing around, dabbling constantly in all the things before you. Sowing wild oats in toxic environments, toxic foods and toxic situations may seem fun. Exposure to constant streams of negative news and vicious social media posts, while wrapped up in personal frustrations may seem like 'life.' Processing constant streams of random thoughts and beliefs; old experiences and wounds; and negative possibilities that are mostly toxic as hell to your bubble, may seem inevitable. While it might seem perfectly natural and even fun to keep doing this, what it's doing to you is ugly under the surface. Even when you can't see the damage, your bubble's feeling the weight.

We can't see what our minds are doing to us. Just as people can't tell when their breath stinks, we get used to the problem. Once you've accepted the challenge and have tried what I'm recommending to you here, believe me, you will be shocked by the difference you feel from where you are right now. It's not that Happiness "don't like ugly," Happiness doesn't **see** ugly. Ugly doesn't exist in The Happiness Zone. And while it's all good that you guys are pretty and handsome, it's inside that I'm talking about. Inside your mind. Inside your body. Inside your soul. Ugliness you can't see can hurt you and hold you back from Happiness. But we'll take care of all of that. Prime your mind with these two *medically accepted facts* before we get started.

THE PLACEBO EFFECT

Fact: A person's ***belief can override their biology***.

It's a medical fact, 30 percent of all medical healing is proven to be the sole result of the positive thought/belief that the medicine will heal. In study after study, 30 percent of those who heal didn't actually receive any medication at all, but healed because they "believed" they received curative medicine. But, did we stop to think about the number of people who actually **took** the medication and healed for the same reason? Healed not from the medication, but from the belief that the medication worked? Of course pharmaceutical companies don't like smart asses who point this out. Who knows how many healed after taking the medication **simply because they believed, and not because the medication**

actually healed them? We'll never know, but common sense tells me there's definitely a percentage there. You can play with that math by adding your guess on that percentage to the 30 percent that the pharmaceutical companies and doctors **admit** were healed from the power of belief. The point is clear. There's proven biological power in thought/belief. That power is not reserved for biological situations only.

NEGATIVE, EVERYDAY THOUGHTS

Medical science tells us that the thoughts that make you frustrated, anxious, sad or angry can affect the absorption of nutrients in your body. I'm no worshipper of medical science, but most live by it, so know that negative thoughts are proven by medical science to stop your body from getting the nutrients it needs. Look into it. This applies when you've already done the awesome job of placing the proper nutrients in your body, by the way. Your own thinking can cause a situation in your body that will not allow the nutrients to properly absorb and benefit you. Any negative thoughts you have are, very literally, destructive to you. This is why we have to start with a focus on how to get your mind comfortably in the right zone before focusing on anything else.

Telling you to, "think positive," doesn't work when your ways of thinking negatively are already hard-wired. You can't just think positive if tracks are already laid for negative paths. **You have to lay new tracks**. The science that discovered neuroplasticity has already proven that no matter what tracks you already have, new ones can take their place. No matter what. It's scientific fact. And while we're strictly focused on your brain right now, here's a heads up for later. Your heart can *easily* generate feelings of positivity out of the clear blue and on cue. Unfortunately, your brain has likely rendered any impressions from your heart as 'useless' and shut your line of communication down, much like the 'blocked calls' feature on your phone. Your heart is constantly trying to holla at you with clear and powerful messages. They're just **blocked** by you know who. AI.

So, regarding how your mind has been working up to now? I can't emphasize this enough. Your wonderful brain is a personal computer that comes with your body. Its software is written with every experience you've had since your birth. The way your brain thinks and what you believe is limited to your past and current experiences. The way you think is limited to what **you** focus on in each moment of your life, and how **you** perceive and process it. It's very, very, **very** subjective. Thus, your brain is very, very limited in its power to guide you. And it uses ONLY the information you have gathered to make decisions on your entire life. These limitations are not insignificant. They're ultimately limiting your life and your Happiness. But we're NOT going for that! No can do.

SNATCH THE CONTROLS FROM YOUR AUTO-DEFENSE SYSTEM: "YUREEGO"

I call the brain AI (artificial intelligence) for two reasons. First, **because the heart** (or whatever you want to call it: gut, instinct, intuition, spirit, soul) **is your true intelligence** and I don't want that missed. Secondly, I call it AI because **the brain will take over** in the same way that scientists warn us that AI can take over if we're not careful. Remember *I, Robot*?

The brain is **powerful**, but many mistakes are made from relying on our brain to guide us. **Many**! If there are any glitches in your personal bio-computer system, then the processed results (thoughts, beliefs and feelings) could lead you in the wrong directions. Well, guess what? There ARE glitches in your system, and everyone else's. Unfortunately, little effort is put into maintaining the maximum health of our brains or our thought patterns. Little is invested in understanding how our brains work or in understanding the proper use of our brains. While your brain would have you think it needs no management, you need an optimally functioning brain and it doesn't manage to get that way all by itself. You have to put work in to train your brain to process the right things, letting some things go. Your brain needs to know how to identify what's worth processing and what to scrap. Your brain's awesome ability to sense **real** threats needs to be laser sharp. Some of our brains see everything as a threat of some sort. In these cases, far too much is being processed, and for no reason. This wasted energy is exhausting and very harmful. Your brain should continuously seek out and create thoughts that elevate you and steer you away from needless drama that brings you down. Sadly, far too many of our brains automatically seek out and mull over things that cause negative feelings. **Our brains latch on to thoughts that trigger bad things for our bubbles. If you catch yourself doing that,** STOP, DROP AND ROLL.

 **STOP** any negative thoughts in their tracks, **DROP** that shit like it's *hot*, and **ROLL** on to the next positive thing in your life.

Our brains are our babies. Just as you guys didn't come with *"instructions"* as lil' babies, none of us received instructions for our brains to operate optimally. This, too often, stands solidly in the way of our health and Happiness. There's no maintenance manual, so, there's no proper clearing of cache (old thoughts and experiences) or purging of files to keep us at peak performance. There's no virus software to run. So, we don't clear out dangerous thought programming. There's no protection from the invading negativity from our environment that always exists. We don't even ensure that our beloved processor is properly charged. **We just let it run**. And we let it run our lives, unchecked. AI is *not* mad about it. AI runs with it because it's a computer. Computers just run. Plus, it's smarter than you *and* your heart (or so it 'thinks').

Furthermore, it's not responsible for your Happiness in the first place. Your brain is focused on physical survival, not Happiness.

The next thing I want you to consider is that **your brain is a temporary tool for survival** in this life while **your heart is eternal**. Your body and brain, well, let's just say, "you can't take 'em with you." These temporary tools for living (body/brain) are for this soul journey only. Someday, when this soul journey is a wrap, that awesome computer brain ... I'm just keepin' it real guys ... will shrivel up and decompose. Bye, bye brainy. Your bubble, however, filled with your information and heart energy (intuition, spirit, soul) will be alive and well, soaring off on more journeys. Think about it. That brain that you're allowing to run your entire life will come to an end, but the heart generated energy of your bubble won't. Like I said, your brain's a temporary, **extremely** nifty and amazing tool, but not a guiding force for your life. I need you to see the bigger picture. Your heart, your true center of energy, your true intelligence, is supposed to have the lead role in your life. Your heart is your center for a reason. Your heart lives on, buoyantly, for eternity. This is what you should be most connected to. Your brain, while it's active and working, is super smart, no doubt *(although there are exceptions to this, I've come to realize. Every brain ain't 100 percent equal)*. Our brains tend to be overzealous, arrogant and hold a natural hunger for power. Kinda like in *I, Robot*. Since it's "our" brain and we see it as power for ourselves, we accept it with pride and roll with it. Nevertheless, our brains are very limited in the ability to guide our lives. That's evident by the fact that most are searching for Happiness and health in life. If our brains were so amazing at guiding our lives, we'd all have those things on lock since birth. See the brain, and use it for what it is. Take care of it. Honor its amazing power. Put it in check. Clear it from negative thought wiring. Use it for its most amazing features and keep your brain in its lane, so you can get where you need to be.

*Back to "I, Robot" for one second. Some very impressive human minds have expressed very serious concerns about the technology, the scientifically developed artificial intelligence (AI) that is now present and continues to develop. We're not going to stop developing AI because we have the power to do it and because it truly assists us with living our lives. But we do have to stop it from taking control over our lives. However crazy that sounds, that's the nature of the wonderful AI beast. I know that Stephen Hawking, Nicola Tesla, and Elon Musk have each expressed very real concerns about the dangers of technological AI in our lives. The concerns on that are **very** real. Already there are corporations selling protection against AI. You, on the other hand, are the only protection against your own biological AI. Your AI has likely already taken over your life to your detriment. Here, I'm offering some free, do-it-yourself AI protection techniques ;-).*

"The brain, the three-pound slab of tofu-textured tissue inside our skull, is recognized (by scientists, at least) as the physical source of all that we call mind. If you are having a thought or experiencing an emotion, it's because your brain has done something-specifically, electrical signals crackled along a whole bunch of neurons and those neurons handed off droplets of neurochemicals, like runners handing off a baton in a relay race." – Mindful.com, Mind vs. Brain

You may have noticed "Yureego" in the title of this section. We're about to talk about the part of your brain that's the true culprit in why we need to sit the brain down. Your brain, your personal AI, has a built-in security system. Let's consider this security system as a specialized 'app.' This app is called "Yureego." This is your brain generated **security system** feature, designed to keep you safe. It works hard and relentlessly. Always on the job of keeping you safe. There's just the *tiny* issue that Yureego sees threats even when they don't exist. Yeah, that sucks, right? It's a quirky app with OCD issues. When in doubt, Yureego defends. When *not* in doubt, Yureego defends. Unfortunately, this security feature gets BUSY and can see threats **everywhere**. It overreacts and runs you ragged from the constant stream of identifying and addressing threats to your personal security. Ironically, Yureego leaves you insecure more often than not. You're wiped out of energy from all the unnecessary security work. If Yureego **only** identified real threats, it would be great. Unfortunately, it's mostly setting off false alarms for perceived security threats that aren't real threats at all. What's worse, Yureego is constantly seeking unnecessary validation to try to build a personal sense of power. It's just busy, busy, busy. If it's not identifying and shutting down threats, it's busy using huge expenditures of energy to present impressions of our heightened value and our security. Most people love the sense of personal protection and keep it running 24/7.

Running Yureego 24/7 can be dangerous to your Happiness, though. On top of being a drain on your energy, use of Yureego is apparently quite addictive (**all** addictions are lead weight to your bubble, btw). Some can't get enough! They are ON IT. The feeling of security and power is a rush for some. The reality is that 90 percent of the work of Yureego doesn't bring real power or security, just an illusion of it. And real threats requiring protection seldom occur. Yureego seldom needs to be active. It's like the alarm system on our house. It's just there, more often set off by lots of innocent, false alarms that draw attention away from real life shit. Most of us, if we had the innate power and security that came with a heart-guided life, wouldn't need Yureego in the first place. But when your AI is running the show, Yureego is *all you got*. All too often, Yureego wastes your time and energy. It's always crying wolf, popping off when no threats exist, which signals weakness and insecurity to those who can clearly see your over or improper use of this protection feature. At the end of the day, it's not keeping you safe when misused. With improper use, Yureego can take the "app" out of Happiness, so watch your use of it very carefully.

The key, is to develop an innate sense of security that reduces your need for Yureego use. I wish we had all been given manuals when we got the AI system, but it is what it is. I want to help you guys to figure out how to best use your AI and its hottest feature, Yureego. Let's take a look at some basic instructions for using your brain, because with overuse that "built-in security system," Yureego, can very easily morph into a full-fledged "insecurity system." *That's similar to running with scissors.* **Somebody's** *gonna get hurt.*

Ain't no apps. Back in the day, we had a slang saying for "That's not going to happen." We said, "Ain't nothin' happening." Lol. That slang later shortened to, "Ain't no happs." I want you to get to the point that your "Yureego" app is **so** under control and you're **so secure by nature** that you can say, "Aint no '**apps**'" running your show. At this point, all your security comes straight from your heart, not Yureego. That's a very powerful space that offers 100 percent security, 100 percent of the time. No exhaustion. No false alarms. 100 percent real personal power. Running off Yureego? Naw, ain't no apps.

Heart | Mind Balance

Use the yin-yang symbol as imagery for the perfect balance of heart and mind in your life. The more balanced you are with each, the more you'll benefit from the synergistic force they were meant to provide. Once you learn to balance, it's like riding a bike. You never forget.

"It's simple, man.
Don't make it too *cerebral*."
    - Daddy

Your brain should be focused on sharp memory, managing your body and its functions superbly, having useful thoughts and processing incoming information in ways that help you. That's beautiful brainwork. We're going to get you there. The chances are strong, however, that your mind is the source of your life issues because it's doing much more than it should. For many of us, it's like that little Tasmanian devil, innocently spinning with a force that totally destroys. Your mind doesn't do so on purpose, there's no mal-intent. Still, it's messing things up for you. Sit that mind down, because all too often, instead of the beautiful brainwork, it's doing 'the most.' Being 'extra.'

With very little effort, your mind can be a factory of some seriously heavy, lead-level energy. When you feel confronted by issues in life, try not to get too 'cerebral.' You can over process unnecessary shit that should have been let go from the start. So much time and energy is wasted processing through unnecessary, unhealthy or old stuff. **It's imperative that you let go of old wounds and find ways to lighten your mind**. You HAVE to do this. You MUST. Your bubble wasn't meant to carry weight. Let the shit go.

Like it or not, how you feel about your life is a reflection of your state of mind. Release your mind from old *(and new)* thought paths that bring discomfort and pain. As I've pointed out, we tend to hold tight to nervous energy. We have to break that tendency! You have to COMMIT to learning how to let go of nervous energy and negative thoughts and emotions. You'll be surprised by what you can accomplish if you commit. **That neuroplasticity thing is real. You can program yourself to think any way that you want**. Start with imagining your worrisome thoughts coming out of you and floating away ... like a bubble. Whatever works run with it, right? No matter how you do it, once you control your thoughts, you'll control your responses to

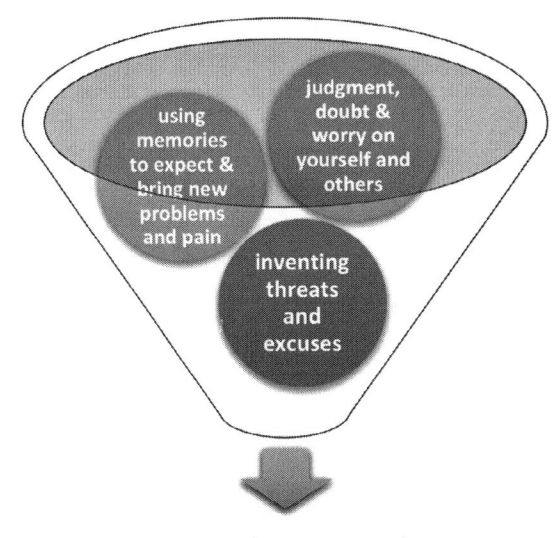

Typical Brainwork

(Gotta love AI. Always doing the most.)

life's situations. You'll control how you feel and what "station" you live your life on. Every thought you have guides you down a path either towards or away from Happiness. Pay attention to how you think and how you feel in every moment of your day. You might be shocked at how often you allow yourself to roll with lead level thoughts and feelings in a typical day. I've, too, been guilty.

Before we move on to what your thoughts are doing to you, I want to make sure you got the point that it's vital that you **take control of that mind of yours and not allow it to roll on auto-pilot**. Do not trust that your thoughts are coming from some wise higher self. Sometimes you can believe a hard-wired thought to be some inspired "message," when it's just a dead wrong automated thought. It takes practice and directed attention to discern an inspiration from the heart, from an auto-generated thought. In general, your thoughts are much more likely to be coming from your survival/security tool, Yureego, than anywhere else. You need to know the difference. I want to show you a way to have a fine-tuned connection to your heart/gut, so that your heart can guide your life and Yureego can be used in the healthy way it was designed to be used, for basic safety.

When uncontrolled thoughts and Yureego run unchecked, you'll miss breathtaking life pleasures and many of the treasures that await you. That makes no sense. So, let's focus on establishing a better partnership between you and your AI brain.

When you pass, your soul with float away from your body and brain. The brain and body will eventually dissolve, and your ego goes with it. Realize now, that your bubble survives this "soul school" we call life. Your brain, body and ego are merely soul school supplies. As sophisticated as these supplies are, they are not you. Your bubble is you, and you are eternal.

25

DO OUR BRAIN-DRIVEN THOUGHTS *REALLY* GOVERN OUR LIVES?

"The first revolution is when you change your mind."
– Gil Scott-Heron

Do our brain-driven thoughts govern our lives? **What**? Hell yeah, they do. Your thoughts are the seeds of 90 percent of what happens in your life.

Everything in the Universe is energy, right? Thoughts too, in case you didn't realize it. Thoughts, especially, are energy. There's actually a theory that your thought energy is comprised of particles that are incredibly microscopic and travel at twice the speed of light, so we can't detect that they're real, physical energy. Thoughts are believed to carry the highest frequency energy known to man. They're believed to have wavelengths so tiny and frequencies so high that they travel through all substances of matter. Imagine how powerful your thoughts and beliefs are to your body and your life. Visualize how they leave you and travel to manifest new realities.

Thoughts create feelings. Feelings spark actions or inaction. Feelings determine our lives. Feelings (emotions) are biochemical, not just psychological. Each feeling that you have involves the release of different chemicals in your body that match **that** emotional state. **Your brain gets wired to the same emotion if you continue to experience it**, which can lead to emotion addiction. Crazy, right? But think about it and you may be able to notice that people tend to revisit the same emotions over and over again. They're hard-wired to them. Doesn't matter if the emotions are good or bad. If they're hard-wired, they're happening again, buddy. And again. A person can find themselves helplessly and *very subconsciously* chasing that same emotion. Even if it's something they hate, everything that happens to that person seems to lead to *that* emotion. They're stuck and don't even realize it, so they certainly can't know **why**. They think it's the outside world coming at them with an endless array of coincidences centered on the same theme that leads them to the same emotion. What's **really** happening is their brain is doing its thing. The subconscious chase after the same old emotion has everything to do with neural peptides, neural hormones, the hypothalamus, receptor cells, biochemical reactions and all kinds of stuff like that. Google it. We have biochemical cravings for the emotions we're addicted to. Good or bad. It all starts with the way that you think. The thoughts that you ALLOW yourself to have. Recognize this so that you can manage to drop any addictions to heavy emotions by re-wiring your brain for thoughts that carry you toward Happiness. If you're lucky, you'll become addicted to positive thoughts and emotions quickly. And when you find you're thinking thoughts that do not tend toward Happiness, time to:

Stop, Drop and Roll

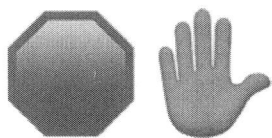

Stop the thought in its tracks. **Drop** it like it's hot. **Roll** forward with your life focused on something that gets you where you want to be.

Our brain-driven thoughts govern our lives because they determine how we feel and how we behave. Our thoughts also govern what we project out to the world, whether we believe it or not. Energy is energy, and your energy can be felt by others even when you try to dress it up as something else. You can smile and be friendly, but if on the inside you are filled with frustrations and anger, believe me, that's what you are projecting. Sometimes you can fool yourself to believe that you are past a certain feeling or thought. You can think, "I'm over that," "I'm not tripping," or "I'm not even thinking about that anymore." Too often, the energy of that emotion is still being held within you. This is why **it's so important to properly 'drop' negative thoughts and feelings so that they are *genuinely* released**. You must be *completely* free of that energy. The energy you hold will be what the world receives from **you**. This will have an impact on your life. You can't fool people. People are energy fields and most of them can sense energy. You sense energy too. You know whether you get a good vibration from a person or not. At the end of the day, your brain-driven thoughts govern your energy and how the world responds to you. Your thoughts govern what happens to you, how you make others feel, and your life. The good news is that, since you **can** control your thoughts, you **can** control your feelings and what you project to the world. No matter what emotional situation you ever find yourself in, you **can** re-wire as necessary. You can re-wire to good thoughts and feelings and move on, wonderfully, with your life. As I suggested before, neuroplasticity proves that the addictions, tendencies and personality traits that are hard-wired in any of us, **can** be re-wired for wonderful emotions and productive behaviors.

"There is nothing either good or bad, but *thinking* makes it so."
    – William Shakespeare

Have you ever noticed that all you have to do, *most times*, is **think** of something fabulous and dreamy to get an amazing feeling? Did you know that that amazing feeling can bring health and healing to your body and raise your vibrational frequency? That state of mind, when consistently held, brings Happiness and dream fulfillment. You'd be smart to figure out how to feel that way *regularly*. This healthy state of mind matches the vibrations of your dreams. Holding on tight to that feeling can make your dreams come true. And did you catch that all you have to do is **think** of something fabulous and dreamy to get the amazing feeling in the first place? Yeah. Don't miss that part.

"When I'm feeling sad, I simply remember my favorite things and then I don't feel so bad."
**– My Favorite Things,
Julie Andrews.**

There are ways of thinking *(I'll share my favorites with you shortly)* that can guide your mind to peaceful spaces in **any** situation. I'm giving you mine, but be creative to develop your own ways to see challenging situations in new and uplifting ways. As you practice seeing almost everything in a light that elevates you, eventually, one by one, these thought processes become habit. I encourage you to develop new, original ways that work for you. Practice makes perfect. Practice a little, every time you are confronted with a challenging situation or opportunity. Never miss an opportunity to test your skills. Use your new, uplifting ways of thinking at every turn, to get yourself where you need to be.

"In everyone' life, there's the need to Happy, yeah."
– Earth, Wind and Fire, Devotion.

ONE UPLIFTING SKILL:

Recognizing beauty elevates you. Do it as much as you can, in as diverse a range as humanly possible for you. See beauty in things that you didn't before. Attempt to see beauty in everything you come across. The broader and more widespread that your "beholder" eye can see beauty, the more elevated you've become.

> **A little note**: This is an excerpt of a poem *(song lyrics)* that Grandma Haywood, at one hundred years and four months, read to me as we chatted by phone during the Coronavirus of 2020. We were thinking of all the blessings of the moment, even though we couldn't see and hug each other and the world was in a state. She said, "I'm drinking from my saucer," then, told me to hold on for a minute, and she found this poem. She wanted me to include this for you. Hear her voice as you read it. Let it be a bit of helium for your bubble.
>
> **"Oh, remember times when things went wrong my faith wore somewhat thin; but, all at once the dark clouds broke and sun peeped through again. So, Lord help me not to**

gripe about the tough rows that I've hoed; I'm drinking from my saucer 'cause my cup has overflowed."

- Inspired by Psalm 95:6-7, Song lyrics by Michael Combs.

Now, let's reflect again on some bubble science by looking at the 'Stations of Energetic Frequencies' to help you to identify which station you're on and where you're going.

Stay Tuned! to the Stations of The Happiness Zone.
Happiness is just the beginning. Few ever leave the buoyant, lightness
of energy found on the stations of HAPPY, LIVING THE DREAM and CLOUD NINE.

...Meanwhile, Outside The Happiness Zone

It's business as usual. What else is new? Always something, right? These dense stations are like quicksand, requiring some lightness of mind just to stay on the ALL GOOD and SURVIVING stations. You'll feel like you're treading water just to hang on the MISERABLE Station. By following what I will outline for you, you have 100% chance of transcending these dense stations. Once you are determined, continuous helium energy will lift you from station to station, then out of there and into The Happiness Zone.

all good
surviving
miserable
toxic
vile

As you enter The Happiness Zone, your thoughts and feelings will remain in an incredible, constant state of Happiness. The HAPPY Station is the first you'll reach, but it gets better from there as you master the art of a buoyant mind, body and soul. Meanwhile, the denser stations outside of the Happiness Zone are chock full of bubbles, most of them feeling stuck there. Bless their hearts. These bubbles are largely unaware of the fact that they control their stations in life. The bubble stations at these lower energy frequencies range from the ALL GOOD Station *(my old stomping grounds)*, to SURVIVING *(been there too)*, then down to MISERABLE *(peeped this one while enveloped in grief)*, and even lower. The lower stations get some kind of shady! I've never been, but I've come across bubbles who, apparently, live there. Those bubbles aren't fun, not by a long shot, but they have the same opportunity to rise up and head towards The Happiness Zone as any one of us.

The thought processes, and therefore feelings, on these lower energetic frequencies are not the best, to put it mildly. Some absolutely suck. And for heaven's sake, your ***feelings are everything***! How you feel determines your whole life, right? Up until now, you may have thought that your feelings were determined by outside forces. You have probably felt that the people and circumstances of your life, however random, ***made you feel certain ways***. I'm telling you, your brain-generated thoughts are what make you feel whatever feelings you have. It's always the case. **It's not your circumstances, but how *you* think, how you process them**, that has determined what station you're tuned to throughout your entire life. Real talk. Get with the program and claim responsibility *(turn off Yureego, first, for optimal results)*.

To help you with this concept, I want to highlight something you've heard from me many times: **This game of life is a school. Learning lessons, sometimes hard ones, is the name of the game. Tests and pop quizzes coming out of nowhere are part of the game. Mid-terms and finals are part of the game. If you are a good student, you whiz through life, perfectly challenged, but able to excel. Good students get the most out of life. Poor students hate on the game and get their asses handed to them in countless ways**. Learn how to be a good student in the game of life. Start by taking 100 percent responsibility for how you think and feel. This is the number one trait of a good student of life.

Watch what you think because your feelings are a force of nature, like magnetism. Think of it in scientific terms. With a magnetic-like force, you attract energy that exists on the same frequency as your feelings. **Imagine that when you are feeling happy, a force emits from you that's magnetic. That force you emit, attracts uplifting thoughts and uplifting occurrences to you. On the other hand, when you are feeling negative, you emit an opposite force that attracts negative actions and events**. The scientific equipment doesn't exist to prove or disprove this (yet), but you can conduct your own studies. You can pay close attention and see if you notice how true this is in your own life. **Please test it.** You will see, firsthand, that it's true. I promise you will! So, be patient. Test over the long term because you probably won't get good at projecting sustained positivity overnight.

Happiness is a no-brainer (you don't need your brain to get it).

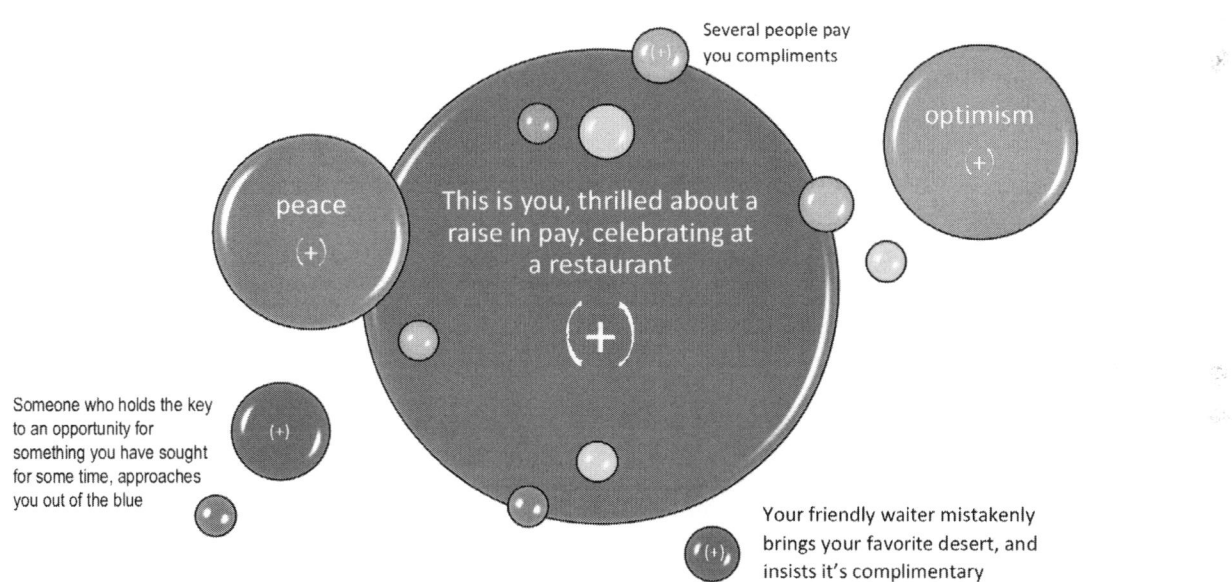

We all can attest that when it rains it pours. Somehow, when we're feeling bad, we've all experienced a subsequent series of bad events. It's *so* irritating! And that's exactly what happens, we get irritated and frustrated by the downpour. This irritation means that you are emitting more magnetic energy to attract more messed up stuff. It's more challenging NOT to get irritated, so put work in. 💪 Check yourself and slow down when you are feeling down. Don't push forward at full speed. Do not take it lightly that you are upset, or you *may* regret it. Feeling upset, frustrated, anxious, or downright depressed about something and pushing at full speed ahead *(without dealing with and releasing that negative energy, first)* can lead to brand new problems. Your low energetic frequency has placed you on the station where shit *really*

happens. This is why 'when it rains, it pours.' **When you've unintentionally put yourself on the station where the 'hits' keep coming, stop**. Deep breathe and release. It's time for some mental push-ups to bring buoyancy back into your consciousness when you find yourself in that situation. Otherwise, you'll make it rain, then pour. Our goal is always to "stay tuned" to the zones that bring us joy and Happiness. I cannot say it enough, you have to learn the skill of being able to:

 ## Stop, drop and roll. And how to stay tuned.

As hard as it is to enter a mental state of positivity in the midst of sadness and negativity, it is a *mandatory skill for your survival and progress in life*. No excuses! You can't say that you **would** think more positively if shit wasn't happening to bring you down. It doesn't work like that. You have to pivot your thoughts when the chips are down. It's much easier to dwell on problems and crisis. Easy as pie, actually. But life ain't for sissies. Toughen up! Step up. Learn to watch what you dwell on and take control of it. If you dwell on anything, dwell on how to achieve a mental state of positivity in the face of disappointment and crisis. Dwelling should, immediately, be followed by action in the form of lots of practice, until practice makes perfect. Challenge yourself to "stay tuned" to where you WANT to be. Doesn't that make sense?

Pay attention to how you think (and feel), day to day. If you're not thinking great, you're not feeling great. Don't accept that. You deserve nothing less than feeling good. Begin to treasure your thoughts. Listen to them. Be very, very careful to keep them at their highest point, as uplifting and positive as possible. You have to work hard to re-wire your brain. You will have to think different thoughts, *many, many* times in order to override old ways of thinking.

Remember what I pointed out to you guys in the book I gave you years ago by Louise Hay, *Excuse Me, Your Life is Waiting?* I was so intrigued that in a stadium full of people, each holding tuning forks to different pitches, once one person rings their tuning fork, tuned to a particular pitch, every fork in the stadium matching that pitch will ring. The ones tuned to a different pitch will not. They won't vibrate *at all*. Science is amazing and it extends through every aspect of our lives. The energy of our thoughts connect with all the things that are on the same vibration, similar to the tuning forks. So if you're thinking inspiring thoughts constantly, no matter what is going on around you, that's good stuff. What goes around eventually comes back to you.

We're starting this journey to Happiness with a focus on peace of mind. I've targeted some common pitfalls that you probably didn't realize your auto-pilot mind could fall into without you even realizing it. You'll have the opportunity to train your mind to avoid them or deal with them in a way that allows your mind to stay at peace. Use the upcoming philosophies and concepts to process situations that you face in everyday life, so that you can be unfazed by the things that truly don't even count. Your thoughts will be full of good energy that lead you to great feelings, no matter what's happening around you.

> "If there are still people here in 200 years, they will not be thinking the way we think."
> **– Daniel Quinn,**
> **Author of** *Ishmael*

GOT SENSE?

I hope so because it's your ace in the hole. I'm referring to your intuitive 'sense' as in **feeling** something without being able to explain exactly how. How good is your intuition without relying on your brainwork?

Your intuitions have surely been dulled from years of your brain dismissing them for its logical, brain-based solutions. Your busy AI will virtually shut down your ability to sense the instinctive, heart-based intuitions *(senses,)* that were meant to flow naturally through you. Chances are, if you rely heavily on your brain thinking, your intuitions are rarely getting through. You may not even get intuitions at all, anymore. AI has laid nice tracks of thought for you to use, convincing you to compute instead of taking chances with intuition. Your brain sees your intuition as flighty and impulsive, not computer-driven and precise ... and you follow right along, as if you have no 'sense.' Use it or lose it! Eventually, from lack of use, your intuitive 'sense' is so weak, it's as if it doesn't exist. Your natural sense, your intuition, your heart, your gut, whatever you call it, it doesn't stand a chance against your brain. As a result, you're probably slowly losing your ability to have a true sense about the most important things in your life. Just as easily as you breathe, your brain will override your instincts before you know what happened. That's got to change. Your ability to 'sense' is more valuable, intelligent and more accurate than you ever thought. Sensing things without the use of brain-powered thought is actually a function of your heart. When you get a 'sense' about something or someone, you're tapping into a universal consciousness exponentially more powerful than that awesome brain of yours. So, tell your brain to go sit down somewhere and turn your ability to sense (your intuition) back on. Having a clear ability to identify when your intuition is sending you a message is a priceless skill. So, fine tune that thing. Get it back in the game. Your intuition will guide and elevate you in ways your AI never, ever could.

Like I've said, most of us take an "auto-programmed" thought and believe we have a *sense* about something from some higher intuition. A brain-generated thought and a heart-generated sense about something are two **entirely** different things. You'll have to practice and pay attention to yourself in order to recognize the difference, but I can tell you that the heart-generated sense is most valuable to you and your life. Once you figure out the difference, start noticing when your intuitions are wrong and you will be shocked. Real intuition, by the way, is **never** wrong. Once you become an expert at recognizing your intuition, you'll have an invaluable tool for life. It's your best friend in the world. Treat it like the beautiful gift it is. Recognize that it exists just for you. Pay more attention to it. Give your intuition some love and energy. Intuition should be your new *Boo*.

If you feel something, but have no information to base that feeling, stop and wonder if it's an intuition? Remember what you felt, and watch to see if something materializes to prove whether you were right or not. Was the feeling an intuition? Keep testing in an effort to identify your true intuitions. It takes a process of trial and error to develop and recognize your intuitive impulses. By simply giving attention to your intuition, it will flourish. It's that simple. No longer being ignored, your intuition will appreciate the love and will begin to step up for you.

When developing your intuition, remember that it is strongest when you are not totally wrapped up in logical thought processing. Offer yourself moments of peace here and there with some nature-filled time to stop and smell the roses. These things will help quieten your mind and allow your senses and intuition to have its day in the sun. Remember the yin-yang imagery. As soon as you begin to work on your heart/mind balance, you're already on your way up.

EMBRACE YOUR NEW BUOYANT STATE OF MIND

The concepts in this section get your mind primed and ready for liftoff. The first thing I want you to do is pay full attention to the titles in this section. Each is titled specifically for the purpose of *you* reading them aloud to yourself. Say them with conviction. **Believe them**. Insist that your AI accepts them as your new reality. Insist! Don't let that AI punk you. This is the first step on your path to The Happiness Zone. I'm excited for you :-)

"I'M 'BOUT TO RETRAIN THIS BRAIN!"

The first step in retraining your brain is to identify which bubble station you're currently on and the station you goal to reach. This is the first step because when I say your mind is hard-wired, what I mean is that your mind is already made up. It's not easy to change a mind that's already made up. **You'll have to make up your mind that you're going to change it, or absolutely *nothing* will happen**. Most things worth having in life come with determined effort. Re-wiring your brain for new trains of thought is no different. Setting a goal is your best chance at succeeding. Have you identified where you are *now*, and where you want to be? If not, think on that before moving forward. Stop and take this part seriously, please. It makes a difference. It's called visualization.

So, now, assuming you have a goal to reach, give focus to your goal every day. Every day, envision your bubble looming on your station. Keep envisioning it rising buoyantly every time you adjust your heavy thoughts to light ones. The thoughts you currently have are what keep you from rising. You'll have to switch some up. You'll need to notice and be mildly alarmed when you feel yourself pulling farther away from The Happiness Zone. You're about to step up and take full responsibility for your 'mind over matter' management.

Start by recognizing and identifying *every* unpleasant emotion you have. Recognize each and every moment that *you* are caught in an unpleasant thought or emotion. Don't just run with that anymore. Those days are gone. Now, notice it when it's happening. I've identified some **helium energy** and **lead energy** thoughts, feelings, practices, etc. for you on the "Rise to Happiness" chart. This was just to get you to start thinking. There are countless thoughts, feelings, practices and beliefs that aren't listed. You can fill in the blanks because each of us instinctively knows the difference between negative and positive energy. We don't need a chart for that.

Each time a bad feeling pops up, try to identify the thought at its root. Literally, name the thought. Name the emotion, too, every time they creep up on you. Calling out your negative thoughts and emotions by name will help you to pivot away from them. It's a distraction, at the very least. It's similar to deep breathing in that it helps you slow the roll of that emotion. At the same time, calling out your negative thoughts is part of the re-wire process. As you identify the thought you identify the **source of where the rewire work needs to take place**. Lastly, identifying and calling your emotions by name lets your brain know that there's a new sheriff in town. It puts your wackiest thoughts and emotions on alert to stand down, lest they be exposed.

For example, let's imagine you just had an incident that caused you to be angry. Recognize that you are angry and admit the emotion to yourself, "I'm pissed the _____ off." Then, take the time to admit to yourself the *reason* why you are angry. Oftentimes, you're caught in a habitual reaction of anger from which you can emerge quickly if you think through it.

But, let's say today you're pissed because … someone just spilled red wine on your new, white, *designer* suit ten minutes after you arrived at an all-white event. Then, without saying a word, chuckled under their breath and walked off with what looked, to you, like a smirk. You heard someone laugh in the distance, to make matters worse. Your AI has tracks already laid for this one. Adrenaline began to rush through you before you ever saw that smirk. Your reaction wasn't even a decision. AI auto-engaged. But let's look at this situation more closely. We'll break this down, so you can use this example to identify and work through future emotions.

The reasons for your emotions are not as clear cut as you might think. Why are you pissed? Is it because your perfect moment is no longer perfect? If so, we want you to have a broader view of what a perfect moment looks like. Your joy is not an option left open for others to take. On top of that, if your belief is strong that a suit is not worth losing your joy, not even for a minute, you'd still be in a perfect moment, wine spots and all. If you had mastered the art of "Stop, drop & roll," you'd still be in a perfect moment.

Are you pissed because your new suit is ruined by red wine? If so, tell your brain to chill out and Google next time, before allowing yourself to get pissed and drop your energy to a lower level. There is always a solution to every problem. Sometimes the only solution within your power is how you think about it. And that's cool, because there is always a way to see a situation that brings peace to your mind. If not immediately, peace will eventually settle in if you allow it. Don't allow hard-wiring to keep you hardened. Allow some "light" energy in. A tiny bit of Tide mixed with hydrogen peroxide will get it right out, by the way, even when done the next day.

Are you pissed because you no longer look as sharp as you had planned? That shouldn't evoke anger. A little disappointment is understandable, but get over it, and do it quickly. Quickly means 90 seconds, tops. You cannot afford to drop your bubble over wine stains. You still look marvelous and now you have a story to tell. You are way too confident to be worried about anyone judging you. Rock your wine stain and keep stepping. Life is so much bigger than that. Open your mind to the possibilities of enjoyment that exist as you move through the event. Even if you simply observe the nuances of the event. Let your level of sharpness be reflected by your confidence and overall positive mentality. Show 'em what you're working with. Rock the stain.

Are you pissed because you think the person was careless? If so, seriously? Getting angry because *someone else* was careless? Why would you be bothered about how others live their lives when you have your hands full with yours? You don't know if they're having trouble with their balance because Multiple Sclerosis runs in their family. You don't know. You don't even know whether they were being careless or not. You never will know. And it doesn't matter anyway. It especially isn't worth the negative effect the anger has inside your body. It's not worth throwing off your Happiness game. **Someone else's carelessness should never be a reason for you to have anger.** Your AI knows little about other people and what drives them, but it'll tout itself as an expert. I'm telling you, it's not. If you trust your judgment on knowing what drives other people, bet money that you're the clown on the scene. You can cause havoc to yourself when you allow yourself to place qualities, thoughts, abilities and emotions on others. Those other people are God's creations, living their lives with incredibly different circumstances than you are aware of. You're walking on thin ice when you believe or even try to surmise what is behind others' behavior. Please, please, please, let that one go. You don't know what's going on with other people. You don't know whether they're hard-wired from unimaginable experiences that they can't work through, and you shouldn't care. You certainly don't jump into negativity as if it strengthens *your* position. Negativity won't ever strengthen your position. No matter what your brain or your prevailing culture tells you. If that person comes back and throws wine in your face, all bets are off! ... I'm just kidding ;-) Seriously, though, even if that happened, when you feel powerful because you are filled with the energy we're talking about now, you would not feel threatened. You would see their baggage as immense. You would see that they are daring you to come into their negative world of energy. You would see that their bubble is toxic. We want to get to the point where in the face of negativity, you are seeing all of this. The ability to see this way, *in the moment*, that's **real** power. Until you get there, realize that you hold the power NOT to descend into negativity when you feel it coming over you. When you have the power to rise in the face of situations like this, you have no fear and ***that*** will be written all over your face. Your persona will speak volumes. You will have no worries about the situation facing you. That will be seen too. You have no time, not for that type of thing. And you're not the one, not because you can whip this clown and get more toxic than they are, but because you're beyond pettiness. Your mind is successfully re-wiring new thought processes that make you more powerful, fearless, peaceful and in control of your life. No one, especially not aggressive clowns, can mess with you (police can mess with *them*, though, *just sayin'*). Imagine that you are in a space, so amazing, that you can shake your head at the issue, but not be shaken. In this space, you'd fully experience, in the face of crisis, that having power over your thoughts is the greatest power in the world. That's next to love, of course. Imagine the power you hold if you can still feel good, genuinely good, within 5 minutes of this happening. That's where I'm taking you guys.

But, let's get back to a more reasonable scenario and finish up here. Are you pissed because their smirk indicated that they didn't care about ruining your suit or because you think they did it on purpose? If you are still running "Yureego," by the way, that self-defense system is going NUTS. It's filling your mind with self-defensive, self-destructive thoughts, for sure. Yureego takes **no risk**. It wants to squash all beefs in order to ensure your safety. Yureego will have you thinking a purposeful wine spill, followed by a smirk could be a life or death situation. The perpetrator must be annihilated or you are at risk. Don't fall for this. This is why I hipped you to Yureego as a faulty app. **Do not** fall for it! The biggest danger you face is being stuck on a station where this kind of thing happens to you ALL the time. Don't take the actions that keep you there. Get off this station! If mal-intent or disrespect actually occurred, that's still NOT worth allowing *your* bubble to drop. I'll admit, where I'm from, that would be grounds for dropping bubbles, book bags, purses, earrings and some science on why you are not the one. So, don't think I don't get it. I totally do. I would have to process for a few seconds myself, ***today***, because of old wiring. But do the math guys. When you add negativity to negativity you get too damn negative. "Keeping it real" behavior is the problem, not the solution. Grow beyond that mentality. If the person who spilled the wine doesn't care or did it on purpose, that person needs a Happiness Hookup in the worst way. That bubble's a little dense, and ***that*** isn't your problem. It's ***theirs***. The only thought or feeling you should have towards them is mercy. If they had been met, their entire lives, with your beautiful energy, they wouldn't be like that. You, on the other hand, have something to lose, your Happiness. *Your job is to stop any of your energy from flowing into this situation they've presented*. Stay focused on where you're trying to go. Get back to enjoying yourself.

Aside from making you feel emotionally awful, anger destroys your body. It creates stress functioning in your body that can lead to disease, heart-attack and stroke. What? Yes! The miserable, bubble-dropping, disease-friendly state that you put yourself in when you feel these ways is simply not worth it. It's literally foolish. Wine stains are not worth dropping your bubble's energy to lower vibrational levels. They're not worth the additional negativity you'll attract from being on a lower energy level. No possible way. Anger is an emotion to stop, drop and roll from. Stop the foolishness in its tracks, as you pivot to thoughts of staying on your level and moving up from there. It's all about your self-preservation. As that begins to sink in, you will start to catch and control your thoughts and feelings, instead of just running with them. There will always be forces and events in your life that are beyond your control, but how you respond to them is all YOU, Boo. All YOU. **Is spoiling your life moment, draining your energy level, pulling yourself away from your dreams and injuring your body worth holding onto thoughts that bring misery?** Will you buckle under the pressure of trying to make positive changes and just stick with what you're used to? Please say no.

While, naturally, you'll want to blame that person and those wine stains on your gorgeous new white, suit for your anger, I need you to see that you actually created your anger. What? Yes, that's exactly right. Never forget that it is your thought pattern that angered you, not the situation, but the way you processed it. You may have had an accomplice, but by allowing anger to be your thought of choice, **you** created the anger within you. It's all in how you see things. This may be hard to see at first, but try to see what I'm saying. You can think whatever you want to think. It's your choice. Why not think in the ways that bring health and Happiness? It's your choice. Once you lay new wiring, thinking this way becomes automatic. Your life has changed.

*Changing the wiring is a process of awareness, commitment and **repetition**.* You will get good at controlling the rush of adrenaline caused by bubbles stuck on the denser stations. My, oh my, can these bubbles tempt. Bless their hearts. But don't judge. Never forget that they are bubbles too. Created by God just like you. They're just caught up in faulty wiring and a lower energy station. Instead of tangling up with them, help them by way of your example. When people see how genuinely unfazed you are by negativity, they'll realize that state of mind is possible. It's a start. Recognize that few things, not wine spilling incidents or people buckling under the weight of their own baggage are worth your anger. Even if people are lurking with bad intentions, you are much more protected from negativity if your mind is in a well-controlled state of peace.

You absolutely **can** learn to pivot when your mind goes there. One easy pivot for *all* challenging life situations is to **pivot your attention to you and your goals**. When shit hits the fan, divert your attention to your current blessings, then to where you're going next in life. Real life is lived in the moment, so outthink the situation so you can maximize each moment for yourself. Spending time mulling over something you cannot change is not the answer. It's the problem. Solve the problem, not by changing the world around you, but by changing your mind. **Master the pivot.**

It's incredibly important to continue to work on pivoting your mind. Try your best. Remember that your anger and unresolved issues tend to linger, hiding inside your bubble, weighing you down. Left unchecked, your mind processes scenarios that have already passed. Your mind will be busy buffering old shit. It may start with something as minor as a hurt feeling or being offended. From there, it can morph into anger, defensive behavior, withdrawal and a host of other behaviors that you may not even notice yourself doing. Over time, these behaviors turn into negative energy trapped inside *your* bubble. You won't even know it. You were never meant to live like this. **Stop the madness**. You MUST recognize, process and **eliminate** emotional baggage **completely** out of your mind and body before it dulls your vibration; clouds your vision; poisons your body and mind; and limits your life.

As you re-train your brain, your mind becomes peaceful even when splashed with red wine at a white party. You're able to use your brain to process the beauty and lessons of the moment *(and yes, you can learn lessons from people on what **not** to do)*. Instead of being wrapped up in a low energy thought or feeling, you could be using your mind to make your life and/or the world around you a better place. Your thoughts are not harmless (*they can whip your ass!*), so keep working to re-train your brain in the best way you possibly can. It's a show of love to yourself. Think about **you**. Once you begin to recognize when your thoughts have ventured into dangerous territory, you've made an amazing accomplishment and are well on your way to a rewired brain.

Your life experiences, good or bad, are like fuel for your soul. The *so-called*, bad or more challenging experiences may be unpopular, but they usually carry more of what I call "nutrients." The "nutrients" are the lessons that nourish and elevate your soul. Think of it like this, the good experiences, the experiences we enjoy most, are like candy. The challenging, bad, unpopular experiences are like cod liver oil. In the right state of mind, you'll see the challenges as good, often offering transformational impact. These "bad" experiences are simply a part of the life package. We're to receive and digest them. It's a process. Accept them (imagine consuming them). Process them by breaking down the experience, extracting the lessons (envision yourself receiving the nutrients through digestion). Then, release the waste (elimination). Get what you need from the lessons. You can't hold onto the waste. This gives new meaning to the phrase, "let that shit go."

Imagine if **everything** you ate was held inside. Imagine the funky, unhealthy mess you would become. It would be hard, actually it would be impossible, for your system to function properly. That's you, mentally, if you don't manage your thoughts, process them and let the wasteful shit go. Controlling your thoughts is not only 100 percent necessary, 100 percent possible as a natural human ability (neuroplasticity), it's also easier than you might think. You just have to PRACTICE.

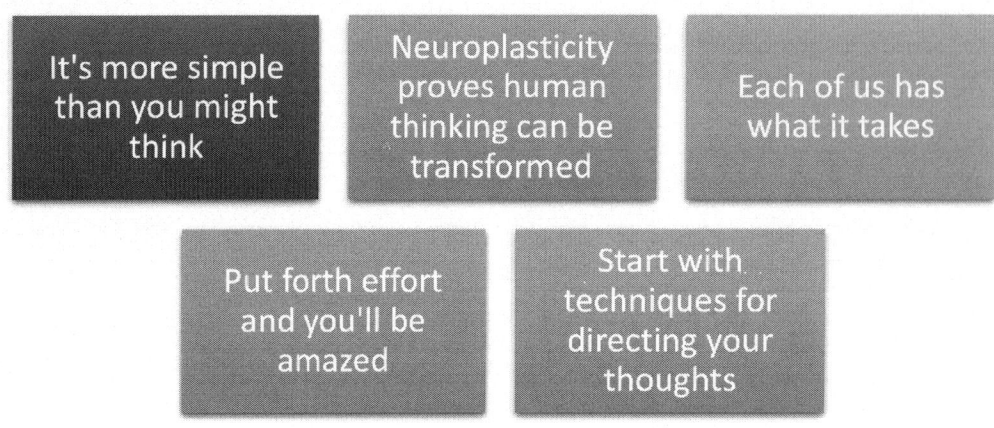

We're going to lay fresh, new tracks for brand new trains of thought that will send your bubble soaring. I recommend using the following techniques to keep your thoughts elevated:

INSPIRATIONAL TRIGGERS –

From this point forward, **let every life challenge be a signal to you** reminding you to push your mind past the negative to higher energy thoughts. Tough shit should be an inspirational trigger for the "*no pain, no gain*" or "*change is the nature of the universe*" mindset. Let each tough situation serve as an inspiration for something new that you will achieve. Remember, it's school. Tough situations are tests. Be reminded that that's all it is and work on passing with flying colors. My suggestions for how to pass some of your life challenges, in the moment, may be a little unconventional. They've worked for me, though, so give it a try. First, recognize and identify low-energy thoughts as negative when they crop up. Then sub-out every low-level, negative thought with buoyant ones. **Keep an arsenal of thought substitutions for every challenging situation**. I have some suggestions coming up. So, when the going gets tough, just let that be a **reminder** or an **inspirational trigger** to get to work, that's all. Get to work on dropping those heavy, low-energy thoughts with increasing quickness. Imagine it as a video game called, "Mind Lift." You win each time you successfully convert a negative energy thought. Keep your thoughts at the absolute highest energy you can to get (and keep) your bubble in The Happiness Zone. Whenever your mind moves quickly past a negative thought, hear the sounds of achievement in your mind [*like when Pac Man eats the fruit* ;-)]. Whatever works! Play this game for at least two weeks after you read the book. Trust me, the experience and increasing skill will be worth it.

PIVOTS –

Recognize, immediately, when you are mulling over something that you shouldn't. Whether it's a past situation that upset you or **any** negative thought, recognize it in the moment. Then, learn to pivot your mind to an image of something that brings joy, personally, to YOU. Feel that good feeling. See yourself as a clown to be allowing yourself to think in ways that harm your precious self. **Never** put up with that! Never just sit back and allow YOUR bubble to *descend to the depths* for **any** reason. It makes no sense! Fight as hard as you can to pivot your thought away, until you win the fight. This fight is for your health and Happiness.

You have all the basics now. From this point forward, everything is for the purpose of planting seeds in your mind that lead to higher level thinking. First, we'll plant seeds for a buoyant frame of mind. Then, we'll review a host of inspirational triggers and pivots for your use. Don't try to remember anything. Everything you read will go into your subconscious mind, and will be accessible to you as you move away from constant brain-led thinking. As you allow more intuition to guide you, you'll remember everything you need to know instinctively. In the meantime, you'll have the book to refer to at any time. No worries, just relax and read to plant those seeds.

"I AM PERFECT"

Please read that out loud. And yes, you are! You were created by a magnificent force to live the role of "you" in the story of humanity. With the knowledge that you were perfectly made by a force with an infinite wisdom more powerful than yours, be confident, courageous, fearless and free to live your life story. When this mentality truly grips your mind, you spontaneously rise.

"The only thing to fear is fear itself."
– FDR, in his first Inaugural address

I want you guys to connect **deeply** with FDR's quote. Since fear is the opposite of love, we want to stay far, far away from it.

"Have faith in *you* and the things you do. You won't go wrong."
– We are Family, Sister Sledge

BE FEARLESS

Break through the fears and trust your life story. This is your story, your soul journey, written for you by God. Fear is just your mind "doin' the most." Your mind calls itself protecting you, but most fear is just your mind on overdrive. Fear has been called the polar opposite of love. You can **fill** yourself with one, but not both. Choose carefully. Fear is seldom the mechanism to protect us that we want to believe it is. Fear is more commonly a sign of lack of confidence and faith. Safety concerns are always *totally* understandable. If instinct is telling you "no" because you might die or lose a limb, I can feel where you're coming from. I'd advise that you think on that one. However, if you are fearing something like disappointment or embarrassment, that's not worth stopping yourself, just go for it. Record it on video so I can see your concerns, though ... *Just kidding.* I'm not trying to talk you into being the next viral meme or video clip on the Internet, but don't let fear hold you back from living YOU. I'm talking about the fearlessness to strive for a personal goal, particular career path or financial status that may seem out of your reach. I'm referring to the fearlessness to take the first step towards a whole new life path or a new home, new career, business or creative project. I'm talking about letting go of fears that limit your expression of yourself or your potential in life. Let fear go. Replace fear with determination.

Fearlessly follow your loftiest of dreams. Dreams are like clues on a personal treasure hunt. No matter what happens, following them always brings you closer to finding personal treasures.

BE FREE TO BE YOU

I don't have to talk much on this one because if there's anything you guys got, it's the fearlessness to be yourself no matter what, and not care what others think. I taught you that better than I practiced it myself, and I love that about you guys. It's such a part of you that it will never, ever change. I think it's beautiful.

For any of my loved ones who read this and could use a word about being free to be yourself, remember that most of us were **trained** to set the goal of being impressive. We were trained to make ourselves attractive to teachers, colleges, employers and future mates. Most of us were trained to be cautious and safe. We were trained not to stand out in the crowd, unless to be recognized as superlative. This was taught to us for our safety. It's safer in a pack, following paths that have already been charted for success. It's safer to be considered "valuable" and "normal" by the masses. This helps to ensure that we sustain ourselves through gainful employment. We also avoid resistance from others if we fit neatly into the mainstream. The problem is that the freedom to be truly you is missing from that path. You're safe and sound, but not your true self. You're already used to not being your true self. Now what? I'll tell you what ... DO YOU,

NOW. That's what. As long as you are alive in that body, there's more to your story. Start by developing your confidence, then make the commitment, "I'm gonna be my damn self no matter what!"

"Freedom is the oxygen of the soul."
- **Moshe Dayan**

A wise person once said,
"Eff this sh*t, I'm doing ME."
And lived happily ever after.
- **Anonymous**

CONFIDENCE

We're each made perfectly. Then, we go and tell ourselves, "This is wrong," or "That's bad." We sometimes reflect, "Why don't I have this or that? I should have that!" That's where we go wrong. Overthinking. We're calculating. Human values can't be calculated. So, don't go there. That's a lot of bad thinking with very little heart involved. In the process, you drop the ball on your self-worth. Accept that you are great, *as is*. You're the **one** person in this world with the responsibility to love who you *naturally* are. Don't drop **that** ball.

"Love me or hate me,
I swear it won't make or break me."
– **Lil Wayne**

Once you open your heart and realize you're fabulous with every perceived flaw, real confidence will flourish. Confidence is a beautiful, natural state of heart, *not mind*. Confidence can flow like crazy when your heart and mind are balanced. It can't, when they're not. Lack of confidence is unnatural, unhealthy and leads to unhappiness. Sounds bad, so you know Yureego is at it again, right? Surprise, surprise. When confidence is low, your brain's too busy where it has no business or skill. It's busy detecting all the things that it 'thinks' will make you perfect in the eyes of others, *and Yureego*. It's detecting that you don't have these things, and instantly setting off false alarms. While alarms are going off, your confidence is going down. This is NOT natural. Get back to nature! Don't let Yureego hijack your confidence. Put Yureego in check. Set it to recognize "real threats." Elevate away from brain thinking when it comes to people, including yourself. Your heart and soul will recognize you and everyone else as fabulous, with 'flaws' and all. Others can find out that you're fabulous, *or not*. What does it matter? The ones meant for you already know. Go about your life. Continuously self-improve for your own good. Do it because that's a part of life, and because you love yourself. We don't self-improve to build confidence because our confidence can't be built, or torn down. It simply flows through us. If you ever feel your flow of confidence is low, give Yureego the stop sign, and give your heart the green light to take the lead. For added insurance, because Yureego might take control when you least expect, update it with rewiring that will make it nearly impossible to lack confidence.

First, **release all sensitivity to rejection and disapproval**. Having a sensitivity to these will make you insecure. Insecurity is baggage energy. See the huge hole ⬛ ahead. You'll fall in there fast and hard if you're not desensitized to rejection and disapproval in advance. Patch that hole up, *now*. The perfect patch? All you need to do is overflow with self-love and appreciation while flexing your ***tough, thick skin* for all forms of disapproval and rejection**. With a thick skin developed around your bubble, when you encounter forms of disapproval or rejection, you **only absorb the advantages and guidance they provide**. Everything else gently bounces away.

With thick bubble skin, you'll immediately detect and receive the advantages and useful guidance that can be gained from disapproval and/or rejection. You'll use them to be guided away from the person(s)/place/thing, and toward your destiny. You'll clearly see that's all that's happening. Disapproval and/or rejection are simply road signs guiding your life journey. They help to identify what's ***not*** for you. They're blessings that appear to be in disguise only because your mind had different ideas. It's all good. More signs mean more guidance to get you where you need to be. Graciously receive your directions, bouncing disappointment away as you keep pushing ahead.

A soft no, constructive criticism or disapproval, should be seen as a *'bear right'* sign ⬛. Consider making constructive adjustments that enhance your life. A hard rejection or disapproval could be viewed as a sign to make a hard left ⬛. Time to change course away from the source either permanently or temporarily. Take every effort to enhance your situation in the meantime, then try a new direction or try the same one again. Follow your instincts. If at first you don't succeed, try again, right? Finally, see a strait out awful form of disapproval or rejection as a U-turn ⬛ away from that asshole. ⬛ Emit vapors of love as you speed on your way. All negativity bounced off because you already know that you can't control the station of other people's bubbles. You're thankful for the heads up to change direction. That's good intel! Keep pushing along your journey until the signs start indicating "keep straight," "destination ahead," and "you've arrived." Since nothing harmful got through your thick, bubble skin, you're left only with advantages from every disapproval or rejection. No harm, no foul. Good directions, and good advice is all you receive.

Secondly, **don't idolize physical appearance or financial/status-driven measures of success.** It's unfortunate, but understandable that we do this. Mainstream ideals of beauty and success have been fed to us as the 'heights of life,' infecting popular culture, media sources and minds for a long, long time. Yureego always seeks whatever's held as most desirable, so pitfalls always lurk ⬗ when you don't reach the heights of attractiveness, wealth and status. You'll need to patch those holes up too, or you'll fall in and hurt yourself. Yeah, looks matter, mostly to those governed by ego. Your wealth and status are more ego accessories. Accessories rock, when they're not the backbone of your confidence. Don't get it twisted. Your physical appearance has been divine since birth. It's unique. It's you. **Those *meant* for you in this life will see your appearance as magnetically attractive, even when the ego tripping folks don't**. Tune out those who are not for you. Rock what your maker gave you, and rock wherever you are in life, financially or status-wise. This is you. Change things if you want, but *only* if you want. Otherwise, refuse to let your brain guide your confidence. Work on your heart|mind balance. Whenever you're feeling inadequate, you've lost sight of real beauty. Crank up that heart so you can see real beauty again. Keep focused on the things that truly make you elevated. If you want to have fun with the aesthetics of external beauty, go for it. Rock that thang! There's nothing wrong with it as long as it has no bearing on your confidence or self-worth. If you want to chase mainstream measures of success, like financial wealth or job titles, get going. There's absolutely nothing wrong with that. Nothing! Never get it twisted, though, **the true beauty of a person is measured by the beauty and lightness of the energy they project, and the depth of real love they have for themselves and others**. When you lack confidence, you're looking through the Yureego brand glasses. Take those off. You don't need glasses. **The things you *can't* see should be the constitution of your confidence.** As you build a true heart|mind balance your interest in comparing yourself to anyone else's measure of beauty and success *faaades awaaay*.

If you do decide to chase mainstream images of wealth and beauty for Happiness, you'll only get fleeting hits of happy from it, and that's if you're lucky. Most who chase the mainstream images of beauty and wealth tend to feel inferior when they don't have more of it than the next person. You'll catch fleeting moments of lift when others admire all your shiny ego accessories. An evolved soul and a deep self-love, on the other hand, will bring sustained lift and true confidence.

One thing's for sure, your soul is here for a reason. You were created to fill a spot. There has never been a ***you***, exactly like ***you, in the whole of humanity***. The beautiful thing is that all you have to do to fulfill your role on earth is to be ***you with confidence***. How cool is that?

Please don't fall for a societal value system that holds academic and financial success, beauty, popularity and status as measures of your worth. Society didn't create you. People didn't create you. I'm your mother and even I can't take credit for creating you. Your soul and everything about you was created by a much higher force, so how on earth can people know what you're here to do and be? Nobody knows that. You are the only one with that answer.

The only way to connect with what you're here to do and be is to flow with being your natural self and not care what anyone thinks! Those moments spent worrying about what anyone thinks of you are THE most wasted moments of a lifetime. Even if you get caught with a funny look *(uncle DNZL or weeping MJ for example)* and you didn't realize it, but others did and laughed at you, so what?! Let 'em "hee, hee, hee," but keep being YOU. Don't give a flying ... *care* ;-). Pivot your mind when you catch yourself worried about what someone else thinks of you. Pivot! Embracing your own individuality and nurturing your own confidence is the more constructive use of your time.

The only way to know what you're here to do and be is to flow with being your natural self and not care what anyone thinks. **Yes, I said it again**, because it's so important that you get that! When you're being your natural self without caring about what others think, that's when you are truly fulfilling the reasons you were created. Your creator will be happy. People? Well, we don't know or care what they think in their hard-wired minds. Do we? Nor do we care whether they are impressed or whether they approve. When you are being your natural self without concern for what others think, you've got true confidence. **Your confidence attracts the people who were meant *for you***. The people who were meant to be in your life will magnetize to your confidence. These are the people that matter for you. They'll love you just as you are. Forget the rest. Solid confidence in being your natural self will make you fulfilled and invincible. It will make your bubble lift in the direction of Happiness. So, be naturally you and flow on with your bad self!

"Do I contradict myself?
Very well then, I contradict myself.
I am large.
I have multitudes."
– Walt Whitman, Leaves of Grass

This is one of my favorite poem excerpts. It connected with me as I read *Leaves of Grass* in college. Walt Whitman was DEEP. I was just nineteen years old. I couldn't process everything then, but I related to this excerpt even more as my spirituality evolved. Embrace who you truly are, and recognize that you are bigger than and deeper than what's on your surface. Be unapologetically you.

Finally, people can't hold you down. Nothing can hold you down. Not if you won't allow it. If you do allow it, then, it's really **you** holding **yourself** down and blaming others for it. Don't be that bubble.

"I'M IMMUNE TO NEGATIVITY"

Say it loud. Your best defense against negativity is managing how you think. Envisioning yourself as immune is a perfect first step. Visualize all forms of negativity bouncing off your bubble.

"I am protected from anxiety and immune to negativity."
– Amy Zerner & Monte Farber, from their Chakra Meditation Kit.

Negativity comes first for your brain. Crazy, right? It's for our survival that our brains recognize and process negativity **before** anything else. Since negativity's **always** lurking, it's super challenging for our brains to free up and focus on the positivity that exists around us. Missing positivity while focusing on non-threatening negativity? Lol, on that one.

No doubt, we want our brains to be on alert to protect us from physical threats. As it turns out, most of the negativity we perceive are not **physical** threats. Think about it for a minute. You might be surprised to realize that most of what your brain spots as negativity was never a threat to you at all. Most negativity comes in the form of attitude, pettiness and/or actions from others that *possibly could* lead to a disadvantage to us. It seldom does. We usually hurt ourselves at the end of the day. Still, Yureego's on the case. Watch it go! Even when we're not **truly** threatened, **our brains activate a response as if a real live threat exists**. Somebody snapped at us, rolled their eyes and made a condescending remark, or they're *slickly* trying to undermine us! Not here, buddy! And not today! Our body courses with adrenaline. Our muscles tense and our pulse rates increase all because a slick, dense bubble needs a hookup? The reality you may not want to hear, is that your reaction to that negativity was an indication of the health of your own Yureego. The chances are extremely high that **98 percent of the negativity you have felt in your life was merely a *perceived* affront to Yureego.** Otherwise, it wouldn't bother you. It would simply be something you witnessed and worked your way around to get where you needed to be. This is life guys. Negativity exists. We knew that. It's a real part of our existence. But let's respond **only** when we're in danger, ok? Other people's drama can NOT activate Yureego. You can't be subject to feeling the effects of a full on Yureego onslaught every time someone else has a moment in **their** personal bubble. It makes no sense. We're not letting that happen. I know you want freedom from that drama, and I got your vaccine right here.

First, remind yourself that negativity from others is not about you. Then, accept that fragile, unhealthy egos are the **first** to go berserk when threatened by negativity. It's true. Healthy egos only respond to real threats. There's no false alarm BS with the healthy ego. **Healthy egos are a form of immunization to negativity**. If you felt any defensive emotions while reading this, it's because your ego heard it was in question and your defense system automatically engaged. Stand down, soldier. It happens so automatically, we're not even consciously aware of our feelings when they're triggered. It's true, though. A healthy ego immunizes you. So, let's adjust the settings on Yureego to recognize that negativity's simply an indication of the space that people are in at the moment. Set it to the '**don't deploy for natural human responses and occurrences, just because they're not 100 percent in peaceful synch with me**' setting. **Click.** Now, click the '**detect and ignore false alarms**' setting. **Click**. That's it. 🐾 Sometimes it takes a minute to fully update, but soon, you'll no longer be upset by someone else's negativity. You'll slowly begin to feel that 'negativity' from others is no longer a threat to you. It's just a big threat to the person displaying it. Watch it, though. Yureego is subject to automatically take control and revert to old settings, so you have to keep your eye on the settings for a while.

There's never a need to internalize the negativity of another person or a moment. Life's just '**happening**.' People are dealing with life 'happening' in their own personal ways. Much of it is a struggle. Sometimes we can see that struggle in the ways that people respond with what we call negativity. Just like life happens, negativity happens too. Recognize negativity the way you would a bird flying by. Don't draw it into your bubble. You immunize yourself with this view. It's particularly important to put these protections in place because processing irrelevant negativity is heavy duty work. It distracts you from the better things in life and drops your bubble. Having a *denser* bubble is just the tip of the iceberg. When you're not immune, you 'catch' negativity, which leads to the release of serious stress chemicals that raise your blood pressure; negatively alter your immune function; suppresses optimal digestion; and suppresses the growth and *reproductive functions*. All this for no reason? I hope you're thinking what I'm thinking.

When we make the adjustments and get immunized, our egos evolve. **Formerly perceived moments of negativity and offense, transform to moments of peaceful 'observation' from a space of protection and safety.** Whew! That's much better. Once Yureego's adjusted, it enters a restful state where it only detects *real* threats. You'll be able to observe more, no longer internalizing the negativity of others. You'll draw so much more from your life moments and the world around you because you're not distracted away from it. As you envision your immunity, negativity will begin to roll off your bubble like water off a duck's back. You'll be in a better space. Immune to nonsense. It no longer shakes you. If you ever detect negativity from now on, visualize it as being unable to penetrate the beautiful film of your bubble skin. You will become stronger and more powerful. More energy for what matters and better vision lift you up and away.

If you're *still* experiencing steady or increased negativity around you after trying your best to immunize, it's time to do a deeper diagnostic. You may have fallen onto the Miserable Station where this kind of thing is quite normal. If you've drifted, even for a minute, onto the Miserable Station, **your** state of mind will find misery in even the most positively intended words and actions. You won't see things except through misery colored glasses. Add in all the real negativity that **must** be occurring around you and that's a tough spot. Be honest with yourself. If you've taken a little dip, **it's all good, recognizing it means you're about to bring that bubble back up**!

Lay wiring for the type of thoughts that protect you from picking up negativity in the first place. I'll close this out with **7 Steps to Building Your Immunity to Negativity**:

1. Laser focus on your goals. You won't even pick up on negativity when your mind is focused steadfastly on your goals.

2. Open up a can of helium on that negativity and bounce outta there.

3. Remember that what anyone says or does has roots with *that individual* and *their state of mind*. How people think of you and behave toward you has more to do with *them*. Even when someone lavishes you with love, adoration and compliments, it's a reflection on them. Stay out of other people's heads.

4. Pivot your focus away from the negativity. Focus instead on puppies or addressing climate change for that matter. Whatever distracts your mind.

5. Never EVER show reluctance to question yourself. Sit your brain down and feel with your *heart* if the person is truly being negative. It could **easily** be that your brain received a different message than was intended by the supposed offender.

6. **Imagine that ALL things that happen to you were by design. The dense bubbles and tough situations provide experience and ultimately a stronger, wiser you. No blaming, no negativity, just excitement to step up *your* game and elevate *yourself*.**

7. Lastly, pure confidence and understanding are the kinds of thought patterns that immunize you from negativity. Increasing your confidence and developing your sense of understanding of others is key. Everyone is dealing with life the best way that they can! Hopefully, realizing that might help you to let some negativity slide off and away. That's real immunization. However you accomplish it, please get immunized.

"I CONNECT WITH LIKE MINDS"

Connect with Minds Like Yours. It's much more powerful to be surrounded by like-minded people who are on your wavelength, than powerful people who aren't.

"Any pessimists, I ain't talk to them.

Plus I ain't have no phone in my apartment then."
   – Kanye West, Touch the Sky, Late Registration.

Each of us is so different. We tend not to notice just how incredibly different each of us is. We mix in with the masses and blend, often led by popular culture, until our individualities fade into the mix. All the while, our individualities are very significant. Each of us has a purpose. Too much blending can mean humanity loses out on some of the unique qualities that were planted in us for very significant reasons. Each of us has contributions. When we connect with like minds, our individuality is encouraged to shine. In an environment of like minds, there's often a comfort that is both reassuring and stimulating. This kind of environment allows your mind to flourish. Your mind deserves that. Your individuality is encouraged. It's a beautiful thing for you, and humanity.

The Internet and social media has really opened our eyes to the vastly different fields of interest, talents and contributions that exist in our society. Science has opened our minds to the different types of personalities and psychological profiles that exist. Wherever we each fit in, we now know that there are lots of others who share our mindsets and interests.

I recently stumbled on some new science that has determined that 20 percent of the human (and animal) population has an increased sensory processing capability over the rest of the population. Who knew? Then again, it's not surprising that 80 percent aren't highly sensing *(to varying degrees)*, given what we see in the world. For those in that 20 percent, however, noticing things that others miss; reacting more to experiences whether positive or negative; processing information more often and processing more deeply could have made them feel isolated from the rest. If they already connected with like minds, their individuality as a higher sensory processing person would have been encouraged to shine. They may have found an increased comfort and reassurance in being who they naturally are. The result of connecting with like minds might be honing natural skills as the gifts to the world they were meant to be. If these highly sensing people only connected with the 80 percent of the population that's less sensitive, they may have felt odd, misunderstood or may **not** have seen their sensitivity as a gift to humanity, thus allowing those precious skills to wither.

Connecting with like minds is a form of fuel for your bubble. It's like a support group for living life. Actually, that's exactly what support groups are usually comprised of, minds that have become like one another as a result of their life experiences. I recommend that you find and connect with folks who share your frame of mind, as well as those who goal to be on the same bubble station you goal for. Like minds may not be easy to find. Keep your eyes and mind open for them. With your mind set on making the connections, it will happen. And as alluded to in Kanye's quote on the previous page, as you keep laser focused and away from opposing views, you set yourself up to rise.

"I CAN'T LOSE"

"I never lose, I either win or learn."
– Nelson Mandela

Say that one out loud, for sure. When you learn something of value to your life, you move ahead in the same way that you **feel** you do when you win. **A learn is a win**, so you never lose as long as you identify what you have learned. Get good at finding the lessons built into every so-called loss. Each lesson learned is pure helium for your bubble. Use that to rise up to the next level.

When life gives you lemons, learn the countless ways that lemons are good for you and you've found your win. Always see things in a way that makes the most sense for you and your Happiness. Remember Mandela's quote **every** time you think you have lost **anything**. Even when the whole world labels it as a loss, re-think that. Life is so much bigger than people think. It's not just about wins, it's mostly about evolving souls. 'Learns' evolve your soul way more than wins do, by the way. Take those wins all day long! Just become really good at identifying and appreciating the valuable life 'learns' that come your way. Constantly remind yourself that you can't lose.

"GRATITUDE'S MY ATTITUDE"

"You may not have a car at all,
but remember brothers and sisters,
you can still stand tall.
Just be thankful for what you got."
     – Be Thankful for What You Got, William DeVaughn.

"Stop looking at what you *ain't* got.
Start being thankful for what you *do* got.
You know what I'm sayin."
     – T.I. lyrics from Live Your Life

Please say "Gratitude's my attitude" aloud! It's important that you count your blessings each day, as a humble show of appreciation for everything you have. I mean literally counting, like 1, 2, 3, 4. It's easier to count in your head, which makes it more likely that you'll do it. Just count the first 4 that pop into your head. Do this at least once, every single solitary day. As a matter of fact, **count 4 now**.

Easy, right? It's hard to stop at just 4, but do. Do this at traffic lights, in the bed when you wake up, on an elevator, standing outside in nature while taking a deep breath of fresh air, and while praying or meditating. Whenever, wherever. Tiny acts of gratitude will lift you. It'll also bring more blessings. I believe that's because gratitude is a helium level energy. According to *Psychology Today*, scientific studies have found that gratitude is associated with a lot of what I call helium for your bubble. The act of gratitude or counting your blessings has been proven to bring increased Happiness and optimism. Gratitude is a seed for positive emotions and increased determination. Studies have also found that gratitude can lead to better sleep and more alertness. What's more, it's been scientifically found to improve health, self-esteem, relationships and progress toward your personal goals. What's not to love about gratitude? Gratitude's the attitude to take not just on a good day, but when facing all of life's crazy situations. There's always something to be thankful for. Finding the silver linings in each cloud is not easy. It's a real life skill. Don't say you don't have the skill. If you don't have it, it's because **you never wired it in** from the start. Rewire! It's **never** too late. In the meantime, make it a habit to "be thankful for what you **do** got." Gratitude is the attitude that can lift your bubble like magic.

(Psychology Today, The Healing Power of Gratitude. The many ways being grateful benefits us, available at https://www.psychologytoday.com/us/blog/compassion-matters/201511/the-healing-power-gratitude, posted on November 19, 2015.)

"NOW, IS WHAT'S UP!"

Say it loud. **Now, is what's up!** What I'm saying here is that the present moment is not only the only moment that's real, but **living with your attention directed to the present moment will make your life more wonderful**. Keep your mind focused in the present moment. The past and the future exist only in your mind, anyway. When you devote energy to the past or the future, you are taking away from your ability to process the present moment that has been laid out for your soul journey. Stay as focused as you can on your **present**. It's a gift from your Creator that you weren't meant to miss. It's even called, "the present!" Duh. There are all kinds of life lessons, experiences and bubble fuel wrapped up into every present moment.

The past, no matter how much we want to mull over it, is no longer real live stuff, so don't live there. The future's a dream. Dream big, but don't LIVE in dreams. The ONLY thing that's **real** is the present moment. The here and now, that's what's up! If you could ignore the present moment and attain Happiness, I would have skipped this part. But you cannot. So, figure out how to reflect on the past, learn from it, dream and drive for the future you want, while living solidly in the now. It always was, and will forever be the truth that right **now**, is what's up.

"Give me my flowers *now*, while I can smell 'em!"
– Grandma Haywood

That's not only humor, it's getting in the moment. Appreciating the moment and not living in the future. That's why Grandma has enjoyed such a rich and wonderful century, filled with life and Happiness.

"ON ERYTHING I LOVE ME"

DC slang translation: *I'd bet my life on the fact that my self-love is at its peak and fully encompassing.*

Say it out loud, please. I thought you'd get a kick out of the language, and it might encourage you to think and speak it more. Whatever you do, love you some YOU. Being true to yourself means filling yourself with so much self-love that you got all the love you need. Bam! **When you have an abundance of love and care for yourself, AND you feel the natural love energy from your Creator, you are power personified.** Appreciating and understanding yourself, then treating and honoring yourself as a perfect creation of nature, will prime your mind for any and everything that life has to offer.

"Learning to love yourself is the greatest love of all."
- Lyrics from The Greatest

Love is the most natural and wonderful thing there is in life. It was meant to blossom inside each of us and emanate out. The strength of our self-love has a magnetic quality. The stronger the force of your self-love, the more love that's attracted to you from others. What a cool perk. The stronger the force of your self-love, the more that love pours out of you to positively affect others. It all starts with the strength of your self-love. Never ever, ever, ever forget that one.

"Beauty begins the moment you decided to be yourself."
– Coco Chanel

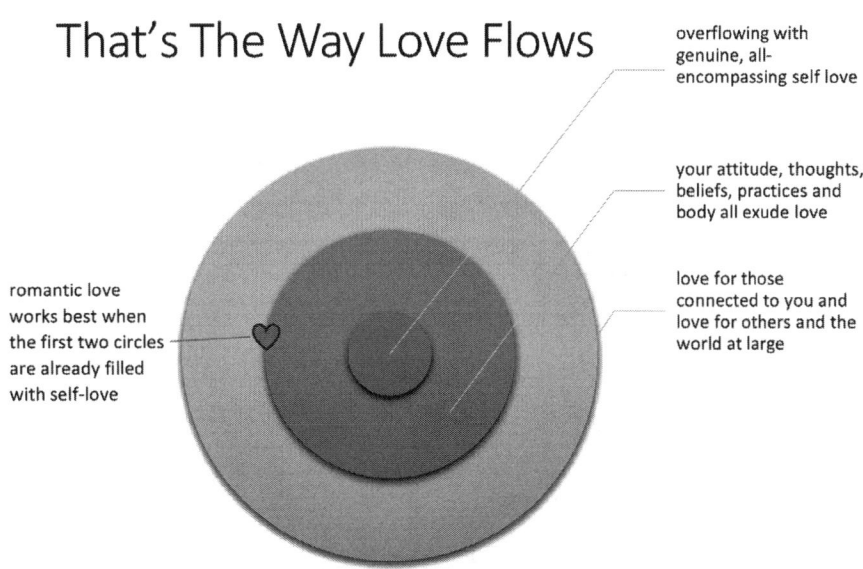

That's The Way Love Flows

overflowing with genuine, all-encompassing self love

your attitude, thoughts, beliefs, practices and body all exude love

love for those connected to you and love for others and the world at large

romantic love works best when the first two circles are already filled with self-love

Love flows from within. You must be able to generate a feeling of love from yourself without the need for love from others. **The love of yourself and the love from your Creator is *all* you *ever* truly need.** Fill up on those. Then, your love will spill over to fill your thoughts, attitude, beliefs, your body and your actions. As each level fills, love spills over into the next one. Your self-love continues to grow and flows into love for those connected to you, then love for people to whom you have no known connections, and finally to the world at large. Loving those who have no known connection to you, especially in an unconditional way, is a VERY powerful and elevated form of love. Few have enough love within themselves to go there, but I know you do. This level of love is the highest. I want this for you. You already have love for the world. I just don't want you to forget that **you have to be filled and overflowing with love for yourself first**. To try to love others without the love spilling over from genuine self-love, will leave you drained. *It don't work like that*. Love for yourself comes first. That's just the way love flows.

"You can't give what you never had."
– Earth, Wind and Fire, You Can't Hide Love.

Self-love doesn't require the approval, respect, recognition, admiration, care, concern or love of others. Your self-love should be generated straight from you. **You should always feel blissful and truly loved, if only by yourself and God. That should feel like more than enough. Feel that love filling you until it brings contentment and smiles to your face.** Love from others is a wonderful thing, but you don't *need* it. There's *no need to rely on love from others*. Just appreciate and enjoy it when you receive and feel it. When you love like this, there will always be more than enough love for you. That's the way love flows. When the strength of your self-love is so solid and real that you feel it can't be contained, you'll find that you're loving your weaknesses, your mistakes, quirks, everything about you! You are truly filled with the greatest love of all. And you stand *zero* chance of losing it.

"How deep is your love? I really need your love, cause we're livin' in a world of fools, breaking us down, when they all should let us be."
– The Doobie Brothers, lyrics from the song, How Deep is Your Love.

I know you guys must be saying, "Huh? **I LOVE myself**. Ha, ha! What's not to love?" But how **deep** is your love? Superficial or egotistical self-love doesn't count. Do you see yourself as a perfect, tiny particle of God? Do you honor yourself regardless of your appearance or accomplishments or popularity? How real, how deep is your self-love?

"So many people are on this journey to live a perfect life. I personally think it's stupid. The reason why I say it's stupid is because you have no idea what perfection is, unless you've experienced imperfection. You should embrace your flaws and fuck-ups because they help make you who you're supposed to be. Don't run away from your bullshit. Embrace it and become better."
– Kevin Hart: Irresponsible.

Developing a love for yourself, independent of anything outside of yourself, is the same skill needed to acquire Happiness independently of what's going on in your life. I hope you can see what I mean. Being filled with love for your truest self might sound like a given, in the same way that having Happiness might, but neither are given. Learning to maintain a strong flow of love within yourself, without outside forces playing into it, uses the same muscles that are required for maintaining Happiness through thick and thin. On top of that, you can't have true Happiness without loving and being true to yourself. You can get some **hits of happy**, but not sustained Happiness. Be true to yourself, making sacrifices when necessary, but never sacrifice yourself by not being true to you.

"You gotta put *your* mask on first."
– Shervonne *[humorous reference to airplane instructions, while emphasizing the fact that you have to help yourself to effectively help others :-)]*

"God wants **you** to take care of YOU!" Grandma Haywood told me this, *rather forcefully,* one day. It changed my life. I thought God wanted me to take care of others. I remembered at that moment what I instinctively knew, but had lost sight of. I needed to prioritize myself in order to be able to take care of others. Good looking out, Grandma.

Love the hand you were dealt. Love your family and your appearance. Love your talents, personality and the unique life experiences crafted for the purpose of evolving *your* soul.

SEE DENSE BUBBLES IN A BRIGHTER LIGHT

Aunt Geraldine had a sign in the basement that read, "it's hard to soar like eagles when you work with turkeys." Funny, right? Truth be told, some bubbles truly are dense and **tough** to work with. Real talk. So, how on earth do you reach Happiness when you're constantly bumping into dense bubbles? There are lots of them, I'm sad to say. Some are so rock heavy and constipated with baggage energy that they may never float up. But they could, if they wanted to and knew how. Every bubble has the ability to release heavyweight energy and rise. Every bubble has a light at the center, no matter how dim it is at the moment. Those dim bubbles might be unlikely to shine in this lifetime, but life goes on. You'll have to deal with them at some point. You'll be ready, though. The key is for you to **have a thick skin and a long fuse**. And as you might guess, it's all in how your brain processes the situation. With practice, you will eventually see the denser bubbles differently, which will help to alleviate that awful pain that comes from feeling their toxicity. With determination and practice, you'll be amazed at how well you are handling situations with dense bubbles. This skill, alone, could raise you one whole bubble station. We'll get you able to view those rock solid bubbles, and the circumstances they bring, in a much brighter light.

SOME JUST NEED A NEW "LEASH" ON LIFE

This is a play on the phrase, "A new lease on life." Look it up, millennials.

Ok, so there are some dense bubbles that are just plain vile out there. We hear about them on the news, Internet and Investigation Discovery. Sometimes evil characters exist right in our midst. It's so easy to label them as nasty or evil, throw shade in the form of disgust and turn away. Sometimes we have to cross paths with folks that don't seem to have one good thing running through their minds. It's natural to be disturbed by them. If you can steer clear of these bubbleheads, do that, but keep your energy in the right zone by recognizing that they are people too.

The last thing I want you to do is to see people as creations of anything other than God, no matter how sinister or vile *(evil)* they appear. Regardless of how wonderful or disgusting one behaves, we share a Creator. It's as simple as that. Goodness and/or vile behavior are all about how near or far one is to the **heart** of God. I like to envision each connection in terms of how long the "leash" is, so to speak, from an individual to the loving, heart energy of the Creator. The distance between vile bubbles *(who show no signs of God's love within them)* and God's 'heart energy,' is simply too darn long. Their connection is weak. Sometimes it's extremely weak. Think of it like a cell phone. It's like they have only a tiny fraction of the smallest bar of reception. While their connections are almost non-existent, there still is always some slight connection. These difficult, sometimes vile bubbles give new meaning to "off the leash," but know that, *they too,* still have a connection to our shared Creator. I never want you to ever envision anyone as completely detached from God's loving energy. Some connections are close and strong, others can be distant and crazy weak. Everyone's connection is different. What is most important is that you see everyone as a creation of God, attached to God's energy. Keep the fact that we are all connected at the forefront of your mind when you witness the longer leashes. And yes, it's fair to recognize that some need a *new* leash on life.

They Just Need A New Leash

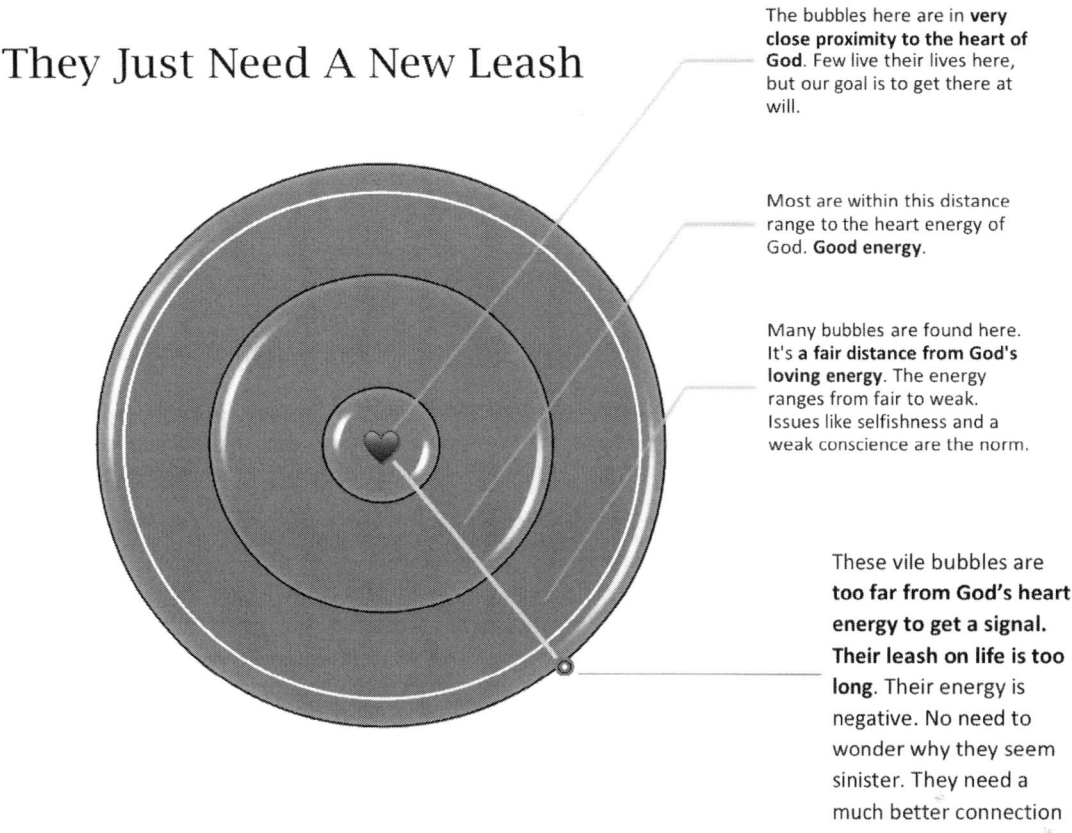

The bubbles here are in **very close proximity to the heart of God**. Few live their lives here, but our goal is to get there at will.

Most are within this distance range to the heart energy of God. **Good energy**.

Many bubbles are found here. It's **a fair distance from God's loving energy**. The energy ranges from fair to weak. Issues like selfishness and a weak conscience are the norm.

These vile bubbles are **too far from God's heart energy to get a signal. Their leash on life is too long**. Their energy is negative. No need to wonder why they seem sinister. They need a much better connection

Imagine someone walking their dog and the dog is close to them, feeling the love from their human parent. Easily receiving love, guidance and encouraging messages. Then, imagine an extremely long leash. The dog is so far from his human parent that he/she can't hear or see to receive instructions. With a ridiculously longer leash, the connection to the parent seems as if it doesn't exist. This pup can get tangled up, confused, into mischief and stands the chance of getting lost. Or worse.

Those folks with the extra-long leashes *(like those who would spill wine on your new white suit and smirk on their merry way)* are simply way too far from the heart of God. Goodness and vileness exist, yes. And they **do** have a relationship with each other. Goodness comes from the source, the heart of God. Vileness is determined by how far away something is from the heart of God. Always center everything and everyone with the force we all share. We are all brothers and sisters in this thing called life. It's not cliché, it's a natural fact. See it this way.

I believe it's healthier for *your worldview* not to give thought power to an opposing, completely separate force of evil. I try to refer to anything with an energy level *that* low, as "vile", instead. No power is given to anything but God energy, here. And *everyone* is within God's loving reach. I don't want you to fuel evil as a power source, or stand in judgment, seeing others as separate from you. Yeah, there are some real assholes out there. But, by assessing people and things as part of a separate opposing force, you blind yourself to your connectedness to them. You also pull yourself into an unhealthy mentality of superiority, however tiny it is. That doesn't feel good to me. It's more important to remember that there is no person, no thing to which you can feel completely separate. Even someone to whom you have attributed aspects of, (gasp) 'evil,' is well within God's love. As are you. A worldview of connectedness that extends to **all**, keeps everything real, and provides a helium effect to your bubble.

It's ok to pray that people will find a way to clear out their crusty, heavy bubbles, connect to God's heart and move on with their lives. They may be far from the Creator's heart at the time, but all they have to do is tighten up and shorten that leash to lighten up.

And remember to keep in mind that you only get to see a little piece of a person's soul at a time, just a slice, so don't try to judge our longer leashed friends. They may someday awaken and end up spending their next lifetime as a religious leader. We don't know! Just spread love and blessings and move on out of their way and on with your life.

"Never look down on anybody unless you're helping them up."
– Jesse Jackson

BAGGAGE HANDLERS AND OTHER CLOSE EN*CLOWN*TERS

Oops. You somehow ended up having to deal with a person who is difficult for no apparent reason. You wonder what is making them act this way. This means you're wasting time! Don't try to figure out **why**! Don't take it personally! Send them a silent prayer. Move on and let that shit go. I have to quote Sweet Brown on this one.

"Ain't nobody got time for that."
– Sweet Brown

There are people who have amazing goodness within, but they carry emotional baggage from journeys past. I read, years ago, in *The Untethered Soul* by Michael Singer, that you can imagine these folks *(and that includes you, because it could be you too)* to have thorns under their skin from experiences and perceived offenses of the past. The imaginary thorns sit just under their skin where you *can't* see them. Heaven forbid you accidentally and innocently stroke their invisible thorns. Let's say you were giving them a loving, gentle hug *(in your mind)*, maybe an innocent comment or even an intended compliment. Lo and behold, they respond with an anguished scream in the form of attitude, sarcasm or worse. You have somehow hurt them with your loving, gentle hug. Now, it's getting **real**, *fast*, and you're like, "Wait, what? No!"

The absolute first thing to remember is that this person may be filled with goodness. Don't judge. Don't label them. And do NOT get offended by their response. It **ain't** personal! They have thorns beneath the skin, that's all. When you respond by getting offended, you're exposing the baggage that **you** still need to release. You got thorns too, Boo. Now there's two of you. Don't get sucked into that drama. Just understand that they're still handling baggage from past experiences. They have not released their pains from the past. Everything they see and experience passes through the lens of pain colored glasses. It's not you. Unfortunately, they're the only ones who can help themselves by letting their own shit go. The problem is that they don't know they're carrying baggage or how to let it go. They think YOU are the problem. That's no reason to judge them. Since they don't know they have baggage, nor do they know how to release the baggage, the chances of them losing their thorns any time soon are remote. You can give them a copy of the Hookup, but your first responsibility is looking out for *you*. Is tangling up with their drama a helium-effect energy for your bubble? No, it's absolutely not. The **last** thing to do is to imagine that the source or true target of their energy is you. It's not. Don't accept that in your mind. To take it personally would be opening the door to allow unexpected, unwelcomed lead energy straight into your bubble. How doofus and self-destructive is that? When you realize you are talking to a baggage handler, also realize that there's nothing you can do to make their thorns fall off. If you keep talking, you're going to keep hurting them and hit more thorns. I'm telling you. If you want to stay engaged because it's someone you love, respect or care about, all that you can do is **listen**. Listen to understand their point of view, without making any judgments. How on God's earth can you judge a person whose life you have not lived? The only response that avoids upsetting them, and ultimately yourself, is showing that you **hear** them, understand or can relate, if you truly can. Always be honest, only say that you understand if you truly do. If you don't understand, just say, "I hear you" or maybe, "I see." It's always helpful for people to vent. If that's not an option, bow out gracefully leaving some form of positivity behind. It's ok to share any positive, uplifting words of wisdom. You can speak your mind, but don't expect it to be well received. A nod, a smile, a hug, a 'virtual text' of love and healing, a message of no worries or just a wish for a blessed day is a beautiful thing to provide.

Trying to talk through things and help folks to see that they're overreacting hardly ever works right away. When it does work, it happens over time. Most handlers don't know they're carrying baggage; have hidden thorns; are hyper-sensitive, or are being difficult to deal with as a result of the old negative energies they hold. All they know is that they were filled with goodness and you came along and said or did something hurtful for no reason. So, if it's someone you know, you can actually help soothe their hurting thorn by listening and indicating that you care and are willing to try to understand their point of view. That's often helpful. By giving them the chance to think about the interaction *(which they **will** mull over at length)*, those truly seeking to elevate will absorb some positivity from the interaction in their own time.

The chances that those *not seeking* to elevate will recognize their overreaction and identify the underlying cause of it are so razor thin that it's a waste to think about it. They will probably always think that the cause of their pain in that interaction was you. Take it on the chin, keep it moving, and by all means don't take it personally. You got your own bubble to keep afloat. Hopefully you learned something from all the listening and had an overall positive effect on them. You practiced the art of effectively handling a baggage handler at the very least. That skill is absolutely invaluable. Now, put in the extra work to make doubly sure *you're* not carrying hidden baggage, or thorns ;-).

"Don't play no silly games with me baby. No, no, no, no, it's just not my thing ... Nooo. No, no."
– Keith Sweat, lyrics from Right and a Wrong Way.

Then, you have the en*clown*ters with the 100 percent natural clowns. The difference between baggage handlers and clowns is that clowns set out to entertain. Baggage handlers don't purposely act out dramas. Their drama may come out very easily, but they're not intending to do it. It just blurts out in response to the pain of carrying the baggage. Baggage handlers are just responding to too much baggage, that's all. They're **good** people dealing with life the best way they can. Clowns, on the other hand, are in **the business**. They **seek** opportunities to engage their skills. I'm not talking about true, professional clowns, of course. We have nothing against good, wholesome clowns. I'm talking about the "downright fool" type of clown. Would you get in the car with someone dressed up as a clown, tears painted on their face, aggressively daring you to ride with them? Hell to the no! By the same token, would you let some clown mess up your chances of getting and keeping your bubble floating? My prayer is so strong that you wouldn't because if messing with clowns sounds or feels refreshing, it's because you're a clown too, needing playtime with your peeps. No judgment. Each of us is at a different stage of life, and a different bubble station. Now could be your "wrestle with clowns" stage. Do what you gotta do, but that's a tough life.

"It's your thing. Do what you wanna do. I can't tell you who to sock it to."
– The Isley Brothers.

When you get tired of that, you know what to do when confronted by a clown. STOP, DROP & ROLL. In your mind, **offer them the sign of peace**, as in, "Peace out, friend." Then, buoyantly rise.

Your bubble's dense, my friend. Gotta bounce, but catch the vapors of love! Peace out.

"They caught the vapors."
– Biz Markie, Vapors

Clowns ain't no joke. Life is too tough to bounce with clowns that challenge you. When you feel you've been directly challenged by dense, polluted bubbles, don't get sucked onto that icky, toxic, dense, constipated bubble station with them. Why would you do that? Sense that clown face with painted on tears under the mask of a normal face. Note the time, and time yourself as you exercise your skills of raising your bubble in the face of being challenged. When you go low and get down with the clown, **you're** hurtin' nothing but yourself. You're just going low. That clowns are already there! You can *descend in the clowns* if you want, but you're the one who pays.

By going low, you aren't hurting them and you're not helping either of you. You are just dropping your own bubble and feeding them with the negativity they've become addicted to. Don't feed the clowns! I'm begging you to say, "no" to that. And let me tell you, it's not easy sometimes. My SE DC raised AI manufactures adrenaline like the best of 'em, but if "I" can feel peace and control when challenged by clowns now, you can too. Let me tell you, when you master how to rise in the face of being baited by a heavy bubble clown, your lift game is strong! And don't forget to note how long it takes you to release any negative feelings from your enclownter. Once focused, each new enclownter will continuously reduce in the time it takes for you to feel completely at peace again. Go for the gold every time! They'll lose their power to upset you. You'll get good at clown spotting and shutting their game down, fast, with vapors of love. You will feel a sense of power over your life that you will never let go. Least of all for a clown.

Now. If the clown is connected with your means of making a living or an important project, you can still peep their clown status and give vapors of love while working with them. **You can.** Apparently, the ultimate challenge has been written into your story. This might mean that you are on a bubble station that you must elevate from (with the quickness)! Whatever the case may be, it's time to rise to the challenge and see what your bubble is made of. Are you capable of controlling your thoughts under pressure? Probably not **yet**, but you will be. Don't lose this challenge. Remember that how you feel is generated from your thoughts. See this person as playing the role of inspiring you toward your better self through tough challenge. Picture the clown as a sparring partner, helping you to become stronger and better through tough challenge. Picture the clown as me, testing and teaching you how to handle the toughest of challenges. Show me what you got! That may be funny, but since they're actually helping you to increase your ability to control your own thoughts, it's fair to imagine. See this as their role. Forget the clown face because this is serious, but fully accept that the person or persons *(some environments can have a real Barnum and Bailey vibe)* are on their own stations, and it's not personal to you. They're simply playing their role in helping you to improve your state of mind, through their series of performances. When negativity creeps into your thoughts, acknowledge that YOU are thinking the negative thought. It is your thought. Your feelings. Your bubble. If you can control your thoughts, you'll be feeling just fine. Focus more on YOUR desired station and how to get there. Focus on your skill to rise, and less on your clown.

Witness how your mind attracts to negativity. It's amazing. Sometimes you try and try to forget enclownters and it's hard. Just be aware that this is happening when it happens. Then, PIVOT! Direct your mind toward your well-being, your work, and the beauty that is in your life at that moment in time. Those focus areas need you! Give them your love and attention. With practice, you might feel completely indifferent or mildly amused by the clown show. Shit, it **could** get entertaining! Or you may even start to appreciate their support in helping you elevate. With practice, practice and more practice, you will hard-wire new tracks for new trains of thought. This will allow you so much peace that busy clowns will find you to be a positively boring audience. They follow energy that feeds them. If you don't feed them by being "shook" by their energy, you'll be catching **their** vapors. Odds are that they won't change, but knowing they can't get reactions from you will limit your private performances. That's a start. And sometimes, just sometimes, your positivity can provide a model of what's possible. There **are** times, rare as they are, when clown behavior is adjusted by extremely genuine, not feigned, positivity (feigned positivity is clown bait, by the way). Some can be inspired, out of the blue, by the example of someone who has control of their thoughts and emotions. It is not impossible for a clown to hang up those shoes and begin the work of evolving to higher stations. There is ALWAYS hope.

FULL DISCLOSURE:

Just because you thought you had a situation with a baggage handler or a clown, doesn't mean that it wasn't in your mind. You could have misinterpreted something and you could be the baggage handler. It's all good, though. Either way, our goal is to get you able to control your thoughts, thus able to control your feelings and your life. If you **were** the culprit, you'll be past all of that very soon. No worries.

ASSHOLES ARE PEOPLE TOO

Never judge a person by the space they're in.

By my definition, an "asshole" is a person who is unable to process their emotions/life experiences *(especially when things don't go their way)* in a way that is healthy to themselves. Therefore, they get backed up with emotional waste that should have been processed and released long ago. Unable to hold all of that in, they randomly ooze out their toxic, funky, unusable, unstable, emotional waste toward others. Assholes are baggage handlers on steroids. Their bubbles are so densely packed with old shit that they're spilling shit everywhere. But don't get mad and let your bubble drop over *their* shit. Self-preserve! But please keep in mind that they are God's creations. They're simply having a tough time with life, no matter what they try to project. Life is tough. Happy people aren't assholes, but assholes are people too.

Assholes aren't born, though. Shit builds up over time. They have no option but to release the toxic emotional waste that can no longer be contained. The baggage handler waits for stimulation, but the asshole shits freely wherever they may be. The clown, on the other hand, wants to perform. Assholes and baggage handlers and clowns, oh my! The asshole isn't trying to perform, their shit is everywhere because they can't hold it. They can't help it and never intended to be in this situation, it's just happening as a condition of too much shit in their system. As a result of emotional pain, frustration, not getting their way, and toxic exposures, their vibrational energy built up negatively and became stagnant. There's no flow to release their emotional baggage from the heart. Voila! We got a new asshole in the world. Recognize, but never judge.

They usually become trapped on the Miserable or Toxic Station, so they always find and bump heads with other assholes. This keeps them going strong. **These are mostly good, loving, wonderful, hardworking people, by the way**, who have zero idea, ZERO, that they're now another asshole. Most would be flabbergasted to see themselves on film and realize they're an asshole. Most are too pride filled to truly see themselves at all. There are some exceptions. There are assholes out there that know they are assholes and are proud of it, but *those* assholes have just been assholes for way too long. They're comfortable now. It's all they know. Their bubbles are rock solid and that's some energy to steer clear of. Still, nobody was born an asshole. If somehow, they could process their experiences and emotions and ultimately release the emotional waste (aka "shit"), that asshole would vanish. You'd be able to see the beautiful soul they truly are. Try to remember, a beautiful soul is in there under the muck. Remember, too, that if you're not hooked up with Happiness there's a chance that you too can show some asshole tendencies. Just another example of why processing your own stuff and letting shit go has immense value to the world. Please help stop the production of assholes by not becoming one. Just as important as not becoming an asshole is having the ability to release any intolerance of them. Replace intolerance with an understanding that life is tough. And relax … assholes can't burst your bubble.

BE A REAL SOLDIER, TAKE IT ON THE CHIN

What's interesting is that you, actually, are a soldier in a sense. You've been deployed to life in the physical realm for an undisclosed duration. We're each a bubble on a mission to experience life lessons and love in the physical realm. Your body is your camouflage (masking the fact that you're really a bubble of energetic information and consciousness.) Once here on Earth, many take the mission for granted, go rouge, and lose the power of the military force (figuratively, God) that sent them.

Your mission, should you choose to accept it, is to live-learn-love, as much as you can throughout the duration of your tour of duty *(not one of us humans knows the duration of anyone's tour. That's God's little secret),* and be completely you. Your role has been militarily crafted for very specific and strategic reasons. You've been given the natural skills to do your job of being **you** throughout your tour of duty. Instinct is your commander. Your heart is your communication tool to speak back to base. Stay true to who you are and your designated role, soldier. Don't yearn for or try to take the positions of others. You're a soldier! Focus on your role. You gravitate to where you're supposed to be simply by being yourself. Doing otherwise jeopardizes the **whole** mission. Experiencing every moment to the fullest and not getting all flustered is what you're expected to do. You're a soldier for heaven's sake! Take any combat you face on the chin until your tour is up. Enjoy the peacetime moments. Serve every chance you can.

By definition, to take it on the chin means to accept something unpleasant in a brave way without complaining. What I want you to do is to learn, through determination and practice, how to course through your life without being worried, bothered, angered, confused, offended, frustrated or shaken by others. People are either obviously going through or not *obviously* going through life battles. Everyone's already got battles going on of some kind. Don't engage in more with them. A true soldier doesn't engage in unnecessary battles. Pick your battles like a ***real*** soldier. And take the fake battles on the chin and keep stepping. Soldiers would ***not*** pull out the stops on a clown, for example. They respond to real threats. Learn the difference, soldier.

Accept most of your life issues in a brave way, learning from them without complaining. Don't waste your energy or your can of whoopass. We all know you're not the one ;-). Use your whoopass to whip your own ass into buoyancy and higher heights. If you pour all of that energy back into yourself instead of wasting it on unnecessary battles, you will enter a cycle of self-improvement that will force me to salute you as General. Cool, strategically on your mission and in control. That's what I'm talking about.

USE BUOYANT PERSPECTIVES AND "HELIUM-EFFECT" PRACTICES

Constantly challenged by life's ups and downs, we have to fight to keep afloat and navigate the storms. Your core philosophies are your float. Keep 'em handy and use them. When life weighs on your bubble, make helium! The right perspectives and practices for everyday life will have a helium effect on your bubble. Here's some of my secret helium recipes, just for you.

CONSTANT CHANGE IS THE NATURE OF THE UNIVERSE

"Everything must change ... That's the way of time.
Nothing and no one goes unchanged."

**– Everything Must Change,
Written by Benard Ighner, Quincy Jones/Body and Soul**

"Everything Must Change," I used to think that was the **saddest** song! It was beautiful, absolutely! But it made me tear up. Change, I hadn't really noticed, was something I connected with loss. Many of us do. Thankfully, I realized this was all wrong. Change is the nature of the Universe and when it is not embraced, anticipated, welcomed as a natural process of life, we suffer from that lack of understanding. Resistance to change brings extra strength pain to your life.

Change is one of the most basic aspects of nature. It's crazy not to embrace it. Nature, life, they flow. They flow in ever evolving patterns. There's no stopping the continuous changes of the flow of life, but we can absorb every moment of its fleeting beauty. Learn to flow with nature. Flow with the fact that everything comes and goes, by design. Embrace the change process. **The best way to be prepared for change is to live every moment fully, absorbing the beauty and lessons in each snapshot moment of your life.** Then let go and flow into the next moment. Once you accept and respond to life this way, your eyes begin to open to the beauty of the flow of change. For every door that you feel has closed, I promise you that another one opened. That's just how it is. Another door opens, full of life. You are only able to see this once you embrace the beautiful nature of life, the present moment and constant change.

It's ok to love certain moments and certain life situations. Hopefully you lived the hell out of it when it happened! That's ALL any of us can do. Live fully in our moments. Let go willingly to go live the next moment. Much of the pain of change comes from the feeling that you didn't get all that you wanted to experience out of a person, place or a situation. If you're living your life in the present moment, the chances are high that you will get everything intended for you out of every person, place or thing. Then, when the inevitable changes come, however unexpected they may be, guess who's much more ready to accept it?

Holding on to past moments is a form of resistance. Your resistance will make any pain you may have stronger, in the same way that weight resistance increases your muscles. Holding on to old situations, wishing they were current, will give you Terminator strength pain. Learn to accept, and eventually embrace the change. It's just the nature of the Universe. Flow with it.

KNOW THAT NO ONE CAN BURST YOUR BUBBLE

That bubble of yours always was and always will be. You didn't create it. It was created by a divine force. It might take on many forms on many journeys, but it can't be burst. It CAN be lowered or raised, but only by you. **You are the one who affects your bubble by how you process what happens throughout your life, and by the degree of your connection with divine energy.** As tough as life may be, it's up to you whether that bubble rises or falls. No one, absolutely no one can burst that bubble. You're indestructible. Identify more with your bubble, not your temporary *(albeit fabulous)* body and brain. Glide through life knowing you are infinitely bigger than what you see in the mirror or in those selfies. Live with the confidence that no one can burst your bubble.

LIFE IS BUT A DREAM

What if what we call life is actually more like a dream state, and once we pass from this life, we wake up to reality?

"Life is actually a dream, but we don't notice it."
– Deepak Chopra

I'm saying, "what if," but quantum physics keeps delivering evidence that this may very well be the case. As I looked for some easily understandable ways to describe this notion through quantum physics, I found an article written by Deepak, called *Is Life Really a Dream?* I was like, what? It's not just me who wondered? Before I share a couple of his excerpts, consider that accepted science tells us that we are mostly space. That all matter, including us and everything else we see is mostly empty space that's been brought into form by consciousness. This thing called life ends, like a dream does, then we likely have another one, and so on. I promise I won't put you to sleep with quantum physics talk, but let's listen to the wise Mr. Chopra for *just* a moment. I think the "life is but a dream" perspective can come in handy.

"Is life really a dream? The bald fact is that matter can be reduced to invisible waves that have no definite location in time and space."
- Chopra

Referencing the experience of those who have had near death experiences, waking (dying for a few minutes) and then coming back into the "dream" (life), Chopra expressed, "the common testimony given by those who have awakened is very significant: They no longer fear death. They identify with a self that is timeless and unbounded. They stop experiencing extremes of emotion. Their minds aren't riddled with extraneous thoughts but feel calm, alert, and open. Wounds and traumas in their past no longer return to haunt them. They tend to feel detached, as if witnessing how life unfolds rather than being tossed and tumbled in the chaotic stream of daily events ;-). At the height of the experience of waking up, they feel liberated and blissful." I had to add these quotes in because they support some of my theories. The fact that after near death experiences, people instinctively follow the Happiness Hookup is a good sign for this stuff I'm pushing to you. Whatever experience they had taught them what I'm trying to tell you. Sit that brain down. Don't you worry 'bout a thing. Let shit go. And eat popcorn and watch the movie. I promise I'm not steering you wrong.

Use the "life is but a dream" perspective to lift you when it works. What's most important about the way you think is that you think in ways that get you through this life as happy and fulfilled and spiritually evolved as possible. This concept of "life is but a dream," while it can't be proven, has no proof against it. All evidence, so far, points to life's temporary nature and that we 'wake up' to a larger, peaceful reality when we complete life. When you look at it from that perspective, it can help you to not take life too seriously. You can get into it without worrying about the small stuff because it's just a dream anyway. This perspective wasn't to be taken literally, although hey, it could literally be the case. We don't know! But it's a perspective that can be used to lighten the load on your bubble when you need it. Why would you sweat the small stuff in a dream?

Chopra, in the article entitled *Is Life Really A Dream?* goes on to say, "A skeptic would shrug these experiences off as subjective and therefore unreliable—we're all in the habit, in fact, of equating transcendent experiences with abnormality, social dysfunction, even madness. People who are different upset the social norm, which is actually evidence that the social norm is quite insecure at bottom." (Deepak Chopra, Is Life Really a Dream? Available at Choprafoundation.org).

Nobody knows exactly what life **really** is in the first place. I honestly don't care. It's liberating to imagine that life is a super lucid dream and we wake to another even more beautiful reality when we pass. Whatever the case may be, don't take life too seriously, guys. Catch yourself when you do. Whether life is but a dream or not, **merrily rowing your boat gently down the stream** and not tripping too much on anything sounds like the move.

THE ANT CONTEMPLATES GOD

I saw a piece of art with this title over twenty years ago. The title stuck with me. I believe it plays off of a bible verse from Proverbs.

> "Go to the ant, thou sluggard;
> consider her ways, and be wise."
> **– Proverbs 6:6**

Scientists now believe that **consciousness is universal and carried within each particle of matter.** That means consciousness exists, *on some level*, in every last thing in the Universe.

It's perplexing to hear, "the ant contemplates God," because how's that little sucker gonna contemplate anything without a brain? But, if there's some form of universal consciousness within them, they wouldn't need a brain. All they would have to do is be. Just by being, they might have built-in understanding of God. Maybe the message in the phrase is not that the ant contemplates God, but that the thought is silly because the ant doesn't HAVE to contemplate God. Meanwhile, we humans toil over theology trying to define, describe and understand the mind of God. Nature, on the other hand, direct-connects, skipping all the brainwork.

POINT #1: DON'T OVERTHINK SHIT. TAP YOUR INSTINCT.

There's a universal consciousness within you. You have a direct-connect, hotline to Universal wisdom as does every person and everything. Even the ant has a direct-connect to universal consciousness. Ants don't have to contemplate God. Nor do we. Each one of us has an innate ability to tap universal wisdom and a direct-connection to our creative force. Your intuition holds a lot of power for you. For lightness of mind, lift up off the brain and tap into your intuition a little more. The ant probably has a better understanding of God than we do. We're too busy trying fit God into our minds.

We live in an infinite universe of which we know very, very little. We're learning every day, but that knowledge could be pale in comparison to the universal consciousness we already carry within us. The consciousness that exists naturally within each of us may have the power to guide us if we allow ourselves to flow. Imagine information, provided by nature/the divine/God embedded in your bubble that you can tap. *(Hee, hee, hee, you might laugh at this. But you don't laugh when you see those movies showing people reaching into the thin air and swiping their hands left and right to see information and videos on invisible computers in real time, do you? No. You're waiting for that. I'm saying, a biological equivalent to that already exists).*

Information is embedded in your bubble. Seriously. So, don't rely on understanding the most important things in life with your brain. Have a little more confidence that you have innate access to the most important things you need to know, and an innate understanding of life. We all do. We just need to tap it. Tap into your instinct, then use it.

POINT #2: BE HUMBLED. THERE'S A BIGGER PICTURE IN PLAY. JUST DO YOUR WORK.

We're limited in our ability to know all. It's never going to happen. We'll never know **all**. It's a little arrogant to think our brains have that capacity. We should accept our limitations on that, and be cool with it. I'm just as likely to comprehend ALL as the ant. I'm totally cool with that. We don't need to know everything. We just need to hustle. Consider her ways and be wise ;-).

Be humbled by the big picture. This will allow you to be as content as the ant appears to be with life. The knowledge you need to be happy is already within you, embedded in the fiber of your being, as it is in each of us, ants and clowns alike. We don't have to know every darn thing and figure out everything with our AI. Our hearts are already connected to the truth and have a direct connection to the Universal consciousness. And just as an ant farm is a small part of life on earth, earth and humanity is an infinitesimally small part of a really, really big picture. When you think big, astrophysics big, where do we fit in? If you go big enough, you'd need an electron microscope to see the Milky Way! Earth is like a microscopic speck in the Universe, and there are **billions of universes,** y'all! Einstein has tried to hip us to the fact that there are parallel universes in the same space of the billions of universes we know exist. You got all that? I don't. But to put it in other words: It's not that serious. Just chill on all that brain power when it comes to your Happiness (I'm purposely repeating this for your rewiring ;-). Be guided by your intuition and keep it moving like the ant. Consider her ways, thou sluggard!

WORDS TO LIVE BY

I saw this on a documentary and it stuck with me. If I could remember which one, I'd surely share. It touted that these words can release negativity and generate positive emotional energy.

I apologize

This one was actually, "I'm sorry," but Daddy insisted a long time ago, that I not use this form of apology saying, "Ey, man. Ain't nothin' sorry **'bout** you! I don't like it. Find somethin' else to say." He was so, so serious. So, we agreed on "my apologies" or "I apologize," the latter being for more intimate situations only. Lol. Daddy was a pistol, but his wisdom was (is) always real and invaluable.

Please forgive me

Thank you

I love you

Simply typing these words made me smile. Every chance that you have to say them aloud, **do it**. Get in the habit of using them, daily. These are words to live by. Use them without hesitation. Each is absolutely perfect for your daily prayer.

WHEN LIFE'S A BLUR YOU CAN'T FOCUS ON WHAT COUNTS

Focus is powerful. Very powerful. A spray can't touch the power of a laser. Focus counts. When you are all over the place, and speeding your way through life, you can't truly focus on anything. It's all a blur! Don't live a blurred life. *Slowww* down partner. Have one *important* thing to focus on at a time, *if possible*. Try your best to simplify your life. Simplify until your life is a custom fit, perfectly simplified for **you**. Don't tell yourself, and don't believe that it's not possible. You are the one who's in charge. It's your life. Make time to focus on everything that is important to you. Let life be a blur at your own risk.

IT IS WRITTEN. QUE SERA SERA

"Que sera, sera. Whatever will be, will be.

The future's not ours to see.

Que sera, sera."
– Doris Day

There's a pre-determined code written into every human being that programs our appearance and health (called DNA). I believe a code is also written into our lives somehow (It's not scientifically proven, of course, but ancient wisdom keeps getting proved true. Slowly but surely. So, I'm taking a chance and rolling with my instinct and ancient wisdom on this one. Ancient wisdom calls that life programming, "destiny"). I believe that in some strange way, our stories are written, similarly, to how our DNA is written.

In the same way that DNA can be overwritten and changed, I think our stories can be overwritten and changed too. I'm cool with being like the ant on this. **I don't know**! I can only tell you what I'm sensing. I sense that choice and prayer are **critical** aspects of our lives. We're to actively live, making decisions and choosing paths as we attempt to carve out our lives. At the same time, my sense is that our job is to learn, dream, hustle and very graciously accept destiny.

We get the most bang for our buck from a combination of acceptance (*acceptance for what happens as if it was already written*) **and pushing for our dreams** (*working, dreaming, believing, praying, because you do hold the power to create*). Smart people can clearly see that it's not possible for everything to be already written AND for us to also have the power to create and/or utilize prayer, because it's contrary to the laws of reality. It doesn't make sense. Or does it, smart people? Hmmm. Do we really have the ability to understand reality or is it beyond the ability of our brains? [Look to the ant, you sluggard ;-)] I don't see a contradiction, though. Reality is deep and might **not** fit neatly into our computer brains. We may never know the true nature of reality. We don't have to know. Whatever will be, will be.

There's no contradiction in having a drive for your dreams, praying hard every day, and taking a 'Que, Sera, Sera' attitude about life. I, personally, feel peace with this way of dreaming, pushing and accepting. I recommend it for you. Push, dream, accept … push, dream, accept … then, repeat.

Ps- Grandma Davis had a music box that I would wind up and play as a kid. It played "Que Sera Sera." I would hear her use those words many, many times. As she slowly gestured with her delicate grandma hands, eyebrows gently raised, "Que Sera Sera," she would say. It seemed to give peace to any and every situation. It cemented the phrase and the concept in my mind. "Whatever will be will be. The future's not ours to see. Que Sera Sera." Turns out, that's a powerful belief. And the idea that we shouldn't hope and pray and work tirelessly to achieve positive outcomes **never ever** came to my mind when embracing this philosophy. It meant, to me, that despite our hopes and prayers and tireless work towards the outcomes we want, we should accept and embrace the results. Que Sera Sera. I hope those three little words will bring peace to your life as they have for mine. Whatever will be, will be. Accept the things that happen in your life, while pushing toward your dreams with all you've got. *(It's Kay sir RAH, sir RAH, btw).*

THE ONLY THING TO TAKE PERSONAL IS "PERSONAL TIME"

"When they go low, we go high."
  – Michelle Obama *(She's too cool. Mom's proud to share the name, just sayin')*

Guys, don't take anything personally, except personal time. Please 🙏. I gave you guys *The Four Agreements* by Don Miguel Ruiz, years ago. I'm not even sure if you read it, but one of the agreements was to not take anything personally. I agree **wholeheartedly**, and here's my advice:

Even if someone has blatantly mistreated you, that's just a reflection of how long their leash is. How you process it and move on, reflects the length of yours.

Everything you say, think and do to others is all about **you**. Your thoughts and behaviors speak to your preferences, biases, and character more than anything. If you are angry or jealous, you may respond to others in a way that conveys that, if only through nuances. If you are loving and caring and content, you will reflect that when you deal with others. If you have a highly favorable concept of beauty or success, you may respond to those who possess those qualities differently than you would those who you feel don't. What you think, say and do is all about you.

ON THE OTHER HAND, what others say about you, to you and/or do to you is all about THEM. Good or bad. For God's sake, don't take other people's responses or lack of response as some measure of YOU. On top of the fact that their responses are all about them being them, your ego *(ALWAYS to blame in the "I'm offended" situation. Sorry to hip you.)* could *easily* be misconstruing what was intended. **Easily**. In this case you'd be engaging in self-harm, which is ludicrous. So, let it go. Sit your ego down. Whatever you "think" happened, let it go! I feel petty just *processing* bullshit. Err on the side of caution and let **all** offenses go. Let your bubble be a 'no offense' zone.

If you are busy, laser focused on fulfilling your life dreams and acting on your most positive feelings, there will be **no space** in your life to trip out on how others respond to YOU. Again, how others respond to you, says everything about *them* … not you. Even if someone says you're pretty or handsome, it's because that's how "they" see it. That's technically *their* business, but thanks, right? Compliments are cool, but it's only how **you** feel about **yourself** that matters. Focus there.

After you've mastered the art of not taking things personally, you can listen to people with peace and calm, even when their thoughts, ideas and beliefs differ dramatically from yours. You can listen, and actually understand. Even when you perceive criticism from others (healthy egos know how to benefit from perceived criticism), you'll be unscathed. All benefits go to you as you learn so much more about the world around you.

Every time you even think about taking something personal, "take personal time" to rise above those low level feelings and do something constructive. Rid yourself of the negative energy that you have inadvertently begun to generate just by thinking like that. Go workout or something.

The truth of why you're offended is because Yureego threw a flag on the field before the offending situation even got underway. Yureego's fast as lightning and always looking for an offense. "Flag on the field! 👀 Flag on the field!" Leaving you feeling offended by everyday life situations. That puts you at a disadvantage. A thicker skin can open you up to advantages that may be right in your face. How much constructive criticism is negated and turned into bubble dropping drama? Sometimes the *so-called* criticism that upset you, could've been accepted as a life-changing gift used to move forward in positive ways. With certainty, Yureego would miss it.

This philosophy alone could eliminate 99 percent of drama from your life. I wish everyone lived by this.

NOT GETTING YOUR WAY? WELL, THAT'S OK

I really hate to break this to you, but life is not a "you always get your way" type of program. It's actually more of a "you **ain't** getting your way, on purpose" type of program. Rise to the challenge. Don't sweat it. When things don't go our way, our soul is being challenged. That means some soul growth is in store. That's a good thing. That's what challenge is for. Rise to the challenge instead of whining and feeling sad. Drop two tears in a bucket and ___ it!

Accept it, try to learn something from it and move on to the next thing. Stop, drop and roll. We're supposed to learn and grow in these instances. You're not getting your way? Ok. What's next? Let's go!

Unfortunately, many people don't process it like that, instead, pain, disappointment, anger and frustration are generated and we roll all in it like Diva when she finds a funky patch of something foul in the grass. Stop rolling in negative emotions! I feel like I shouldn't have to tell you this at this point, but since it's a trait of our AI to do this, I have to reiterate. As kids, we could let things "go" much faster. Disappointments would last for a minute, ten minutes tops, then we'd be off playing somewhere. That's what you have to do now. Let the disappointments go. Learn something from it. Go play somewhere and do something you love.

Sometimes things don't go your way because you're being guided in another direction and you won't make the turn. You keep driving down a road that holds a dead end for you. There's always another open road. Pivot to the open road. Keep an open mind to that and stay encouraged.

When you don't get your way and can't let the feelings of disappointment go, those negative emotions carry negative energy that has to go *somewhere*. Sometimes people try to hold it within, but they usually **share** that energy, unfortunately. This is when sharing does not mean caring. And while they're not usually doing it on purpose, that infectious energy is like a virus. It's harmful to those who receive it. Learning to drop disappointments quickly and having the skill to move on without much pause is a life skill worth more than gold.

As you become good at letting disappointments drop away from you, you open up space for awesome energy to fill you. That energy can be used to propel you forward. Dropping disappointments quickly also eliminates the spread of that toxic energy. Don't be that person that lets disappointment fester, then **shares** all the toxic energy. Tolerate that energy for no longer than one hour, tops! Once you get good at it, fifteen to thirty minutes is all the time you need to process and move on. To hold on to that negativity until it infects you, then others, isn't very nice. Be a hero. Save yourself and others. Let the moment that things don't go your way, be the start of feeling ok. Be cool with the fact that the Universe is not under your control.

THE ART OF CONVERSATION: TRYING TO PROVE YOU'RE RIGHT IS *WRONG* (FOR LACK OF A BETTER WORD)

Don't **NEED** to be understood, heard, accepted or believed. Don't be that bubble.

Conversations are sharing sessions. When talking with people, make sure you don't catch yourself **stuck** on proving that you're right about something. If you've made your point, chill, unless your point of view is requested. Instead of a focus on what's right or wrong when it comes to opinions, thoughts, points of view, "facts," feelings or anything else, **it's much more valuable to notice the viewpoints of others as the treasures they are.** Conversations are like live, real-time, hands on sociology lessons. Observe, absorb, learn about the life and mind of someone else. You already know what you think, right? 🧑 Here's an opportunity to learn how others process life. This is good for your growth and exposure. I actually recommend that you see the views of others as works of art. When in conversation, no matter if it's two minutes with a stranger, imagine yourself checking out a piece of art in a museum. The art you are observing is live audio, delivered straight to you, out of all the people in the world. It can be a blessing or simply entertainment. Just take it in. Take in those thought, belief creations and learn about the artist, the person(s) you are communicating with, through their expression with you. Some thoughts might seem realistic, some "facts" might seem a bit abstract, but see each as valuable bits of information. You can pick up on the nuances of their personalities and the depths of their feelings if you pay attention. The intricacies of their perspective might be amazing to you, if you *truly listen* to people.

There is not enough of that going around. The number one reason why there's not enough of that is because it's impossible to get into someone else's point of view while focused on your own. And that's what usually happens. As soon as we hear the first words that connect to a hard-wired thought of our own, our brains go to work. Their words have different roots in their own minds. They're sharing their art with every sentence. But instead of getting into what they are sharing, in an instant, your mind is reaching the conclusions you **already had** before the conversation ensued. You're not even truly hearing the person. You think you are, but you're only glancing with your ears. You are simultaneously processing your own old thoughts, which dilutes the experience. You're in your own museum, looking, again, at your own creations. Stuck in your museum, you're missing out on brand new things and most especially the beautiful art of the conversation. You hear them, but are you listening?

No one else in the whole wide world sees the world the way you do. Just you. Accept your truth as "yours," and give others that same opportunity to have "theirs." Listen to the truths of others to learn more. It's an advantage to your spiritual growth. Your truth could change and that's ok. Even when viewpoints **seem** to be fully shared, there are differences. There are so many ways that your brain can see things differently than the next person. Consider optical illusions. Have you ever been floored by one? Think of a person who is colorblind. They are right about seeing green when you see something else. Our brains produce different outcomes based on our experiences and a whole host of other factors. With everyone genuinely seeing things based on their unique point of view, being "right" is completely relative. Unless it's life or death *(or loss of limb or something super serious)*, if you're not seeing eye to eye, that means you don't see eye to eye. It means nothing except that your experiences, your thoughts and brain wiring is different. You already knew that. You could've had the exact same experience, same information at the same time and still see it completely differently. It's healthy to embrace your own points of view while keeping an open mind. Change is the nature of the Universe. You become richer as you absorb the realities of others. Absorb without having to *correct* the thoughts and beliefs of others. Your viewpoint on the thing that you were *right* about might change over time from exposure to new ideas and information. And that's not just ok, that's actually a beautiful possibility. What beautiful results could be born from humanity sharing themselves in positive ways? Being completely accepting and as understanding as possible of the viewpoints of others is pure elevation for you.

The thing that is unhealthy is closing your mind to other points of view, insisting yours is **the right one**. That's not just unhealthy mentally, but it's unhealthy physically and spiritually. Conversations, when done well, should not be battles. Don't be that person who treats it so. What's happening when you do this, is your brain is trying to "represent." When you do this, you can envision yourself challenging someone in a dance battle, waiting with your arms folded, sometimes not waiting, just busting out some moves, spinning on the floor with your point of view. Come on, man? Don't break your neck. Shut that down, throw in the towel. Instead of doing all the entertaining, be entertained sometimes. Just listen to understand another person.

Do we need to be "right," or do we need to navigate through life in a way that brings love, Happiness and evolution to ourselves and others? You can have both sometimes if you prioritize the art of truly listening, and putting your energy into truly understanding people. Truly listening to others, in itself, is a form of love and positive energy. It holds the potential to bring Happiness to both you and the person sharing their thoughts with you. Everyone stands the chance to evolve from the sharing of themselves through their points of view. Don't spoil this beautiful exchange by needing to be right. It takes peace of mind and tolerance to be able to see the art in the expressions of others. That peace of mind is the key to a vault of treasures about the world we live in. When your mind is humbled and at peace, your auto-defense system won't deploy. You won't end up in disagreements over which artwork is "right." This is much healthier for you. What's more, the beautiful space you are in usually makes the other person feel great to be able to express themselves without being ignored, half-listened to, or worse, rejected as wrong. Offer what you have, but don't push if they're not receptive.

If you're listening to the point of view of someone whose view is in contrast to yours, and it causes a weird feeling of adrenaline flowing or any anxiety, take it as a clue. There's some faulty hard-wiring in your brain that's causing that. Don't ignore that feeling. Recognize it and name it. It'll be tough to pinpoint what's happening, so let me hip you: Your brain had already solidly accepted something as fact and someone is now challenging that, or jeopardizing themselves with false information. Gasp! •• Yureego threw a flag on the field and your defense system auto-engaged. You must defend yourself and/or save that poor soul! You engage to save the day by setting the record straight.

It happens. Since we want to elevate our minds and our lives, it's time to control that. That auto-response is harmful in a few ways. It's harmful to your body for starters. Adrenaline ain't no joke. Harmful effects to your body shouldn't be triggered by the opinions of others. Blame it on your brainwork. But no worries, we're going to get you skilled at controlling Yureego, by first training it to stand down in conversations with people who are just socializing with you. It's time to re-wire tracks for new responses to conversations. Remember that you don't need confirmation of your views. You don't even have to hold onto your views. What's more, you *could* be ... dunt, dunt, dunt, dah ... WRONG. Does that word hurt a little bit? Work on that until you don't give a shit. The quality of what you have to say will immediately elevate. Your world will open up because **you** have. When you *could* be wrong and it's totally cool, you're on your way to Happiness. You'll have a true appreciation of the wonderful diversity of viewpoints and "facts" accepted by others.

You can create new artwork in the museum of your mind, sometimes by the end of a two minute conversation with a stranger. Don't miss your blessings. Your thoughts are right for you at the time that you have them. They are your art. You don't need confirmation! Feel confident about your views, but be totally ok with learning and letting some of them go to create new ones. The thing that undermines your intellect most is holding tight to the notion that you already "got it," and you don't want or need to hear what anyone else has to share. You know the deal and you don't need or want exposure to the rest of humanity's expressions? Really? That not only isn't smart, it's also indicative of insecurity, and we can't have any of that y'all. Always be open to listening and learning from others. Even when you disagree. Listen when possible. In the same way that don't look to win by browsing art in a gallery, even if yours is displayed in there, you don't look to win in conversations. Post your art, appreciate the work of others.

This might not be easy at first. It's the nature of our brains to hold on tight to our thoughts. On top of that, Yureego is always at work fighting to protect our "brand," insisting that our thoughts, ideas and beliefs are right and on point. Your ego builds a house of cards for yourself that can fall at the drop of a hat. That's why we work so hard to prove and believe we are "right," it's the ego protecting the house of belief cards you've built. Knock it down yourself. Abandon the need to prove or control the situation. You'll surely release *some* baggage that you were holding. You'll release baggage that you were in the process of packing.

Another really good reason to be open and relaxed about sharing and learning through conversations is that our brains can EASILY program thoughts that are not in our own best interest. Being open can present an opportunity to change that. Add that to the fact that change is the nature of the world we live in. Even universally accepted facts are relative. Things change on a dime. What was true at one moment can be very different the next. It makes sense to stay open, ESPECIALLY if we desire to be "right" about something.

The best way to start is to walk into conversations as if you're walking into that art gallery. Turn off Yureego the way you might turn off your cell phone. You will enjoy a focus on the art of the conversation more than you think. The skill to do this comes *only* with some determined practice.

As you begin to look deeper into conversations, you might be amazed at how much more you begin to see about people. You may be surprised by the value of what this presents to your life. I caution you not to automatically place more value on "experts" or the words of people with status or education or wealth. That's like only valuing the art of the great masters or notable artists. What? Open your mind. See the words of the homeless person as a Basquiat. Remember when the homeless guy at the shelter went on video to share, "you never know when that little thing you've done means the world to someone else." Taking the time to listen to him, and the fact that he took that moment to share his feelings from his heart, elevated our experience of giving that day. His words had impact in 'my' life, quite frankly. That brief encounter with the homeless man was a gift, equal to the moment when Obama actually responded, "You know I will," when I had the opportunity to tell him to "hang in there," during a handshake in the Rose Garden (cool, right? It took all of **one second, total.** But it was crazy, because I had envisioned telling him to "hang in there," months before that totally unexpected moment actually happened). Don't think I'm kidding when I say that *each* of those moments, the simple sharing of a few words, especially the listening, were like living moments of art. Equally valuable to me.

When you see value in all people and their different points of view as artistic creations of humanity, your mind is primed for lift. You no longer find it necessary for their expressions to match yours. You no longer deploy Yureego and feel all tense for no reason in the middle of someone sharing a message. You no longer assign a right or wrong to the thoughts of others, or your own. You no longer allow your brain to assess the quality of the messenger or the significance of their message, or the things behind their words. You may not understand. You *can* disagree. You should respect. I hope you will appreciate. There are no coincidences. If someone is trying to share a thought with you, don't block it, no matter how much it contradicts your viewpoint. **Valuable clues that could pivot your life path could be embedded in the thoughts and beliefs of others**. The moments in which we share exchanges with people are such beautiful things. Everyone loves to be truly listened to. It's an easy gift that you can give to others to truly listen. Your thoughts are safe and secure. You are smart. Your brand is strong. Don't fall for Yureego's alarms. Lose the need to be right and enjoy diverse dialogue even more.

I've touched on this before, but since it can sometimes be THE thing standing between you and Happiness, let me touch on this again in a slightly different way. It's part of our culture, and many cultures of the world, to associate self-worth with the value of our minds. It starts when we're babies. "Oh, he or she is so smart!" That baby gets extra smiles and attention. Some of us have had the wonderful reinforcement in school and throughout our lives of having our brain abilities heralded as "sharp," "exceptional," "superior," and something to be honored. From this alone, we're hard-wired to the emotion that comes from being right. It can be reassuring and soothing every time we're right. Those who did not receive all the accolades are sometimes just as hard-wired with the need to be right. Being right has been wired in our minds to be the road to self-esteem, respect and achievement. Since we were tots, we've associated being right with good feelings. Throughout schooling it symbolized the power of our brains. Being right brought reward throughout our childhoods and it continues in employment. And that's all very understandable. All well and good. Except when it comes to conversations with other people in life. Those of us who pride ourselves on being smart have tougher times with not being right. When talking with people outside of work or school, get over the need to be right. It's just **not** that serious!

"Facts" are easy to feel "right" about. But when it comes to topics involving people, be aware, our brains have trouble processing things properly. People are **complex** and can't be processed through your brain alone. The same way that Siri and Alexa can't truly "get" you, your brain's a billion times more sophisticated than Siri or Alexa, but it still can't truly "get" where people are coming from. The possibilities of what's going on behind the scenes with people are far too broad to process. When it comes to situations, questions or assessments involving people, never assume that you or anyone else truly KNOWS what's up. People are too complex and there's too many variables we cannot know. All you can do in this case is use your senses and follow your heart.

Once you release the need to be right, that openness and relaxed nature will open up more opportunities for your mind and soul to grow. Accept that people see things completely differently and what's true one day can already be false by some new development that you just don't know about yet. Become determined to enjoy and embrace different beliefs and points of view as the thing that makes each of us unique. Accept varying opinions on things that your brain KNOWS as fact. Be open. Share your point of view with no need to be right or any need to change the points of view of others. If we each understood that and released the need for others to accept or agree with "our truth," we might achieve world peace.

Sometimes you just want to share your viewpoint with someone. Beware, there are those that don't want to hear you. Lol. And it's cool. No worries. They don't mind hearing confirmation of their own viewpoints, but that's it. Perhaps they have good reasons for this. We don't care. Just remember **when**, not **if**, you're in a conversation with someone, and you notice that your differing viewpoint is causing them grief, their defense system has activated and that won't change during the conversation. They are *not* going to listen and care about your viewpoint. Not now. And it's A-OK. No sweat because it's not a big deal. Let them be. Sit your mind down and train it to let that shit go. Just to keep the bubbles in the up direction, let it go. This person may not be a good conversationalist for you, or it could simply be that you're discussing an issue that's sensitive. It could be bad timing. Why? That is so far out of your jurisdiction, we're not going there. All you need to process is that it ain't personal. If someone is, for whatever reason, unable to listen to your point of view, it's probably because they're just *unable* to do it. They have their reasons. Let that shit go. Have respect for their reasons. Don't be the person that lets their defense system activate because someone is not listening to you or is in stark disagreement with your point of view. Don't allow your energy field to shift because someone insists on a different reality. Don't fret because someone doesn't want to hear you right now. Come on guys. It's all good. There are wonderful conversationalists that will listen to you. If you really, really want to talk, strike up that conversation, later, to share your thoughts with someone who listens and enjoys learning about other's points of view.

"Children do not yet know that the world doesn't revolve around them. As grown-ups, dare we admit to ourselves that we, too, have a collective immaturity of view? Dare we admit that our thoughts and behaviors spring from a belief that the world revolves around us? Apparently not. Yet evidence abounds. Part the curtains of society's racial, religious, national, and cultural conflicts, and you find the human ego turning the knobs and pulling the levers." (Neil DeGrasse Tyson, Astrophysics for People in a Hurry.)

So, long story short, develop a genuine comfort with the fact that **if** no one else in the world sees things the way you do or even respects, understands or accepts your point of view, **you're good**. You're comfortable. No defense was evoked. You're incredibly secure, fully enveloped with peace, confidence, assurance and love.

Be so secure in the beauty of the "art" of your thoughts and perspectives that you see the "artwork" of others with an eye for detail. Be open enough to listen with true appreciation that whether it meshes with your mind or not, what others have to say is but another expression of humanity in this moment in time. Be filled with grace and peace of mind, and see being right as wrong when it comes to conversations.

Brainwork doesn't elevate your bubble. All that matters is that you live and learn and love.

DON'T CLAIM THAT BAGGAGE! LOSE "IT" OR BE THE "*LOSER*"

"Sometimes the past should be abandoned, yes.
Life is a journey and you can't carry everything with you."
  - Ha Jin

How can you be "completely" filled with goodness if you have a bubble constipated with heavy, toxic emotional baggage? That math isn't working. Your baggage is YOU. You are a total of your good wondrous energy, plus the weight of your baggage. If you carry around a bunch of unresolved emotions, the chances exist that you're an asshole and don't even know it. Others would though. People can sense baggage. It's like when you can't smell something because your nose became desensitized to the odor. You get used to your funky energy, but others aren't. They're not going to tell you. Daring ones may try, but even from a space of love and courage, they'll only hurt your feelings because your baggage makes you hypersensitive. The only one who can stop this funky cycle is you.

I was watching a Prime series the other evening. One of the characters turned to a group of guys as he's laying out an emergency plan to pull everyone through a crisis situation. He asks very quickly, very seriously, "Ok, who wants to f____ a hobo?" It's an intense and serious moment. The guys all want to do what's necessary, but are looking confused and darting eyes at one another and away, seeing which one steps up. Even to get themselves out of the crisis, no one speaks up. They just look around nervously. Hey look, we know that hobos are having their soul journey. We recognize our connectedness to them and their spiritual equality with us, of course. I didn't write that script and I don't apologize for exploding in laughter at their reaction. The analogy here is that as you carry around your old baggage you halt the progress of your life in ways that you don't see. But others can. You put your life in a state of confusion and limbo. Your bubble is dense and constipated from the baggage. You're likely giving off the same vibes that those guys were getting from thinking about intimacy with a hobo. Put all that shit down and clean up. Until you do Happiness is *just one* of the many great things that won't be attracted to you.

I'll talk more on this in the "When Shit Gets Real" section, but let me introduce here that the emotions and pain that you experience during life's trials and tribulations are real live bundles of negative heaviness inside of you. They **must** be processed and released so that you can lighten up. As I said before, if you don't process and eliminate, your life will be weighed down by that "baggage energy," AKA shit. You'll lug it everywhere you go. And it ain't Gucci luggage. It's embarrassing, dilapidated homemade luggage. While you're strutting, pushing out love and positivity, your whack baggage 👀 is giving off a weird vibe.

"What's wrong with the world mama…I think the whole world addicted to the drama. Only attracted to things that'll bring you trauma."
– Black Eyed Peas, Where is the Love?

Baggage energy hides well. You won't know you have it, unless you pick up on how you truly feel when you think of certain things. The clues to your baggage energy are in your emotions in certain circumstances, certain experiences. Learn to identify whether you truly have great energy when you think of things that have caused you grief. If you feel anything other than peace, understanding and/or acceptance, you're likely harboring baggage. Remember that your baggage is exactly that … **your** baggage. Your baggage sits under your skin like those hidden thorns I spoke of. Nobody can see the thorns, not even you. It's so crazy! You don't even know they're there! But an innocent topic of conversation or a picture or a random comment, anything can trigger an emotion because the thorn is there. You can't do anything without getting hurt! Nobody can do anything around you without taking the chance of accidentally hurting you. You're rendered way too sensitive and fragile because of these thorns. This is a different sensitivity than the sensitivity to perceive more of what's going on in the world. **This sensitivity** is a clear disadvantage to you and everyone you come into contact with. You actually become the problem. Time for all homemade baggage to get checked.

"Spark joy in your world through tidying up!"
– Marie Kondo

It's time to clear out your baggage energy. Start taking the time to notice your feelings and the thoughts that trigger them. This isn't optional, y'all. Once you notice a feeling that you don't enjoy, don't be satisfied with the notion that it's someone else's fault or brought about by situations beyond your control. **YOU are THE ONE who is 100 percent responsible for how you feel.** Wake up to that fact right now. Accept that it's **your** method of processing that caused it. You accept this, right? Well then, behold, a door has already opened and a new chapter of your life is being written, even as you read. Because you accept responsibility, change has already started!

All you have to do now is some serious house cleaning. Your mind is the house, of course. Take time to turn inward with the intention of cleaning up. Use quiet time to yourself and use meditation as primers to get your mind in the right place. Then, STOP, DROP and ROLL this way:

1. Identify the thought that causes the discomfort or pain.
2. Take any possible positive lesson that you can from the experience that triggered the baggage. There is always, always, a lesson that you can take away from **every** experience. Put that AI to some REAL use! Find a positive. Find a lesson. Learn it.
3. Shit the rest out. Flush it away! Keep the lesson and run with it.

I don't enjoy sounding like a broken record, but at the end of the day, it all boils down to the same thing. Hold on to the lessons you can get out of life. Save the things of value and let the rest go. Baggage spreads throughout your bubble, dulling your vibration. It clouds your vision. It poisons your body and mind. It limits your life. Ain't nobody got time for that!

JEALOUSY: <u>J</u>UST. <u>E</u>NVIOUS. <u>A</u>ND. <u>L</u>OUSY

Jealousy spurs from comparing ourselves to others, wanting what someone else has or believing that someone has an advantage over us. A weird feeling can overcome us. We believe that someone will or already has received **something** that we want for ourselves. Nobody likes the feeling of jealousy. The feeling isn't good. **Beneath the surface of jealousy is *always* a sense of inadequacy, loss of some type, a sense of insecurity and/or unhealthy competition**. It sucks talking about jealousy, but it's such a bubble dropping emotion that I have no choice. We must lay tracks for trains of thought that carry you up, up and away from jealousy forever.

The math on jealousy's not hard at all.
Yureego's too big + your heart's too small.

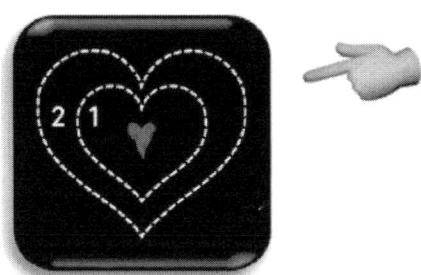

Jealousy is triggered by faulty brain processing. The brain, in some twisted effort to strengthen your position in life, sends out alarms that you're at some form of disadvantage. They're false alarms, of course. That doesn't stop the deployment of your defense system. That's how jealousy gets triggered, but that's not the only cause.

The cause of jealousy is the toxic combination of **insufficient self-love** *(leaving inadequate love for others)*, and a **heart/mind imbalance**. Yureego detects this situation and steps in to save the day. It auto-sets your security alarm. Threats constantly lurk. 👀 There! Someone enters the picture having something you view as desirable *for yourself* and we got a "flag on the field!" Jealousy activates at lightning speed and fills the body with ugly, dangerous stress chemicals. It's always bad, but it can get real ugly. For some, it turns into chronic disease. For most, it just hits in pangs here and there. For all, it's not good. No worries though, we're shutting that system down.

In case of jealousy, you have to adjust Yureego. Click, "**detect *real* threats**" in your Yureego app. You may have already set that before, but Yureego has a mind of its own sometimes and will auto-adjust if your heart/mind balance or self-love slip. Next, start increasing the usage of your heart, as opposed to your mind, to guide your thoughts *when it comes to people*. Visualize your heart energy growing into balance with your mind. Remember the *yin yang* inspired heart/mind symbol. What's happening when jealousy strikes is your heart's not representing its full portion of the swirl. Get that thing balanced! Look back at the "Way Love Flows" chart. Not only do you need to rev up your heart energy to balance it with your overzealous mind, but you also need to generate a LOT more self-love. You're running low when you can muster jealousy. Pump up that volume. Once your self-love is overflowing and the Yureego app is adjusted to detect real threats, your heart will have enough power to be genuinely happy for you *and* for others. Yureego will no longer detect the benefits of others as threats to you. A perfect balance of heart and mind eliminates jealousy altogether. Your heart knows you're perfect exactly as you are *(Your brain doesn't recognize this, by the way. That just doesn't compute for Yureego. Yureego needs all forms of insurance* *and proof. That's why you shouldn't trust your brain to run your life in the first place).* **Your heart always feels energized by the good things held and experienced by others. Your heart would never be jealous of anything or anyone. It's never threatened. Ever.**

It'll take a minute to regroup. Until you're too filled with self-love to muster jealousy, and Yureego only responds to 100 percent real threats, I have a few mindsets that might help control jealousy. Start by imagining that *nothing* you're meant to have, nothing you want, will be missed by you. Nothing. It's literally impossible. You're following me? Imagine that you get a go at *everything*, through the course of many soul journeys. Imagine that even if not in this life, every dream you have, every desire, will *eventually* come through. Deep breathe that in. See all limitations as being placed there to stop you from going in directions **you** weren't meant to travel in this lifetime. Any limitations or "omissions" are **blessings** that guide you to where you need to be. Then, take another look at what role your Creator planned for **you** as you were given everything that you have. Your features, talents, interests, physical abilities or inabilities, family, place and religion of birth, each of these hold clues to your story. **This is your story in this lifetime.** Your bubble is eternal, so it's not a stretch to imagine that you'll get another go with a whole new set of features in the middle of that bubble. With it, comes a new set of circumstances, too. Since you can't know what the next journey will look like, stay focused on *this* one and knock it out of the park. If you're disappointed by this notion, click "**system shut down**," on Yureego for a minute.

Now I want you to imagine seeing those people who possess the things you want, as kindred spirits. They're kindred spirits with you because you'll ultimately share their experiences. You have that in common. They're just taking *their* "go" **now**. Your "go" at the wonderful life treasures **they** have now is coming to **you** one day and you're cool with that. You have things going on in this life right now, anyway. You'll get to that other stuff when the time comes. You recognize that there is a shared spiritual bond between you. Root for the soul spirit that is experiencing the things you want right now. That is your sister or brother in spirit living their life the best way they can. Taking their go at life. Now imagine that you're able to go back to truly appreciating your journey and all of the unique features that came with **it**, but in a more inspired way. You know you'll eventually get a go at having all those things you were jealous about, so there's absolutely no need for jealousy. Free of jealousy, you run with the beautifully challenging life you have.

If that doesn't work, try this. Envision the object of your jealousy as your mom or daughter/father or son for a minute and see if the feeling shifts. You may be able to feel a sense of pride instead of jealousy *(pride carries negativity too since the object of your pride HAS to connect to YOU in order for you to feel the pride. Pride holds some selfishness, but it's a definite jump up from jealousy.)* If the jealousy fades when you think it's your mom/daughter/father/son, then use your imagination until you solve the real issue.

From day one, Yureego determined that you were a separate, individual person with needs that must be filled *(starting with food and nurturing as a baby)*. Yureego picked up very early that you had to get your share of scarce resources *(as a child, if you didn't grab and eat your cake, it could be eaten by someone else and you could be short).* Then, Yureego learned that some people had things that others didn't and *that* presented privileges *(maybe you witnessed a teacher's pet, for example).* Naturally, Yureego stepped up to seek all the things you need for your survival. Unfortunately, it morphed into seeking **all** privileges, luxuries and advantages. Good looking out, Yureego, but there's more to life. **Life's too deep for Yureego to process alone. Life requires a lot of heart**.

Your brain tries. Its best job is to compare you to others, though. Sit that thing down whenever it starts that nonsense. You must override that thinking, immediately, and operate with some heart. There's a bigger picture than what your brain can see. But, it's easy to understand how that comparison BS got started. We ALL got "compared" by teachers and friends as kids. Some folks got compared to others by parents, family members, neighbors, etc. Then, the process of comparing ourselves got hard-wired. We end up doing it to ourselves throughout our lives. Next thing you know, you can't look at others without comparing yourself and your life, whether consciously or not. It's a sad reality. The result is jealousy that touches us in some unwanted way. Nobody wants to admit to possessing the qualities of this ugly word, so it gets covered up and denied that it exists within us. It gets wrapped up into a bunch of excuses as to why you're feeling some kind of way. You may lie to yourself. You can do whatever you want to cover it up, but being just a *little* jealous, or even *envious* of other people or their situations is a clear sign that you have some tidying to do. Time to clean house and clear out old baggage thoughts and energy that open the door to this awful emotion. No matter what you tell yourself, other people, life situations, and general unfairness in the world is not the root of the problem. You'll see that when your heart opens up and Yureego's in check. Until then, try the mindsets I suggested. Come up with your own. Do whatever works for now, and work hard to get to the root of the problem.

So, when a pang of jealousy occurs, release that 'lousy' notion your brain has generated because it's an illusion, a lie. There's absolutely nothing to be jealous of. ***The tiniest hint of jealousy*** should be a reminder that the level of your bubble has dropped too low. Your worldview has become limited and distorted because of the drop. Jealousy is a sign of a weakness of heart, and an unhealthiness within you. Ignore it at your own peril. You can't rise but so high with it. Get working on getting it out of your system for good! Once your heart energy is right, you will rise from jealousy and see things more clearly. The fog of jealousy will fade away. You'll not only never experience jealousy again, but a true sense of connectedness, an intuitive understanding of life and the beauty of your unique journey will replace it and leave you stronger.

OH, WAIT! ... ABOUT THAT RELATIONSHIP JEALOUSY

I believe each bubble has a large number of bubbles *(souls)* to which they are connected on a spiritual level. Kinda like that old Verizon network commercial where a crew of people were walking behind the guy everywhere he went. **Each** of us has a network of souls connected to us. It's a beautiful thing that you want for someone you truly love. If you don't want your loved one to be connected to others, then stop fooling yourself that you truly **love** … you're not in love, you're in need. First, get yourself together. Go back and study "the way love flows." Once you're focused and confident and overflowing with self-love, your need should be satisfied. You should feel incredibly confident and completely unconcerned about anyone else. Problem solved.

When someone with whom you share true love is connected to another soul or vice-versa, don't hate, *appreciate* and respect the connections that exist for each of you. Don't make the connections, between your loved one and others, all about YOU. The only thing that should be ALL ABOUT YOU is your commitment to elevating yourself. You should *both* be confident and free to live your lives. You are **not** in jeopardy when love is real. True love is an unbreakable bond.

You're not even in jeopardy when the love ain't real. You're never in jeopardy of losing anything because everything that is meant for you in this lifetime will be yours. If, by chance, you're sensing that a relationship change is in the equation, you got this! Just don't let it be because of your ego-based jealousy. **Make certain that your self-love and confidence is overflowing, and that you fear nothing.** Since you embrace that change is good, you're ready to flow like water to where you need to be. There's never a reason to worry or be jealous. This thinking can help you to eliminate, in advance, the pain caused by Yureego sounding off all the scary alarms. Sit that thing down and relax. Everyone is responsible for their own commitment to themselves.

Don't **need** to be the center of someone else's world. There's something innately egotistical and needy about that. When a pang of jealousy hits, take that as a sign to focus on **you**. It's Yureego that "needs" to be the all-powerful, reigning king or queen that dominates the life of a loved one. Love, might I remind you, is a function of the heart, not the brain. If you feel in your heart that your love is great, what the heck is the problem? Don't let that brain screw things up. Work on this. Don't let jealousy overcome you and ruin your relationships and your life. The king/queen status that Yureego seeks is some bullshit. When you love regardless of all of that, when your love fills you first, then your Boo and it's not dependent on anything, just pure and strong … that's sexy as shit! *Try* to lose someone when you have *that* attitude. A genuine lack of jealousy indicates a depth of confidence that's magnetic. I'm talking about confidence that comes from an immense self-love, not that bullshit confidence that comes from Yureego. Heart-based confidence is where your feeling of king or queen should originate. Your king/queen status isn't real anyway, unless it emanates from *your* heart. Never rely on the **behavior** of someone else to give you that. *Right?* If you feel a need to be the center of someone's world, **shake that shit off**.

There's a network of souls connected to each of us in ways that we're unaware of. It's part of our journey to interact with these souls. Don't get mad if someone is tantalizing or even if they're **trying** to get next to your Boo. If Boo don't know what to do, then **you** do. You know what I'm saying? It's nothing to worry about. Know in your heart where you need to be, and be there. It's silly to want a loved one NOT to observe, admire, smile, laugh, talk, care about, enjoy, and love members of the opposite sex (or same sex, gender equality!). Get comfortable embracing different connections for your loved one without feeling an egotistically generated sense of loss to you.

So, if you ever feel that a loved one is a possession of yours or that others compromise your love, you know you've got work to do on YOURSELF. Turn moments of jealousy into an opportune time for introspection. When you feel the first sign of jealousy, **relax, deep breathe**. Build up your heart-based love and confidence for yourself. Pivot to something that elevates **you**.

If, on the other hand, you experience jealousy directed at you. Keep in mind that those folks are dealing with a heart/mind imbalance. They're having a hard time with it and may not have any idea how to handle it. They're likely rolling, helplessly, with jealousy. That's all they know to do. It's painful for them no matter how they try to hide it, and it's beyond their control. Don't internalize that! What sense would that make? Under the surface, they're being affected by insufficient self-love and what they perceive as *your advantage or power*. That's *all*. Have enough love to provide some high quality vapors as you keep it moving. ✌️

And a final spoiler: All relationships aren't meant to last forever. Relationships last long enough to experience the things we're to experience for the growth of our souls.

"It's important to understand that you go through levels in life. There's tons of levels, man. As you go through these levels, fucking just understand what they were, and become better."
– Kevin Hart: Irresponsible.

DON'T HATE, ELEVATE

Actually, **meditate until you elevate** if you EVER have an emotion of hate building for *any* reason. You HAVE to elevate from that feeling. Hate is a rock-hard, anvil-weight thought and emotion. I don't even like to **use** this negative word in writing. *I hate to even joke using the word.* Just don't deal in this one. Don't "hate" **anything!** ... Don't even hate ducks! *[private joke :-)]*

NEVER convince yourself that hate is warranted because of offenses to you, or even atrocities to others. It doesn't matter how awful the offenses were. It doesn't matter how much you didn't like, or didn't agree. Let it go. If it's a real offense, let the offender deal with karma on that one, ok? Tangling up with hate for *any* reason will only pull you away from that beautiful, loving universal force that wants to course through you. You need that. But you can't have both. So, let go of any and all feelings of hate. Release it, so you can elevate.

If you ever have a feeling of hate, remind yourself that the world's a LOT bigger than the space your brain is in when you feel hate. Hate is born of narrow and dark thinking. Hate makes you small. You can change that feeling, though. Neuroplasticity proves it. No excuses. Just put in hard work. Do what it takes to lighten your elevation. If you don't change it, the reflection's solely on you. And it ain't pretty.

BE UNAPOLOGETICALLY YOU

God made you different on purpose. Never be more concerned about fitting in or being viewed favorably than flowing with your natural inclinations and natural ways of being. Embarrassment and shame are powerful emotions. People will avoid the feelings of humiliation or the distress that comes from "wrong" or "foolish" behavior, like it's the Plague. Fear of not being accepted or admired, or hired, or loved is fear of being ourselves. Forget all of that!

Who determines what's considered wrong or foolish behavior? Why on earth would your self-confidence be up for grabs in the first place? You know where I stand on this one, already. The only shame that I ever want to you to experience, if ever, is shame for giving a shit what others think about you or what you're doing. You guys heard me loud and clear on this from the time you were very young. I want you to know that I admire how deep your confidence is in being 100 percent you, already. I'm just putting everything in writing for you. I love how confident and shameless you are, even when you *know* you are operating outside of what the world accepts as impressive. You hold such an air of confidence, like, "this is me, folks, and I'm running with it," that has driven me **CRAZY**. But I love what it represents about your self-confidence. I got my money on you guys. As you mature, the experiences of your "leave no stone unturned" youth, and that beautiful confidence to be yourself, will carry you everywhere you need to be.

"There is nothing either good or bad, but thinking makes it so."
- Shakespeare

Who is determining what's right or wrong, anyway? What's right or wrong are completely relative to ever changing circumstances, culture and personal preferences, just for starters. For example, there are people who've been incarcerated on felony charges and did hard time for having weed. Some years later, the exact same act is acknowledged to bring legitimate healing for those who use it and legitimate wealth for those who sell it. What's right and what's wrong are very relative to the hard-wiring in people's minds. As for foolish behavior, come on now. Don't let yourself, much less anyone else, dictate what's foolish for you. You are doing your thing on your path along your soul journey. Don't adjust your game based on the hard-wired thoughts of others. That could stop your flow for no reason. Right or wrong or foolish behavior is all in our heads. I personally say a little foolishness is good. Do what feels good to you. Follow your instincts. Follow your dreams. Have no shame in doing it. Shame on those who spend a moment of their soul journey passing judgment on you. Have no feeling of embarrassment or shame, or feeling apologetic because someone else's sensibilities have been offended. Flow on with your bad self! Your confidence to be unapologetically you is beautiful because it keeps you squarely on your own soul path. Recognizing anyone who doesn't vibe with that is a **gift**. They've waved a friendly flag to identify themselves as someone you probably don't need in your life right now.

What's the worst that can happen? Let's run with the worst being that somebody laughs at how you look. Ok, that **does** sound messed up. I admit. I also apologize for laughing as I think about it. I totally get it, and I don't want that one myself. I'm laughing, imagining Uncle Denzel, as a prime example of why NOT to take it too seriously. Even those held as the most handsome or gorgeous, dapper or fly, even those folks get laughed at sometimes. It's a human thing. Humor is always good, unless we're the subject of it, right? I've done some double takes on myself in the mirror and in pictures before and laughed, "What the HELL, girl? Ha, ha!" So, I **know** others with my sense of humor would have felt the same way, if they had the chance to see me *(like when y'all snap and post those moments when I slip!)*. While I still don't WELCOME being laughed at, as I re-wire my thinking, more and more, I reeeeally don't care.

I'm not putting my self-confidence up for grabs, and I don't want you to either. Learn not to care. Consider the feeling of shame and embarrassment to represent how fragile your confidence and ego are. Be alarmed when you feel them. Be unapologetically you even if you are being laughed at. If you were Dave Chappelle or Kevin Hart, they'd laugh at you in hushed tones because **everyone** knows in those situations that **they got next**! We each have to figure out how not to care about it. If the thought really bothers you, as it does most of us, **literally** imagine people laughing at you. Do this to get used to the idea of the feeling and your response to the feeling. Imagine people laughing at you, and immediately stop to reflect on how you would process that feeling away. If you can get to the point where your thoughts and emotions remain in a space of peace and joy, even in this worst case scenario, you will have achieved a comfort with being yourself that can't be shaken by anyone. That's the mindset that you beautiful souls deserve. Be YOU with no apologies, because as Poppop Mikey would say to me, "Ey, man … I don't want to hear you say, 'I'm sorry,' 'cause ain't **nothin'** sorry 'bout you! Huh? … **HUH!**"

The best reason to be shameless? The guiding force in your life, your Creator, is cool with the creation of you. The force that created you is cool with you doing your thing. You, your behavior, your interests, your trials and even your fashion adventures are A-OK with the force that created you. That knowledge should mean much more to you than the judgment of people. The more I know about how the minds of people work, the more I can't fathom how we would adjust our LIVES to meet the needs of other's **minds**? It's totally senseless! If you put stock into people's judgment of you, **shame on you**! … *Just kidding ;-)*.

It's very liberating showing your whole self, not hiding your flaws at all costs. When people see how happy you are with your flaws, it might foster their confidence to be more comfortable with their own. While folks around you are busy hiding, covering up perceived flaws, and flaunting only the good stuff, I want you to continue to break through that behavior and be immersed in the comfort of your real, full self, funny flaws and all.

Remember this:

If people don't recognize your beauty, talents or value, keep it movin'. It takes one to know one. You just might be in the wrong environments. Keep moving forward with confidence in who you are. Keep beaming with love for yourself and all of your ways. You'll eventually end up in a space surrounded by folks who understand and treasure you.

JUDGMENT IS WAAAY OUT OF YOUR JURISDICTION

"The best of business is to mind your business.
If you got no business, then make it your business
to leave other people's business alone."
 – Lyrics from "To Each His Own" by Faith Hope and Charity.

Remember that everyone is on their own personal soul journey. You know absolutely nothing about the soul journeys of others, so don't judge. Accept others the way they are. Embrace everyone and the things they're into as tiny pieces of a big picture designed by the Creator. Since everyone was created by God, you might as well be judging GOD when you judge others. I wouldn't touch that. We're by no means given life to judge the lives of others. It's a negative thing, because judging others takes your mind off *your* business. I'm thinking the superiority it takes to cast judgment on others can generate some negative karma. Judgment of others tosses you into a weird space. Life and humanity are too complex to judge anyway. Our hands are way too full handling our lives. What's more, any focus on someone else should be for the purposes of recognizing beauty of some kind. Swap judgment with the identification of beauty in others.

Just as dangerous as judging others, is judging yourself. Don't judge yourself and don't compare **yourself** to others. All of that is out of your jurisdiction. It brings the energy of your bubble down. It generates negativity that affects you and the world around you. If you find yourself comparing yourself, comparing others or judging yourself … try to work on that. Instead of judgment, try to pivot your mind to ways to show love to others and focus on the progression of your dreams. **You are an asset to the world. Act like**

it. Each of us has our contribution to this world, and that's all we know. It takes all of our energy just to meet our own obligations. Stay focused.

"To each his own. That's my philosophy. I don't know what's right for you. No, no baby. And you don't know what's right for me. Woo!"

> **– Lyrics from the song "To Each His Own" by Faith Hope and Charity**[*This was my favorite song when I was ten. I still love it! :-)*]

HONESTY AND OPENNESS

"Honesty is the recognition of the fact that the unreal is unreal."

> **– Ayn Rand**

Honesty and openness mean you're flowing with what's real. That's good. **Why create bullshit?** Isn't that the job of an asshole to push shit? You know what that's doing to your bubble, right?

Suppressing our thoughts and emotions, for any reason, means more baggage for us to carry. Stop adding baggage to your bubbles! The thought and belief energy that keeps you stuck on lack of honesty and openness is some dense energy. You can't move toward Happiness with that. If you're confident and filled with faith, why is it necessary to lie or cover up? Just deal with whatever comes from honesty and openness. That's called being **real**. That's flowing with life and letting life flow through you. Despite what Yureego is telling you, lose that fear. Face the music. Deal with the truth. Fear of being honest and open imprisons your spirit. You need **freedom**.

If you feel a need to be dishonest or feel that being closed is necessary, there's something you need to change in your life. We weren't born feeling the need to lie and cover up. It's not our natural state. Feeling a need to lie and cover up becomes hard-wired in our brains as a result of bad experiences. It's time to rewire to return to your most natural state.

I'm not advocating or talking about projecting your business to the world. Don't publish all your passwords! I'm talking about being dishonest with people you know, and/or fearful of the people you know, *"knowing"* things about you. By holding onto fears that cause dishonesty and lack of openness with the intent of protecting yourself and your identity, you're not protecting yourself the way that you think you are. You actually keep yourself imprisoned in a space, labeled as safe, but free from much more than the risks you're avoiding. That space keeps you free from joys in life that you can never reach while imprisoned in the so-called safety space of needing to lie and cover up. If this sounds naïve, don't fall for that. You know better. I'm not being naïve, I'm being **honest and open with y'all** ;-). Dishonesty and secrecy represents fear. Fear is the opposite of love. Don't hold fast to habits that put you on the opposite of love and freedom. Develop a general sense that nothing and no one can hold you down and you have nothing to fear. It won't be an easy habit to break. The intense release you'll feel when you communicate with honesty will be well worth it. You'll release baggage as you increase your free-spiritedness.

Start by taking a chance on honesty and let things fall where they may. If an apology needs to come along with your honesty, give it. Offer honesty and apology and move on to the next chapter of your life story. If a misunderstanding or disappointment results from your honesty, and you end up losing something you wanted, accept it. You're a soldier, remember! Whatever the result, you are shortcutting to a lighter existence, and Happiness. Believe that. Don't be scared to be honest. **Always trust in the long-term outcomes of honesty and openness**. As you use them throughout your life, let them symbolize for you that your life is on the right track.

Openness symbolizes a pure lack of fear, confidence and an innate understanding that there's never truly anything to hide. There's no one in this world who doesn't have "stuff." If you are not one bit worried about what anyone thinks or how things will shake out if your reality is known, that's **true freedom**. Not to mention that your example of confidence and fearlessness will surely inspire others. Anyone who would use your honesty and openness against you in any way has blessed you by revealing themselves. See folks like that as "U-turn" signs. No worries and no judgment! Never believe that anyone can stop you or stand in the way of your destiny and dreams. Be fearlessly honest and comfortably open. The ability to freely speak your truth at all times is a huge step in the direction of lightness and Happiness.

"The truth shall set you free."

TAKE TWO CHILL PILLS

Something or someone has pissed you off. Uh oh, got your bubble down? Nope. At the first signs of anger, take two of those chill pills I gave you with this book *[have two sugar-free gummy vitamins ready in case of emergency, for those who didn't receive the pills or for extra-strength, two valerian root capsules ;-)]*. Chill pills help you to relax as you elevate up and away from the anger and the situation. When something or someone pisses you off, take chill pills. Save that can of whoopass to whip your own ass into shape and to where you need to be. When confronted with someone's toxic energy or when frustrated about something, take the pills with a full bottle/glass of fresh water. Focus on **how you're reacting** to the frustration, and note the time. If you dwell on the situation and are still upset after ten to fifteen minutes, you've become toxic. Detox immediately.

"Ey man, take a chill pill."
– Daddy

Never just roll with disappointment, frustration or anger. By taking the chill pills immediately, you stop the damage to **yourself** in its tracks. The "pills" I've provided for you are all natural, and powerfully effective in my trails ;-). They usually take about five minutes to start to work. Take your dosage. ***Believe in its power to work***. Focus on you and the health of your own mind and body. Master the skill of calming down **fast** because one has to calm down to begin processing the situation. Chill pills slow the rate of breathing as well as your heart rate. They relieve the constrictions to your blood flow and the tensions of the muscles. Taken with water and a few long deep breaths, your brain is now getting increased hydration and oxygen. This process enables you to let go of the turbulence in the mind and body within the short period it takes the pill to work. Try them. The feeling of peace that comes with this level of control is well worth it.

The fact that anger is one letter short of danger gives clues to the dangerous effects of anger on your mind, emotional well-being and your physical body. When chill pills take effect, danger is averted. Chill pills mean your bubble can avoid a hard, unexpected drop. Who has time for drops when you're trying so hard to rise? Until you master the art of controlling your anger without them, the all-natural relief of chill pills can boost your well-being.

Before I share more directions for taking your chill pills, let's put your anger in perspective. Neither life, nor the people in your life, are trying to beat up on you. If that doesn't seem believable to your mind, then just imagine it to be so. Imagine that everyone is just living *their* life the best way they can. Imagine that anyone who seems to have it out for you, or anyone who has caused you pain, frustration or anger, is stuck *(to their own dismay)* in an awful hard-wired cycle of their own misery. You are simply close enough to catch the vibrations of their misery. They may not mind your company on the Miserable Station, but that's no reason to hang out there. Your proximity to that miserable energy is something for YOU to work on. That's YOUR job to float up out of that! Every second that anger grips you, you're descending deeper into spaces where you'll get more of the same. You have a whole LOT more to live for than being pissed off on the Miserable Station. Rise up and out of (d)anger.

Life continuously provides the lessons you need. Every blue moon a person *could* possibly be focused on causing you pain, but the odds are incredibly long on that. If you do run into people who are doing that deliberately, **you** are in the wrong places, at the wrong times and with the wrong peeps. This means YOU have to change something. You're on the wrong vibrational energy station in life. Don't look at them, **it's you** that must adjust. You're accountable for the situations you get in. **Take full responsibility. Time for change may be the only lesson that's being presented to you**. Receive that message. Change is an ever present reality in our lives. Embrace it and begin to sense the changes that need to be made. Consider which changes are easy and which changes must be made no matter how hard.

By taking the chill pills, you not only feel better almost immediately, you're also able to think more clearly. Not one of us can think clearly when under the grips of anger or intense frustration. Don't try. Calm down first! **When angry or upset, your AI and Yureego can descend into a temporary, virtual, storm of dense energy that can be likened to mental illness**. Your body is also compromised. You are in a dangerous, compromised state. Don't ever trust thoughts generated under the grips of anger. Ever! **Always get your mind calm before trying to think your way out of the situation. This is for your own good.** That's why I say to save the can of whoopass to challenge your own ass to get on track. You'll need strength just to fight off your anger, just in case the chill pills take a little longer to work.

Once the chill pills take effect, physical tensions release and your emotions return to a state of peace. It's not uncommon to see things in a different light. It's likely that you'll, now, see steps that you could have taken to avoid the situation in the first place. You may see how to solve and move past the situation. Now with the added power of chill pills to control random declines of your bubble, you'll consistently elevate to where you deserve to be. Any time. All the time.

This world is not all about serving you and making your life wonderful and your dreams come true. There's much more going on. Life is lesson based, not just a race to get to your dreams. Your Happiness is icing on a cake made entirely of life lessons learned by you. Don't try to skip the cake part. Recognize that life is more about learning lessons than appeasing you. Challenges are core experiences of life. YOU HAVE TO SEE CHALLENGES DIFFERENTLY. Look AT them, not past them. Embedded in every situation, there's ALWAYS an opportunity to learn something that can elevate you. You just have to **Keep Calm and Actually Learn Something**.

CHILL PILL SUGGESTED USE:

1. At the *first sign* of anger building, take two chill pills with a glass of water, and three to ten very long deep breaths, depending on the situation.
2. After your deep breaths, STOP for a few moments of meditative peace. Do not drift into the toxicity of thinking about the situation. Think of a *'few of your favorite things.'*
3. Note the time, with the goal of releasing all negative thoughts and feelings within five to fifteen minutes, or the fastest that you can. Try to beat your best time, each time.

These aren't placebos, but they ARE proven to work best to stop the flow of anger for those who believe they will. Taking the time to drink the water is important. Don't skip it. The water hydrates and fuels your brain to handle stressful conditions. Deep breathe a minimum of three times, but as many times as you can after taking the 'pills.' Without too much focus on the issue itself or how it came to pass, search for a positive lesson that can be learned out of the situation. Then, look at how YOU can make changes in a personal and positive way. This focus immediately shifts your attention back to something you have more chance to control, YOU.

Begin **planning your course of action to resolve the issue**. Take the first steps of action right away. If at first you don't succeed in positively resolving the problem, try again. The beautiful thing about chill pills is that they're not only non-addictive, they're curative. Over time, use of chill pills will actually increase your ability to control the powerfully negative force of anger **naturally**. Studies have shown that chill pill users experience fewer opportunities for anger, with less intensity. With the chill pills I provided you with this book, you are now **always** in more control of the situation than you might originally think. You are always on your way up, with no excuses. *(The placebo effect almost ensures the pills will work if you believe they will.)*

DEEP BREATHING

I know, I know. You've heard it a million times and now it means nothing. Breathing happens. It's not something that you have to DO. So what's the "deep breathing" thing about? Well, Oh. My. Goodness. I am glad you asked! Who knew that deep breathing was a little different than regular breathing? Deep breathing accomplishes a deeper cleanse and regeneration of your body than the regular breathing you do without thinking. On top of that, concentration on your breathing helps to clear your mind from the less important things and stresses of life. Oxygen is fuel. It's food for your body. **Oxygen is healing** to you. Remember that. And it's the one thing that you need replenished **every minute of your life**. It makes sense to me that something *that important* to your body is beneficial in larger quantities. Increase your oxygen intake. Deep breathe as much as you possibly can, purifying your body and mind.

While deep breathing, you oxidize the cells of your body, and activate miraculous processes of healing. Your body and mind regenerate from the increased oxygen. Imagine fresh, deep breathed oxygen as energy that creates brand new, healthy cells in your brain and body. Envision deep breathing as clearing out old, toxin carrying oxygen out of your lungs and body. Breathing in brings the healing and cleansing power inside of you. Breathing out releases toxins (CO_2) and toxic energy from your body. The deeper you breathe, the deeper the healing and cleansing effects. The power of healing your body and your mind is packed within every deep breath you take. This is so important, I'll be mentioning this one again.

KNOW WHO TO MESS WITH

When possible, only deal *closely* with people who give you a good feeling. *Whenever possible.* Sometimes you have no choice, but when you do have a choice, deal with people that give you a good feeling. If you get an odd feeling from someone that you can't put your finger on, don't mess with that until you're sure there's nothing to stay away from. That odd feeling could be your instinct guiding you not to stray off your course. That's all. It's not that the person isn't good. We're not going there with it at all. That person is probably awesome, but just not on your best path forward. If you get an odd feeling, take it as a sign to steer in an alternate direction. For now. Don't make excuses. Moving forward with them can be an effort, on your part, not to rush to judgment or hurt someone's feelings. You're being accepting and loving and determined to move beyond a feeling you had no reason to feel. I get it. Believe me. But life has taught me. You were probably given that feeling for a reason. That person may simply be, wonderful as they are, not what you need *right now*. Heed and fine tune your instincts so that they guide you accurately as you move forward in life. Your instincts are invaluable in guiding you to where you need to be and who you should be around. Your instincts will find all the shortcuts.

You're on your way to being an example of the positive change the world needs. The amazing lift that's occurring in your life serves as an example to others. Stay on course. Follow your senses to take advantage of shortcuts that lead you directly to where you were meant to be. Your brain can only compute. It can't possibly know what your instincts can. If your heart is guiding you away from someone, gently heed those feelings. Wonderful feelings from people should be followed, but odd feelings from people should be considered as detour signs along your soul journey path. There's a reason for them. Hopefully, the odd feelings aren't coming from Yureego. They could be. You'll have to figure out how to know the difference. If they're coming from Yureego, you still need to steer clear because problems will still be the result. You could be the source of the problem, unfortunately, but avoid that by steering clear. Just to be safe. While you double check to make sure Yureego is updated, enhanced and running perfectly. Always check yourself.

Someone who was previously perfect for you can expire from your soul journey. You could be faced with processing the fact that your feelings about that person have changed, or that they are no longer flowing with your path forward. That's a natural part of life. Things change. It's not sad, it's totally ok. Don't get trapped by feelings that you **have** to hold on. Be comforted by the fact that real love and/or friendship is never in jeopardy. Branching off might put you both in a better space. The entanglement of your bubbles is solid, but you have to focus on your path forward. This is your life. Holding on to things that stand in the way of your personal progress is not an act of love. Remember how love flows? Holding on in this case can, however, be an act of fear, the fear of loss. Holding on can also be a rejection of your path forward. Everything moves in a constant ebb and flow. Do what you have to do to keep yourself rolling in the right direction.

Look for a good feeling from people. Some people are solidly on their own path to greatness, and meant to cross paths with yours. Sense when you are in the right place at the right time. Sense when you are connecting with the right people for you. By sensing who to mess with and who to miss, you'll shortcut your way to beautiful spaces and places for you. Take the time to learn what you need and what works best for you, so that you will know, with confidence, who to mess with.

SHIT JUST GOT REAL, NOW WHAT?

"Every life is just one damn thing after another."
    – Winston Churchill

"I'm sorry to say so, but sadly, it's true that bang-
ups and hang-ups can happen to you."
    – Dr. Seuss

Trial and tribulation are just necessary parts of life. It doesn't mean that something is wrong when things go wrong. Sounds funny, I know, but **going through some really tough shit is a core part of life. For each of us. Just remember** *this* in the midst of the toughest of times. It's always how you respond that matters. **Focus on your response**.

"No one is immune to life's plight."
    - Mom ;-)

"The resistance to the unpleasant situation
is the root of suffering."
    - Ram Dass

In times of tragedy and crisis, turn inward (quiet time, time to yourself, meditation, prayer) in an effort to cope, grieve, heal and let go. Friends and social time can be beautiful reinforcements of the love and care around you, but the only thing that can truly lift and heal you is having those uplifting feelings and mentality of healing come from **your own mind. It has to generate from** *you* **in order to work**. To generate the positive feelings that lift you from the dread of real life shit, you have to connect directly to the full, creative, loving force. And that takes some quiet time, time to yourself, meditation, and prayer.

In the absolute worst of times, notice kindness, beauty and love. Remember my favorite story of Whoville. The people of Whoville pulled together and sang, expressing their inner joy and love. Their solid connection to what mattered most consumed them, despite the circumstances. The fact that their reaction touched the heart of the Grinch and in-turn blessed them with goodies was just icing on the cake. In the worst of times, always sing a song about the blessings of real love that continue to exist around you.

> "But that can't make me sad, just can't make me
> 'cause I've been there before, don't wanna go no more.
> The world can't take me, won't let it drive me mad.
> **– Earth, Wind & Fire, "On Your Face"**

Seeing things, even crisis situations, in ways that hurt you and bring you down, and not changing your mind to see things differently is self-destructive. Flat out. The thing that stops you from lifting out of the pain of the situation is the hard-wiring in your **mind.** You can easily become stuck on why it *shouldn't be*, or how *wrong and/or unfair the situation is*. Your brain has lots of those swirling circles going. It has you stuck, frozen on a negative loop. Free yourself. Close the Yureego app and open up a new train of thought on how you're going to deal with the situation in the best possible way. When you feel pain, it's usually because you're focused on the things that bring pain, not the solution. **Crisis situations, however traumatic, are ultimate opportunities to train yourself on how to see the bright side.** You can't see the bright side unless you control the way you think. You *can* adjust and control the way you think! It's a skill. **What skill is more important?**

While in the midst of crisis, it can seem impossible to see the bright side. You can feel as if your heart is helplessly crushed by the situation. You associate your "feelings" to be something from your heart, but we've already pointed out that most of your feelings come from your **mind.** The only feelings that come from your heart are the very instinctive, intuitive ones that have no basis in reason. These never bring pain. Usually, when shit gets real, your flood of brain-generated emotions cloud your instincts so well that you don't have a chance at a true heart-felt emotion. Your brain is likely clicking like crazy and taking you into depths of worry, panic, grief or despair. *Those ain't from the heart*. You *can* process the situation and get past the old hard-wired thinking that brings you down. You just have to do the very tough work of changing your mind. Let's look at the process I've outlined for you to get through these times quickly. First, absorb the situation; then, accept it. Next, process what happened and what you can learn from the situation. Finally, what are the actions you can take to rise above it? Focus everything you've got, mind and body, on taking those actions.

"When you're in a slump, you're not in for much fun.
Un-slumping yourself is not easily done."
 – Dr. Seuss

On a very personal note:

In the midst of the most ***serious*** of crisis, I've learned over the years to just accept the situation, and do it ***fast***. The faster, the better. The more thoroughly I accept it, the better. I've also learned that in any crisis, I *must* spend *some* time focusing on "The Shell," engaging myself in trains of thought and actions that are in my own self-interest. Sometimes this comes after no-holds-barred bawling and a scream or two if it's called for. No shame to my game. After that, I immerse myself in constructive projects [like The Toy Drive and The Happiness Hookup ;-)] and the things that I love (plant fuel; stretching; herbal remedies 😎 and red wine; mind/body/spirit literature; science and nature documentaries; art in every form; some *really* good music). A transformation ***always*** takes place. I'm *slowly* able to appreciate the new chapter that has begun in my life. It's a process. When crisis strikes, actively engage in your own process to let the healing begin.

Processing life's shit is a dirty job, but it pays to do it right.

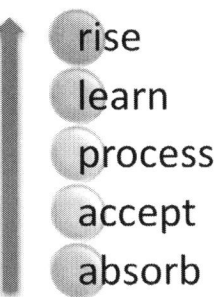

rise
learn
process
accept
absorb

This is so very important. Let's go over this once more. The next time shit gets real, first absorb the reality of what has happened. Fully accept the situation. Don't tell yourself it shouldn't have happened. Don't blame **anyone**, especially not yourself. Don't think about 'what if this' or 'what if that' had happened. Don't tell yourself that your life can't or won't be wonderful in new, unimaginable ways. **Do** say to yourself, "I accept it. I totally accept this shit. Now what?" Do get in the moment. Stop the focus on the painful situation for a minute, and notice some of the beauty that still exists in the world. Think of four wonderful things you still have. Name them to yourself. Take some still time to yourself. Meditate and listen to some *positive* music. Focus on dreams of your future. Cope the best way you can, keeping your mind set on moving beyond the situation. Cry, shout, journal, walk, workout, draw. Do ***something*** that helps you to channel the hurt, frustration, worry, anxiety and/or depressed energy completely out of you. There's **no** value in those emotions, only pain. So, TRY with all your might to quieten your AI. **Learn something that will have a positive effect as you move forward in your life. You HAVE to find** *something* **that you can get out of the situation**. Make that lesson the thing that you will use to change your life. Let the painful memories go. Drop those like they're hot. Just rise with the good stuff gained. There's *always* something positive to gain in the absolute worst of situations. **Don't let your AI win by keeping you blind to the positives and the beautiful ever-changing nature of life.** Find what beauty you can. Turn the page to the new chapter of your life story. Envision your future as you would dream it to be from this point forward. You must lift your own bubble **to get to the space where you can get a clear view of how to live the rest of your life. There's no clear view of it from the depths of despair.**

"Keep on moving, don't stop."
- Soul II Soul, **Keep on Moving**

The emotions and pain of dealing with real shit become negative energy bundles inside you. They must be processed away. That's the process of 'healing.' For optimal healing, simply keep all the benefits of any lessons learned and eliminate all the rest of the shitty situation as waste *(let it go so you can flow again)*. Release it from your mind. If you don't process and eliminate, your life will be negatively affected by what will become "baggage energy" that you carry. *Baggage energy is just another name for unhealed wounds*. While you may not detect it within you unhealed wounds are icky lead energy that hold you down securely. Baggage acts as friction to your flow of life. It'll make it almost impossible for you to truly move beyond the situation. It'll not only affect you, but let me reemphasize here that baggage vibes **can** be felt. Don't tell yourself they can't. While you're pushing out love and positivity, your baggage energy is coming right out with it. You'll have a rancid, funky icing covering all of your love and positivity underneath its muck. *This will affect your life* as others, including those who could bring you joy and good fortune, are repulsed by that icing. *You can repel blessings, and invite more crisis, unintentionally*. It's extremely important that you process thoroughly and let the waste of the situation go. As long as you're actively and healthily processing, it's just a matter of time before all that baggage goes "poof!" The crisis will come to an end, and better days begin to appear in your life. Health and joy can return in abundance.

"It's possible that the things that are happening are actually not negative. That this is all part of a perfect plan, divinely orchestrated, whose purpose ultimately is to guide and shepherd

us into a cracking of the shell that we built around our hearts. An opening of the mind and the body to a greater awareness."
  – David Wilcock

Let's say the situation completely pulls the rug from under your feet, then punches you with an uppercut and *then* a straight right. You've been hit with some serious, serious stuff. You might need to stop and shut down for at least a couple of hours to a couple of days. You'll need to do this just to compose yourself enough to heal and move forward without hurting yourself more. You have sustained injury, but you **will** heal. You can heal more quickly if you attend to yourself.

However you can get time to heal, take it. Don't just run forward with life, full speed ahead, when you have real injuries from shit you just went through. View emotional injuries as you would physical ones. Figure out how much healing you have to do, and heal up before you try to resume normal activities. Ignoring emotional injury and stress can create some deep set damage as all that negative energy you carry draws more negativity to you. All of that unprocessed negative energy, when not released, can make the original injury exponentially worse! Now you got a much bigger, festering wound that won't heal *(eww)*. Don't be that bubble. Keep accepting and letting go until you know that you are more at peace and have begun healing.

"Life is *not* for sissies."
  – Neal Donald Walsch

There's a certain beauty in a person who has come through struggle, because their soul has been the beneficiary of the experience. Give in to the situation with full acceptance of life's trials. Cry a river to release all the toxins that cloud your view of the potential growth that's possible in your life. In the midst of the shit you're going through, you can easily develop into a better person.

"Life for me ain't been no crystal stair,
But all the while, I keeps a climbin', and
reaching landings, and turning corners."
  – Langston Hughes, Life for Me Ain't Been No Crystal Stair.

Grandma Haywood, when facing a tough decision, says, **"God, put it in my head how to help you."** While she asks in an effort to push God's plan forward, she truly believes that the way to serve God is to do what's best for yourself and others. I shared one of the quotes that Grandma told me, "Michelle, God wants

YOU to take care of **YOU**!" That message resonated. After the passing of Daddy and Aunt Joan, writing to record loving messages for you was healing and transformative for **me**. Always try to pivot all the energy of the "shit got real" situation into something meaningful that lifts YOU.

*Side note: While writing **this** section, my AC went out. It was hot (understatement). I deep breathed and called for service. They told me on a Thursday morning that the soonest anyone could come out would be Monday. I took three extremely deep breaths instead of immediately getting upset, and looked up the weather forecast because it was REAL hot at that moment. I immediately saw that the temperatures were going way up over the 89 degrees I was experiencing that Thursday morning. Over the weekend, the DC area would hit temperatures over 100, with humidity levels that allow for swimming in mid-air. Wow. WHAT? I was about to abandon writing The Happiness Hookup because how on earth can I write to tell you guys how to "elevate in the face of crisis," if I'm freaking out about a broken AC system? I could feel some 'reactions' flowing inside, so I tried to process the situation the way I'm asking you guys to. Did I mention that both cars had **just** been picked up from the repair shop, nearly $4K paid, but **both** still had issues and had to go back? Yeah, well, that too. What I can tell you is that those were four days of incredible heat. That's documented. But an attitude came over me, and infectiously caught Dad too. We actually chilled out (that's figuratively) and fully accepted the situation. We were mentally in a tropical paradise. We got three fans in order to be able to sleep at night, and lots of high quality water. We took it on the chin and retreated in peace and comfort of mind, if not body. I looked for something to learn from the situation.*

*I reinforced my belief that once you accept something, you're much more able to deal with it, no matter what. I could see that we were elevating, evidenced by the way we breezed through otherwise horrific, possibly life-threatening heat. On one of the days, Dad enthusiastically suited up and jumped in an Uber to go downtown and landed a new client, no less. That taught us that our frame of mind, tolerance and positivity in the face of adversity, was paying off. Fans, as antiquated as they were in my mind before those few days, were the answer to our prayers. They instantly addressed the issue of juuuuust enough coolness to sleep, and muffled the 'middle of the night barking' of our aging pups. Before the AC system broke (during one of the **worst** heat waves in **American history**, it turned out), we were not getting a full night's sleep, because of the dogs' barking. The AC breakdown experience changed our lives in positive ways. We learned that we could control whether we heard the dogs barking or not, with fans.*

*Four **excruciatingly** hot days later, the AC system was fixed by a pro, within four minutes of arrival, by flipping some switch on the interior of the unit that we didn't have access to (I'm not shitting you, **4 minutes**. He even laughed and said, "There ya' go!"). Four life-threat-*

*ening days over **that**? No sweat :-) I wasn't even mad. I felt blessed to have prevailed in not allowing life's test of wills or endurance to force my thinking, feelings, or bubble down.*

I'm looking at challenges and crisis differently now. They bring a priceless experience to the table. Learn something, and some of the worst situations *(and even some tragedies)* can reveal themselves to be powerful stepping stones. These are the moments that elevate your soul.

"In every mis*fortune*, you'll find *fortune* staring you right in the face.

If you'll just notice it."
– Mom

What I used to see as imperfections *(I'm a **former** perfectionist)* look like art to me now. Everything looks beautiful, like perfect pieces of naturally occurring art. The imperfections now look like aspects of a snapshot in time that make the moment more real. I see the so-called imperfections as "touches" that mark the moment in time. Touches I may miss someday because they marked a moment of such beauty. When the touches change, so will other things. I can see now that with every imperfection there are perfect things tied into the moment. I'm appreciating all of it. Even in tragedy, I'm now able to see design wrapped up in it (more often referred to as destiny). This viewpoint brings comfort, acceptance, and appreciation. Once you begin to see differently, you begin to be filled with excitement about the next chapter of life. Even in the midst of shit.

"When you feel down and out, sing a song, it'll make your day.

You need a time to shout out loud. Sing a song, it'll make a way."
– Earth Wind and Fire, Gratitude, Sing a Song

While processing your way beyond your situation, this may sound silly to you guys, but consider finding a song or two that resonate with you and sing it when you have time to yourself. Sing when others are around, it doesn't matter how you sing it. Singing through tough times is just one more way of actively lifting that bubble of yours off the Miserable Station *(Sometimes when I would be frustrated to have to clean up after you guys, belting out a little "Swing Loooow, Sweet Chariot" would brighten my spirits. Whatever works, right?)* Sing, clean, organize, read, write, workout or stretch. Your options abound. **ACTIVE** engagement in something very personal and positive throughout the process is an excellent way of keeping your thoughts focused in the right direction.

"We can always choose to perceive things differently.
You can focus on what's wrong in your life,
or you can focus on what's right."
     – Marianne Williamson

Remember this example of when shit got real for me, and how the way I processed it made *such a* difference in my life.

"It's Daddy. Give me a call when you get
some free time. Love you." **– Daddy**.

The last time I heard Daddy's voice was on a voicemail **less** than forty-eight hours before he unexpectedly died. It was the best voicemail message of my life because of the timing. Timing is everything. Because of the timing, it stuck with me. It also stuck with me because I didn't get some free time, *in time*. I missed our usual, wonderful, marathon call. Our calls were always filled with love, philosophy and **super**-crude, 'laugh 'til you cry,' humor. But at that exact moment of my life, I was overwhelmed and stressed by pressures of trying to help others. He knew very well that, "Call me," would get an immediate reaction. His mention of "free time" sounded like he wanted me prepared for our usual marathon talk. Folks who know me know what I'm talking about. I put WORK IN on my marathon calls *[This book ain't nothing but a phone conversation for me. Lol ;-)]*. Free time felt impossible for me at that moment. I was leaving a funeral, driving toward work. I was stressed and wanted to get some things behind me to be able to relax and chat with Daddy. I wasn't feeling in my natural space at that time, and *he knew that too*. He had slipped me messages to find free time before. "Ey man, sometimes just go hit or miss," he'd say. He had tried to tell me that I didn't need or deserve to be living the stressed way that I was. I knew, from our past conversations that his last message was loaded. I knew that the moment I got it. That was how we communicated. So, I was going to do what he suggested and was absolutely intent on stealing free time for our talk within the next couple of days. There was zero chance that I wouldn't find the free time for our marathon talk. Did I say zero chance? They say God laughs at plans.

"No matter how far wrong you've gone,
you can always turn around."
     – Gil Scott-Heron

Life gives you lessons in every tragedy, *every one of them*. You are not being beat up on for no reason. Like I've told you guys, many times. Life's toughest challenges are like spankings from God. The same way I've spanked your little buns to try to teach you lessons when nothing else would, life's lessons sting sometimes. But only to get your attention to the very important lessons you **keep** missing. There's love embedded in these tough moments. Thankfully, I saw that immediately.

It took months for me to figure it out, but with his bubble by my side I restructured my life to allow more time for myself and the people I love. I already know Daddy's proud that I heard him and that my life was changed by his words. There's no telling what impact I'll indirectly bring to myself and the world as my life continues to change. I will certainly move forward more empowered. I attribute much of this to his timely and powerful message to me. Shit got real in the moment that I realized he had passed. But, learning something valuable from it and using that to launch the next chapter of my life has been a beautiful thing. The positive changes in my life are in honor of him. When shit gets real, see the opportunity for a new beginning. **Seize it**.

"We all know sometimes life's hates and troubles
can make you wish you were born in another time and space,
but you can bet your lifetime that and twice its double,
that God knew exactly where he wanted you to be placed."
     – Stevie Wonder, As |Songs in the Key of Life

And if shit ever gets so real that you feel hopeless, always, always remember that you are completely and forever enveloped with love that can be used, **ANYTIME**, to lift you right on out. Listen to Stevie's "As," and envision that message coming from not just me, but God too.

"Know through all your joy and pain that I'll
be loving you always ... Alwaaaays!"
     – Stevie, As

Most of us come into this world crying in discomfort, having experienced a trauma, expressing our apparent displeasure as we cringe at the cold reality of birth. Then, we let that experience go and move on with living life. Given that that's how we enter this life, there's no logical reason to expect life to be a heavenly, perfect, strictly pleasurable, discomfort-free experience. There's no reason to hold onto the experiences we don't like. We didn't do it as a baby and we shouldn't now. Let's get that solidly in our heads from the jump. **Waves of challenge are natural occurrences**. Repeatedly get knocked down by them and squeal in frustration and agony, OR learn to surf. Surfing life's waves is an 'on the job training,' self-taught skill. It's in each of our hands to master it all by ourselves. Otherwise, we can live with being battered by these **natural** waves. Whether you stand firm, getting repeatedly knocked down by life's naturally occurring waves of challenge or you learn to surf 'em like a pro, your response reflects the buoyancy of your bubble and who you truly are. Rise to the challenge, because that's who you are!

In surfing slang, "Bitchin'" means awesome, amazing and/ or great. The best surfers live for those bitchin, *most challenging waves*. Find some *good vibrations* in the most **bitchin'** of life's moments. Learn to surf and ride those 'bitchin' waves!

If nothing and no one can hold you down, do the math … you're elevating ;-).

"Life ain't where you *rest in peace*."
Mom

WHEN IT RAINS IT POURS, HUH?

We've all experienced this one. Try to see it as if the author of your life story is trying **hard** to get your attention. You may have been drifting off script. Stop for a moment and pay attention to the things you could change in your life. You're likely stuck in some old behaviors as if on a hamster wheel, and missing a valuable life lesson. You may not be making the changes necessary to move beyond a lesson you're meant to learn. If you can't see or understand what the lesson is? No worries. It happens. There's **something** you can do to stop the downpour.

Changing something is the solution to the "when it rains, it pours" problem. Use both your brain and heart to see what you feel needs to be changed. Try your best to tap an instinct for the changes that would make a difference in your life. You're not looking for the answer to *all* your problems, just a positive change in your life, big or small. Hopefully, you'll make a change that takes you in new and wonderful directions. One good change in your life can stop the downpour.

Whatever you do, make sure it involves real changes in your thinking and actions. Sometimes hard changes are necessary, but start small and go from there. In most cases, you have a pretty good idea of what needs to change, but you're not willing to do it. You may think you're unable, or it's impossible to make a change. Deep down inside, you already know that's not true. But it's all on you. It's your life. Do you really want to stick with what's not working, make it rain, *then* complain? Really? Have at it, then. When you get tired of that and are ready for some sunshine in your life, set a goal and make that change.

When you finally learn the lesson you're supposed to learn, and have made the core life change required, those rain clouds will "poof!" They'll completely disappear leaving the sun shining brilliantly down on you with no forecast for rain. This will last for a while. You'll know what to do when the next drizzle or downpour hits.

Q: Why aren't they playing my songs? 😫

A: Because you're no longer tuned to that station. 🧑 You have to turn to the right station to hear the music you want to hear, right? Such is life (*c'est la vie*). You have to turn your vibration to the station that plays the life situations you want. Your vibration has to be similar to how you'd feel if you had everything you want. THAT feeling carries the vibration that "auto-tunes you" to the station of your dreams. Don't put the cart *(your dreams)* before the horse *(the work that it takes to get on the right vibration despite what's going on around you and in your life)*. Figure it out. Get it done. Let shit go. Sit that brain down. Learn to meditate. Pray. Connect with the source. Feel good as shit, no matter the depth of the challenge you face or the hold it has taken on you *(sometimes debilitating ... we **all** know)*. Get up and fight off that baggage! Don't let your **baggage** whip your ___. Come on, now. You have to fight.

"I don't fold under pressure.
Great athletes perform better under pressure.
So, put pressure on me."
– Floyd Mayweather

FEELING STUCK OR TRAPPED?

"Go ahead and free yourself."
– Fantasia, Free Yourself

If you EVER feel stuck or trapped, go inward. Meditate and ask yourself how you got in the situation? What mindset led you there? Are you really trapped? *Criminal abductions aside*, you're usually not trapped. As in the image of the horse held in place by being tied to a plastic lawn chair, the feeling of being stuck or trapped is mostly self-imposed. It can be so hard-wired in your mind that your brain literally has you trapped. Sometimes you're just so unwilling to make changes in your life. Don't be so risk-averse, that you trap yourself. **Never be afraid to make the tough choices and tough changes** that are necessary for you to feel free. If you ARE trapped, there's still a way out. Freedom always starts with the belief that there's a way out. Change your thinking, first. Sure, you'll have some "dealing" to do to resolve the situation. No doubt about that. So, get at it soldier! Harriet Tubman was

Release thoughts that imprison you.

stuck *and* trapped. Muster courage. Practice hope with equal amounts of fearlessness, determination and hustle. Keep your eyes on the prize of your new life. You deserve freedom. Nothing less. So, have hope and a vision for what you want. Then, go get it.

> "Hope is the thing with feathers that perches in the soul.
>
> And sings the tune without the words.
>
> And never stops at all.
>
> And sweetest in the gale is heard,
>
> and sore must be the storm that could abash
>
> the little bird that kept so many warm.
>
> I've heard it in the chillest land and on the strangest sea.
>
> Yet never in extremity, it asked a crumb of me."
>
> ### – Emily Dickenson, Hope is the Thing with Feathers [Sky's favorite poem ;-)]

I hope you guys are old enough to *truly* get this poem now. Hope comes from the heart. Muster as much hope as you can to get yourself through every situation that grips you with that feeling of being stuck or trapped. Your heart knows that you are not stuck. It will generate hope to guide you where you need to be to get you up outta there. Pay attention to the things you truly hope for and start moving in ***those*** directions.

The key, at the end of the day, is to not miss the lesson that the current challenge (feeling stuck or trapped) is trying to teach you. Most often, you'll have to pay attention and learn something about *yourself*, instead of focus on whatever you 'think' is holding you. Pray for guidance. Constantly generate self-love throughout the process. **Increasing your self-love is *extremely* important** *(it's usually part of the problem)*. Think constantly of what YOU truly want. Visualize it. Claim it. Don't be too scared to go for it. Remind yourself every day that your spirit is boundless and free … and *eventually*, you'll be free and flowing again. **You are not stuck. You are not trapped. But you *do* have to free yourself**.

"A helping hand is at the end of your arm."
– Unknown origin

WORRIED? DON'T

"Worry is prayer for the wrong things."
– Neal Donald Walsch

Worry releases chemicals in your body that negatively affect your health. That sounds like a no-go to me, but wait, there's more! On top of messing up your body with the negative effects of worrying, **you're unintentionally *praying* to receive the things you worry about**. Wait. What?

Worried thoughts are real live energy. Believe it. That energy flows out from you like a text message request **for** the very thing you're worrying about. You're actually ***increasing*** the chances of it materializing by worrying. You're praying ***for*** it. That's the **last** thing you want to do!

Worry is such a low level energy anyway. It's a negative energy in other words. It's lead for your bubble. It's a +82 of unnecessary weight for your bubble, off the break. Let worry go and you'll actually ***increase*** your chances of being guided through whatever it is you were worried about.

"Match the frequency of the reality you want and you cannot help but get to that reality. It can be no other way. This is not philosophy. This is physics."
– Incorrectly attributed to Einstein, but very true!

Instead of worrying, send out some "texts" for a beautiful outcome. Don't dwell on things that make you feel bad. Never ever, **ever** do that! Accept life's harsh realities quickly, then pivot to uplifting thoughts. Accept that there are some things you cannot change. Then, **hope and hustle**.

When you find yourself worrying and don't know how to stop, distract yourself. Distractions include: reorganizing your closet, watching a comedy, working out, listening to music or spending time outdoors surrounded by nature. You guys seem to know how to ignore things that you don't want to deal with, so use that skill to ignore your own mind. Cover your ears and make noises. It doesn't matter **how** you keep those thoughts out, just keep them away!

"I've had a lot of worries in my life, most of which never happened."
– Mark Twain

The crazy thing is that most of the time spent worrying is in vain anyway. It is time spent projecting unwanted possibilities on your life and others. It may be time spent mulling over how awful something is in the present. Or even worse, you could be worried about something that is in the *(gasp)* **past**. None of these options make sense when your mind is at peace. If it makes sense for you to worry, **that's** the root of your problem. Get yourself to the point where worrying makes no sense.

"A frown will bring your spirits down to the ground, and never let you see the good things all around."
– Earth Wind and Fire, On Your Face, Spirit

Why would you think that it makes sense to worry? Are you thinking that worrying means you are actively recognizing the magnitude of the situation and dealing with it through thought energy and processing? If so, wouldn't a more productive way to deal with it be a course of action? If you are thinking, trying to develop a solution, that's not worrying. You are trying to create a course of action in your mind. Something that puts your thoughts or some solution into motion. That's a good thing. Taking constructive action is a good choice. Worry is not that. Worry is not productive. Worry allows the thought of something unwanted to generate bad feelings for you.

Do you think worrying means you care? Show how much you care through constructive action. Show care in the form of genuine faith that things will work out one way or another. Show care through prayer and faith that the divine guidance to solve the problem will fill your mind. Don't worry, push forward with a solution. If it feels beyond your ability to help solve, don't be ashamed to let the universe have that one. You can't solve everything. Accept the things you can't change. Full faith and acceptance that everything will work out never hurts. Everything always works out one way or another. We're not all-powerful creators that can solve the world's problems. The way I see it, life and everything in it, was set in motion by the same force that created us. That force still exists and *obviously* has enough power to handle what needs to be handled.

Perhaps the biggest thing here is learning to let go of insistence on how things "should" be. You are amazing and miraculous and special as all get out, but you don't happen to know how things **should** be *(not one of us does, even though we think we do)*. You just know how you want or envisioned things to be. Your visions are a guide for you, but not the Universal Master Plan. Be a little humble. Do your best to achieve the outcome you hope for, but venture so far as to accept life as it unfolds. Don't worry yourself. Learn something instead. Even if the only thing you learn is how to let go of your worries. Learning how to let go of worries is an extremely powerful skill.

> "Baby, everything is alright, uptight, out of sight."
> **– Stevie Wonder**

> **Note**: When all else fails to rid yourself of the worry, fully **accepting the worst case scenario is a trick that works for me**. Try it. Once you are in full acceptance of the worst case scenario, you're more empowered to deal with whatever happens. You feel more invincible and prepared. Hope and faith start to set in to replace the worry.

FORGIVE AND LET THAT SHIT GO

> "The weak can never forgive. Forgiveness
> is the attribute of the strong."
> **– Mahatma Gandhi**

When something is past, *it's over y'all*! Later, Jack! Speed on before you know what. It's time to take a lesson from it and keep it moving. Drop it like it's hot. Forgive and let that shit go!

"I think we can agree, the past is over."
- President George W. Bush

Somebody hurt or offended you with their actions or inactions? Whether you're feeling froggy or injured, remember that what you're holding onto at this point is called a negative thought. After a brief period of time, any thoughts about the situation become negativity coming from YOU. Thoughts about situations that have already past, particularly thoughts about how you received unjust treatment, are kind of like food in a sense. These thoughts start off as something you need. You needed the thought to understand and process what happened, so you could learn and put a positive solution in play. The moment of need for that thought expires, however. Whether your thought was right and you indeed sustained an offense of some kind, or whether you were wrong and *mistook* a situation as an offense doesn't matter. What's important to understand is that, like food, those thoughts expire and become rotten if not digested and eliminated. You have to process stuff while it's **fresh** to get the value out. You gotta throw it out after a couple of days, guys. Take a long hard look at yourself if you are still mulling over old offenses. The culprit is not someone else, it's you. As you hold onto the anger or the offense itself, the chances are strong that **you** are offending other innocent people with the subtle funk of the old shit you carry. Keep it fresh. Let shit go.

"History is a rock ... can't swim if you're holding it."
– John Malkovich as Walker in *Bullet Head*

When you forgive and let go, you release funky, ugly energy that immediately provides lift to your bubble and allows you to turn the page and float on to the next chapter of your life. When you hold onto hatred, anger, simple thoughts about the situation, or revenge, you keep yourself at the level of the thing you despise. Need I say more? Our attitudes and feelings transfer to our bodies. So get rid of painful memories with forgiveness and understanding. Forgiveness heals **physically**, both you and those you forgive. It **helps you to evolve spiritually**, as well as creates a more buoyant bubble.

It's not easy, I know. But work on it. Be determined. Set goals. You will amaze yourself when you realize that you have let something that you didn't think you could possibly let go, truly go. Once you do, you will keep letting things go. Trust me! Forgiveness will be your forte. You'll notice that the offenses slow down considerably too. Who knows why, but you'll be the better for it.

THAT'S NOT FAIR!

If you're still feeling like life is supposed to be fair, where have you been? News flash, it isn't **supposed** to be anything, much less **fair**. We are each on completely different life paths. Our souls, our bubbles are at different levels. Therefore, how on earth can things be equally distributed? Your experience is what your soul needs to experience. The next person experiences what their soul needs to experience. Yours has nothing to do with theirs. We each have different lessons. We're each a different soul. Stop the nonsense of expecting things to be fair in your mind and deal with what comes in *your* life. Deal with it with acceptance and grace. And keep pushing.

Inequities, and even injustices are realities of life. Whether it's basic human rights, animal rights, or the right of way, no matter how much effort goes into enforcing them, they never shake out with 100 percent fairness. There's a bigger picture in play. Speak up for injustice, but do not allow yourself to be burdened by it. That's baggage. Be cool with the fact that life isn't going to be 'fair.' Fight your way through life when you must. That just means a fight was written into your story. So, fight your way through! The best way to make progress toward your dreams is to release any baggage energy built around the need for 'fairness.' You're more empowered when you accept this. Don't go there with thoughts that what others have is, somehow, not fair to you. That reeks of insecurity, selfishness and a Yureego gone haywire. Nip it in the bud. Adopt a more well-rounded appreciation for the diversity of life. Life is different for each of us. There's security in knowing that you have everything you're meant to have, that nothing meant for you will ever escape you. Run, powerfully, with the hand you were dealt. Figure out how to win with it. See blessings for others as **beautiful**, not something to be measured against *your* holdings. Life is very complex. There are complex lessons in play throughout this game. Life wasn't meant to be fair.

GRIEF

"Happiness is beneficial for the body, but it is grief that develops the powers of the mind."

— **Marcel Proust** *(I do believe that grief, when processed healthily, can mark an elevation in your life.)*

From childhood, most of us have been hard-wired to process grief in the worst way. We learned to process grief in the way that brings the PAIN. We usually focus our attentions on loss; NEVER having the loved one again; painful replays of moments that will never be recaptured; sadness and despair. Sometimes the pain is so strong and crippling that it affects our lives in negative ways and delays healing. Since the experience of losing loved ones is a normal, inevitable part of *everyone's* life, I want you to have the healthiest, smoothest, no-baggage healing process possible. It'll require some re-wiring, which is a big challenge, but it's worth it.

Bawl for as long as you need when a loved one makes their exit. It's healthy to release tears as you absorb the 'exit' as your new reality. After the initial bawling period, the pain may feel just as intense, but the healing process has begun. Now, it's time to begin processing how you're going to move forward from this without baggage. I have suggestions for re-wiring your thoughts to ease the healing process.

GRIEF RE-WIRING IS AS EASY AS 1, 2, 3, 4

Before you get to the next 'exit,' train your brain. Acceptance, understanding of how our bubbles flow, and turning Yureego off for a minute, can work wonders for freeing any baggage from grief. Read this before an exit occurs, or read it following an exit *(after the bawling session subsides)*.

1. **Humbly accept, from the heart.** Accept and embrace the change. Do not resist what has already happened. Every exit is a great, great thing for the person who has moved to the next level. This change is a part of THEIR life. Do NOT miss that they are having a new journey experience. Their parting is a glorious life change for them. **Focus there. Death is *not* negative.** Process that. Release the need to know why the timing or method didn't match your ideas of perfection. The timing and method are now in the past. Let go. The here and now is much more beautiful than you "think." Let all the brainwork go. "Feel" a sense of acceptance and a humble trust in the creative force that brought you together in the first place. You didn't arrange for the loved one to be in your life. Many factors beyond your control had to fall into place for you to have been connected. See this, and recognize that you *also* don't arrange when your loved ones leave *(with few exceptions, of course)*. The same creative force that brought them to you is still, very much in play. That force has insured that they are still available to you in a different form. Humbly accept this with gratitude. **Learn**: Our time with *every* loved one is limited. From the start, there is a set amount of time that you will have with *everyone*. Neither of you know the amount of time you will have. Get all the beauty you can out of *every* moment. Be prepared to let go if their exit comes before yours, knowing that you knocked the moments of your relationship out of the park when you had the chance.

2. **Genuinely celebrate their beautiful and natural transition**. I want your first thought for every exit to be of a celebration that highlights the beautiful, new existence for those who cross over. See it more like a graduation celebration. Regardless of how they crossed, the transition to the next realm is believed to be a beautiful experience for them. DO NOT miss out on that part. They got the chance to release all of the struggles of this life and enter into pure love and light. You **can** actually stay focused there, instead of on yourself. Imagine that, right? This seems impossible to do, but all things are possible. Remember that you're faced with the choice of hurting with painful

thoughts of **your** loss, or being filled with awe and joy about how wonderful their new experience must be for **them**.

You could choose to be filled only with thoughts of the wondrous Cloud 100 experience of graduation that your loved one is experiencing. True, they can't experience life in the physical realm right now. At least not the way you can. But is that sad? If you think it's sad that they can't experience life here and now, then all the more reason for you to let go of thoughts that bring pain, and go LIVE while you can. Your loved one will take joy in seeing you do this, by the way. **Learn**: You can be so entangled with their spirit, that you can feel their elation, the elevation and joy of the exit for *them*. Sense that everything is wonderful for them *(which it is)*, and try not to center their beautiful exit on your personal pain. That would be a gift to them and a feat of some amazing brain and heart work.

3. **Develop a heightened connection that you can feel.** Here's a scientifically unproven fact that I know in my heart to be true. Evidence exists, but it's not considered proven. Your loved one still exists as a bubble, and has heightened abilities now. Their abilities are above and beyond anything we can imagine ourselves able to do. They're at a vibrational frequency only reached without the denseness of our bodies and brains. We couldn't reach those levels if we tried, but it's nothing for them to reach ours. Imagine them with access to God level technology and the happiest of vibrations. They're just as surprised as you would be to realize that after the exit, they can still hear, see, and be near you whenever they want or whenever you need. The only problem is that you have them completely tuned out. Grief fades when you are tuned-in to them. Belief that they're gone prevents you from building a reception. It's not **their** reception that's compromised, it's yours. Believe this one guys. I promise I would never steer you wrong. Increase your connection. Loosen up on all the bye-byes, and enjoy the new relationship. **Learn**: If you swap out thoughts of loss and woe with thoughts of their, very tangible, new existence, you can start the process of developing a heightened connection that might shock you.

"They won't leave in the night, I've no fear that they might desert me."
– Shirley Bassey, *Diamonds are Forever*

4. **Bubbles are forever** ;-) Energy can only change form, it can't end. Although we know this from science, it's a bit too abstract for us. We're believers of our eyes and ears and what we can touch. We rely on our eyes and ears for **everything**. That's how we determine what's real. Even though we know full well that we are bundles of swirling atoms, it's too abstract, so we ignore it and see

ourselves the way that our brains can easily process. Even though we know there exist sounds that we can't hear *(dog whistle is just **one** example)*, we stick with the notion that we can hear everything. Even though science tells us there are many spectrums of light that we can't see, it still doesn't exist in our minds if we can't see it. Most, unable to wrap minds around our limitations to perceive reality, base beliefs only on what can be seen and heard. It's mind-boggling that we do this, but we're the ones being boggled by our minds. We don't have the eye and ear power of most animals on this earth. We know this, but that doesn't stop us from 'feeling the power.' Our instincts can't compare to that of animals, but that doesn't stop us from feeling that we "know" everything. We should be a little more humble about the power of our brain. We should recognize that our brains aren't equipped to perceive what's going on with entries and exits. We're unable to perceive **many** things that are very real. See the people you love in a different way from the start. Instead of seeing only with your eyes, and seeing only their bodies, start to 'see and feel' their bubble and recognize that the most significant parts of their being are held there. If the love is real, it's the bubble you're feeling. Establish a connection with who they truly are. Recognize that their bubble holds their consciousness, their heart and soul. These are the eternal parts of them that exist well after they exit our 'Life Channel.' You see, while we think everything revolves around this 'Life Channel' we're on, it doesn't. This is just one space for bubbles to hang out on. There are more. The good news is that when your loved one leaves the 'Life Channel,' they still exist in a way perhaps more real than **you**. They know all of this hookup stuff once they exit. Without the strain of processing with a brain, they're tapped into pure consciousness. You, too, should avoid figuring all of this out with your brain. Give the processing of exits to your heart. Establish a connection with the bubbles of your loved ones while they're alive. Don't focus so much on the physical, constantly changing part of them. Try not to overly focus on the physical aspects of *anyone* for that matter. We're all infinite bubbles of energy. Yes, our bubbles are forever! When an exit comes, after you've already identified with the "infinitely live" part of the person you love, grief will come, but the grief won't take too long before giving way to an amazing feeling of comfort. I pray that you can re-wire to experience that. You'll feel that you still have them in, yes, a very different, but very wonderful way. I **pray** you experience this. **Learn**: Connect with the eternal parts of your loved ones. What's truly real is our field of consciousness, the heart and the soul of each of us. These are the things that we take with us. This is what we call our bubble, and it never disappears. Our ability to perceive the bubble after the 'exists' is heightened if we relate to this concept while they are *living*. But it's never too late because bubbles are forever. You can never lose someone you love. So, don't "think" you do.

Grief can be **such** a rock solid barrier to Happiness, it's worth chatting more on this before we move on.

No matter your perspectives or how prepared you are, there's an immediate emotional wound that occurs when you feel you've lost someone you love. Something comes over you that's **heavy**. Expect it. Don't try to make it go away too fast. This is grief. It's part of the human experience. The pain of grief is as natural a reaction as if you had been stung by a bee. Or a swarm of bees, in some cases. Or punched in the gut by a heavyweight champ. Or, in the most traumatic cases, it can feel like you were shot out of nowhere by a sniper. Each loss *has* its impact. Immediately following impact, however, the healing process begins. Your healing process can be impacted by how healthy you were in the first place. Whether you're hit with the loss at a time when you're perfectly happy and healthy, or at a time when you're *not* (unhappy, stressed, etc.), it's time to let shit go and be completely convinced that you WILL fully heal. Commit to a full, miraculous recovery. **Remind yourself that the biggest show of love and respect to your loved one is to feel their presence, to show them that their presence in your life actually *elevates* you. Give 'them' happy vibes. Move forward, uplifted, because they're sharing every step of the way with you. Commit to healing beautifully to 'show off' how much positive impact they still have in your life**! Happiness WILL return to your life more quickly. You *can* emerge miraculously healed and happier than ever. You can and you will if you're 100 percent committed.

The big problem is that when a loved one makes an exit, we're already hard-wired to thoughts and feelings of deep loss and mourning. It's automatic. Those feelings of loss are compounded by all the changes that will occur in your life. Most of us aren't too keen on life changes in the first place. While we mull over all the ways that our dreams have been shattered, however, our loved one is having the time of their "lives." We're so wrapped up in our own feelings that we're unable to connect with *that*. It's a natural reaction, but you have to try your best to break out of the concept of loss. Lose the "me, me, me," focus and accept that everything is ok. Nature is at the helm. Some sadness is perfectly natural. You sustained an injury. You're healing. Prolonged sadness, however, identifies a wound that won't heal. That's not natural. We'll need to build up some healthy thought processes to get you healed up. The natural return to the spiritual realm of our loved ones is not supposed to land us on the Miserable Station. Timing, cause, and manner of passing have to be accepted, just as timing, cause and manner of birth do. Accept **everything**. Your loved one must be going nuts to see you unhappy. Commit to healing quickly for them. You're missing the new relationship with them! We can't have that. Heal your wounds by latching on to the perspectives that help you. You don't have to roll with painful, hard-wired thoughts.

Using your brain to process life's exits will bring the pain for several reasons. It's not capable of sensing beyond the physical. It's already hard-wired to be sad about exits, and when the Yureego feature senses *any* disadvantage, it automatically locks onto its "woe is me" mode, which has unlimited capabilities of dread. With our AI/Yureego at the helm, our hearts don't stand a chance to weigh in. If our hearts were at the helm, we'd be better able to connect with the universal wisdom that reveals that it's all a natural and beautiful life transition. Set a goal for yourself to see death to be as beautiful and transformational as birth. Start now, on building a perspective of death positivity that better connects you to reality and Happiness.

As hard as it is to perceive, humans change form from having a bubble with a body at the center, to having a bubble without the body at the center. We go from physical to non-physical, physical to non-physical and the beat goes on. The bubble goes on. Bubbles are forever. That's it. Use your heart's instinctive, intuitive energy to sense that the same bubble you loved, still exists beyond your five, limited senses. If your eyes and ears had powers well beyond the human spectrum, you'd realize this is true right now. Wherever their new home base is, your loved one can be with you in an **instant** when needed. They're probably with you right now. Their ability to be with you at a moment's notice is kinda like texting to us, it doesn't take them from their "new life." They can group text lots of people all at once. Their technology's more advanced. You can't bother them ;-). So, don't hesitate to connect. If their new form could be enough for you, you'd be rolling right now. Fortunately for them, we don't have the power to snatch them back from the Cloud 100 Station they're on. If we *could* snatch them from Cloud 100 back to our dense reality, they'd be in some kind of trouble.

Wouldn't it be a show of the ultimate love to be happy about this new chapter for you both? You loved them when they had a body in their bubble. Now that they have an angelic high flying bubble unbound by the body, you can't act like they don't exist! Come on now. **Let their new presence be more than enough for you**. You're still a team IF you can feel and accept the new situation. Share the next chapters of your stories, together. It's straight from heart to heart now. You are forever intertwined, so no worries! Enjoy the new soul mate relationship.

"We are healed from suffering only by experiencing it to the full."
– Proust

Never forget that it's scientific fact that the energy that's writing these messages for you cannot end. Energy can only change form, it cannot end. Although we know this, it's just too abstract for us. Believers of only what the eyes can see and the ears can hear and what can be touched or felt, have the **hardest** time with grief. Just as atoms are real, yet impossible to see with our eyes, there are many things that we can't see, hear or touch that are very, **very** real.

There are atoms swirling throughout our bodies that we can't see or feel. Our bodies are mostly empty space, but we can't perceive that. We're on a spinning ball, hurling through space at a phenomenal speed, but we can't perceive that either. We know we're not perceiving realities that we accept as real. Is it so much of a stretch to accept this one? If you believe, you *might* be able sense your loved one. It's your responsibility to *try*. They're probably waiting.

Notice nature's example of how to deal with grief as you witness how animals deal with it. They miss their loved ones. They absolutely do. You can see their grief, but perhaps because they don't have the luxury of being captivated by their AI or Yureego, they're able to process from their hearts. Their hearts, as all hearts, are more aware of life's perpetual motion. They recognize the loss, grieve, accept, then move on. Maybe after the initial shock, they instinctively understand that the exit is not a bad thing, just an unwelcome, natural part of a bigger process? Who knows, but it would be very healthy to believe a bigger process is in play and to roll **happily** with it.

Change your core beliefs about life's "exits" now. The hard reality is that everyone comes with an expiration date. Never take for granted that you know that date. That's the first thing to do. Treasure, not take for granted, every single moment of life that you have with any of your loved ones **while they are living**. Make the most of every moment that you have with every person that means anything to you. This makes the grief process easier when it comes. If you lose a loved one and regret not having said or done some things, remember that you can STILL tell the person everything you want to say *after* they've passed. Their consciousness still exists as real as yours right now. I don't doubt that the ability of their bubbles to receive your messages is even *better* than it was when they were here. There's no AI in the way to distort, nor will they be too busy for your message. That might not be scientific, but that's cash money you can take to the bank. Just talk to them. Never carry baggage about something unsaid or undone. Their bubbles are floating so high now, trust me that they are NOT tripping on any of that. That's just your issue now. Let that shit go. Say and do all that you can with those who are still here. Your loved one, in particular, would be so happy to see you moving forward in such a beautiful way.

If grief lingers to the point that your bubble is sitting low for extended periods of time, don't be too proud to admit that your state of mind has become unhealthy and must be healed. Extended periods of grief indicate that you're carrying a lil' emotional baggage. It's ok! We just have to get to work on releasing the baggage thoughts and feelings. Please remember that extended grief does not indicate depth of love for the loved one. Never believe in a million years that it is positive; required as a show of true love, or highly regarded in **any** way, for you to mourn at length. That unhealthy perspective does not originate from love or the heart of God. To the contrary, that theory is constructed by the ego. With that said, let's continue to look at a few more ways of thinking that might bring healing and lightness of mind.

What we call death is a beautiful transition of life. Beautiful things should come from it. What's even more beautiful is that we never lose the ones we love.

You never lose someone you love. Not in the way that matters most. It just looks like you do. They witness what happens in your life after they have moved on from their body. Seriously. Look into what I'm saying. You can Google for information on out of body experiences by people who have been under anesthesia. You can look into the accounts of those who were clinically dead, then came back. Every story is like the next. Inspiring. Add to it the overwhelming evidence in the form of the unexplained and **you have to have brain wiring of steel not to accept that your loved one is still around and accessible to you in bubble form. Open up. They're right there for you.**

Never lose focus that this is *your* life. Your challenge is always to keep your energies as high as you possibly can. Whatever you choose to believe, your bubble *does* get out of this life alive and well. You **CAN** take the most important things with you (love and soul lessons). Fill up with so much love that there's no room left for grief. You have soul lessons to knock out of the park.

THIS PLAY NEVER ENDS

Imagine that life is a Broadway play called, *The Circle of Life*. Every actor/actress is on stage learning life lessons from acting out their roles. Each has a different role to play, but learns from not just their role, but everyone else's. Everyone learns from the plot and the set and every aspect of the play. Learning is the whole point of the play, but everybody is getting deep into their roles and having fun with it. Some portions of the play are purely entertaining and comedy based, but the most significant lessons are learned during the tragic portions of the play. The play was written by the greatest teacher and playwright that ever existed in the world.

"All the world's a stage. And all the men and women merely players; they have their exits and their entrances, and one man in his time plays many parts."
 – William Shakespeare

When a person has completed their role, they exit, stage left. They go backstage and remove their costume. Backstage is AMAZING! It's luxurious and peaceful and gorgeous. Everyone's happy as can be. They're filled with love and excitement as they dap up (handshakes, fist bumps, etc.) all the others who've completed their roles. Backstage, they reflect on what they've learned. They share soul lessons with each other. They rest and enjoy being out of those costumes and back to their natural selves. They grab refreshments and celebrate. While enjoying their break, they also watch the ongoing play being live streamed whenever they choose. Some go off and work on other important projects as they wait to be called back for a new role in *The Circle of Life*.

Now, imagine that when one of the actors' role ended and they went backstage to get refreshments. They turn to watch some of the play from backstage, resting and enjoying themselves. Then, they see that one of their very close actor friends, who instead of moving forward with their role, is stuck in a personal tragedy and messing up their performance. Turns out their personal tragedy is that they're grieving the loss of the actor friend who's now backstage. They're stuck and hurt and depressed and not able to move forward with their role in the way they were before. They didn't agree with the change. Although it was perfectly written, they can't see that. They are devastated by losing their stage friend. The pain they feel over the perceived loss is intense and damaging. They're mentally and physically damaged now, AND unable to perform their role. The backstage friend, filled with concern, is now talking at the live-streaming monitor encouragingly saying, "I'm right here! It's no big deal! Just keep acting out your role and I'll see you when you wrap up!" But the friend on stage can't hear them and keeps thinking over and over that they've lost them forever. They're going through the motions, but not handling their role the way they usually do. This doesn't heighten the play or the backstage celebration of their friend. Unfortunately, it does initiate an unnecessarily painful period for the actor that's still on stage, unhappy and unable to knock their role out of the park. All the while, the backstage friend wishes their on-stage friend would realize that there's not a thing to worry about. The backstage friend wants their on-stage friend to get on with knocking their role out of the park. "Aw, come on! **I'm right here**. Everything is great! I'm trying to watch you do your thing! We'll dap up and party backstage when you finish!" The on-stage friend can't hear or see them, so the backstage friend might as well not exist at all. But the show, of course, goes on.

Believe it or not, **the things you can't see or hear are the most powerful things and the most real.** For example a thought, you can't see or hear a thought. Secondly, love, you cannot see or hear the feeling of love. And my third example is your soul, that part of you, aside from your body, which makes you who you are. We can see and hear your body, but we can only 'feel' your soul. When a person passes from this life, their soul detaches from the body. You can't see them, or hear them, but believe me, their energy, their consciousness, still exists and it is in fact very, very real. And while you have limitations on seeing and hearing them, they're still seeing and hearing you. They're just as real as when you could see them in bodily form. You still have them! They're just backstage. Once you realize this, you can begin to get used to the new form of the relationship and you might even "feel" their presence. While religions have tried to tell us this for eons, science is getting closer to convincing us of this. But don't wait for science! Life's too short.

So, as we lust for life, we should celebrate the exits when they come. Each one of us is living a life cycle that ends in rebirth. Each person has a different cycle with different experiences and different lengths of time. Leaving the body for the next journey is a part of the cycle of life and a reality to be embraced, not mourned. Live each moment to the fullest. Never put off sharing words and actions of love. Life is short, y'all!! There's only room for goodness [and greatness ;-)] in your life. Conduct your life in a way that eliminates regret when life transitions come. And throughout your life, know with every particle of your bubble that death is not final, just a transition to another realm. See the exits of your loved ones as similar to when a teen goes off to college. You miss the way it used to be, but you know they're still there … just in a different way that's better for them. Your loved ones are still THERE for you. I don't mean this figuratively. I mean this so very literally. We don't lose their souls, just their roles (in this reality). You'd sense their presence, if your mind didn't rule it out. REWIRE. A healthy understanding and an embrace of the cycle of life is transformative and keeps you in the rising flow toward Happiness.

The brain *grieves*. The heart *savors the new relationship status*. You *have to choose*.

A perspective of "death positivity" is a basic human need. The soul is infinite and death should be celebrated. There's no such thing as death when it comes to energy … and energy is all we truly are. Think about it. Celebrate death as a beginning and the completion of a story full of meaning. That meaning plays out in ways that we may or may not see. Focus on the beauty of the story that just played out. Celebrate genuinely, as you pull away from ego's selfish perspective of loss. Go live.

IN CASE OF DEPRESSION OR ANXIETY

"That's life. That's what all the people say.
You're riding high in April, shot down in May."
– **Frank Sinatra**, **That's Life**.

Life comes at you, *whew*, and the absolute strongest and wisest of us can get smacked with a touch of anxiety or a feeling of depression. Shit just happens, man.

BE POSITIVE.

That's in my blood (type B+), literally and figuratively. I couldn't make it up. But the words "be positive," don't work for me when I'm *not* feelin' it. Sometimes life's grip squeezes so tight, nothing can get between us and life's grip. I'm not immune to life's plights. I just know how to wrestle out 🐿. From my experience, here's how to wrestle out of a slump.

FOOD FOR THOUGHT: NATURE HOLDS THE CURE

You guys laugh when I talk about vegetables and water as if they're cures for practically everything. Trust that I know how funny it sounds. I do. Stop and ask yourselves though, why would **man** hold more power to heal you than the force that created you? I mean, wth? Am I tripping? That's what you're believing when you laugh at nature as a solution. Natural foods and cures were created by the **exact** same force that poofed you into existence. No middleman. I would think before laughing, if I were you. I've looked at this thing very, very seriously. I've read a lot of science. I've tested all kinds of things. Here's what I've deduced, from all of that extensive research and experience.

Nature has provided everything we need to naturally heal. Man upgrades with medicines and procedures. We then rely on the medicines and procedures *(you'd be shocked to understand how we came to rely on medicine, but it wasn't by accident, nor was it the widespread 'will of the people').* Then, we have a health crisis that extends to the health of our brains. It's outrageous how many suffer from anxiety and depression.

I have **NOTHING** against emergency medicine! After I broke down *twice* and accepted a last minute Epidural during labor, I wasn't mad about it. Disappointed that I broke down, but not mad. At least I tried my very best. Man has come up with some drugs! Do you hear me? And I was NOT mad about it! Water and veggies were NOT going to have the effect I received from that Epidural. **Unbelievable.**

There's some confusion about the cycle of health, medicine, and nature. And there's apparently some confusion about the fact that the brain is a body part and subject to the same health needs as your stomach, liver, heart or ligaments. We're quick to associate food intake with the health of other parts of the body: "I can't drink that champagne, it gives me a headache!" "That dairy doesn't sit well with my stomach." "I can't eat salt because of my heart." "Sugar will drive my glucose up." But, I have never, ever heard anyone mention what is good or bad for their brain. It could be argued that the brain's an even MORE vital body part! Right? Not sure where the confusion came from, but news flash, your brain is a body part. If you're feeling down, maybe your brain isn't getting everything it needs? Or maybe it's getting things it doesn't need. Think about it and treat your brain with a little more focused love.

Can you answer the question as to whether or not depression, anxiety and mental health issues diminish or disappear when exclusively consuming the things nature designed for us to consume? Do feelings of depression or anxiety diminish or disappear when a diverse range of raw, organic plants, ample amounts of fresh water and increased oxygen are consumed daily? Add a body in motion and a mind exposed to positivity and meditation to that equation. While your hard-wired brain tells you it's hogwash that these things could make a difference in lieu of medications, the answer, as studies have shown, is a resounding *yes*. Yes. As proven by scientific, medical studies, these things make all the difference.

If you ever feel like any form of depression and/or anxiety has paid you a visit, **focus on the body** section of the book, **first.** Those feelings are not your true nature, they're brought to life by imbalances in your body and quite possibly a tad of baggage energy held by your mind. Don't jump to (or fall for) the medical profession's outlook and answers until you've tried what I'm telling you. Medical science's answer is toxic medications, **without** addressing the source of the problem. You need detoxification and nutrient therapy, meditation and exercise ... and sunlight. Add in a bunch of helium-level philosophies to top it off and voila! On the other hand, those medications create dependency, toxicity and mask symptoms, as you continue the subtle abuses to your body and mind that caused the problem. If you want real change in your life and want to eradicate anxiety or feelings of depression, you CAN do it. It takes detoxification, nutrient therapy, meditation, exercise and inspiration whenever and wherever you find it. That's proven.

The absolute first thing to do is **cleanse and properly fuel your body** by infusing it with nature *(lots and lots of live, raw plant energy; deep breathing fresh outdoor oxygen; drinking lots of fresh water, two liters a day of the purest water you can get your hands on)*. It's likely that you're exposing your body to something that your body is intolerant of AND/OR you are deficient in some mineral or nutrient *(a low body pH will lead to mineral imbalances, which have been linked to depression, so eat alkaline foods and avoid acidic foods for a bit)*. Cleanse your body with a flush of live, organic plants and water, and take food-based vitamins and minerals. Secondly, begin to lightly stretch and/or walk. Keep active. Do the natural things you love to do. Every day, make certain that you involve yourself in some motion. If you don't feel like doing anything, **you must force yourself to do something**! Touch the sky. Touch your toes. Light stretching of your body and walking around the house is way better than being stationary. There's healing in that motion! If you feel you can do more physical exercise, do it, but if not, *which is often the case when you're down*, then just do **something**. Start with two sit ups, two pushups, **something** **every day**. Try it! This is what we all need to do anyway. A body in motion is a healing gift to your mind. Stay at the movement and the infusion of nature for your body for a good, long while. Over time, it WILL transform. Stay at it until you feel the difference. **90 days is the minimum**! You are *so* worth the effort.

To cleanse your mind, write, draw, shout, talk, cry out your feelings, because you gotta get rid of those baggage thoughts and worries. Keep in mind that your hard-wired negative thoughts are likely on a continuous "loop" that you can't seem to break. Distracting yourself with new actions could break the chain, and break that pain. The continuous negative thought loop is bringing your bubble down to the ground. Now, on the Miserable, or even Toxic Station, you're in a space that isn't healthy for any of us. We gotta get you out of there!

The good news, is that even for folks who are dealing with clinical depression and serious anxiety, there have been revolutionary advances and research that prove that you **can** be healed with proper nutrients provided to your brain as opposed to drugs *(you know how I roll. I have evidence ;-)* Dr. William J. Walsh, PhD, for example, has worked with thirty thousand individuals and developed an effective nutrient therapy that has produced thousands of reports of recovery from serious issues *including schizophrenia and autism*. The anxiety or depression is temporary and very healable, but this a situation that only YOU can get out of. This is YOUR life challenge. It's the game of life and **it's your go**. No matter which way you play it, your bubble will be intact and will learn from the whole experience. You're perfect, even as you work through your life issues. You're perfectly created, perfectly challenged, and now perfectly advised that nature holds the cure for you.

"Nutrient therapy can have a powerful impact on mental functioning,

but several weeks or months are usually
needed to achieve full effect."

Patience and belief are virtues here. Get

with the program because,

"the need for drug therapies will gradually
fade away as science advances."

– Dr. William J. Walsh, PhD,
Nutrient Power, Heal Your Biochemistry and Heal Your Brain.

I strongly believe that all of your answers are in *Chapter Three: Your Bubble is Your Temple*. So, let me reiterate. Your brain is a part of your body in the same way that your stomach is. Your brain is a body part. You know that your stomach doesn't like certain things and that it needs certain things, but you don't consider fueling your brain with what it needs. **There may be things that you are consuming or exposing yourself to that your brain does not like, and doesn't respond well to.** There are substances in some foods that are known to be detrimental to *your* optimal brain function. Everybody is different. Make sure you are getting what's good for *your* brain.

It's well known that lots of oxygen, water, exercise and meditation are excellent for optimal brain function. On the other hand, there are things that are **known contributors to anxiety and depression, including sugar, wheat gluten, dairy products, lectins (from beans and wheat), food additives like monosodium glutamate, pesticides and fluoride.** An improper balance of minerals is another suspected cause. Anything that causes inflammation in your body can possibly cause inflammation in the tissues of the brain, which could lead to these issues. It's worth eliminating these substances to see if it makes a difference.

So, ask yourself, are you giving your brain what it truly needs? If you want the icky feeling of anxiety and/or depression to go away, infuse your body (ultimately your brain) with the highest forms of life energy fuels that you can find. Do this religiously for several weeks, months, actually. If you don't notice a dramatic change after ninety days, I will let you slap me.

Made you laugh! ;-) Skip to Chapter Three if you're feeling anxious or down, and keep cranking. What may seem like the hardest thing to do is the most important. It's most important that you keep cranking. Like the crank flashlights we give to the homeless, every crank *(motion or action to you)* in a particular direction can lead to a dramatic energetic effect. Every action you take builds towards something. You generate energy with every action until some form of light is achieved. Motion, action, is the crank. Keeping in motion can help connect you to God energy. I have said this before. I have no idea why, but there's something to it! Stay physically in motion, *especially* when you're feeling down. If you're feeling down right now, the motion for you is flipping to Chapter Three. Oh! And listening to some Earth, Wind and Fire ;-) That never hurts. Just keep cranking.

Your new mantra:

"I" make *Happiness* out of whatever *happens*.

TAKE LIFE'S CHALLENGES HEAD ON: LEARN

"Life is not for sissies."
- Neal Donald Walsch

Yeah. I quoted Neal Donald Walsch *again*, on purpose. Life ain't for sissies, y'all. Don't forget it! Life is school for your soul. The challenges in life are like classes. The fun stuff is like recess.

You are supposed to learn a lesson, pass the class, then move on to the next class. **You'll get credits for the lessons you've actually learned, not from simply sitting through the class**. If you actually learn, the credits will add up and the next thing you know, you're graduating to the next level. Those super fun, dream-like moments of life can be likened to recess. They're fun and you can still learn some valuable lessons on the playground, no doubt. Even then, the lessons that elevate you to the next level usually come from challenge. Challenges are opportunities for your soul to evolve. See the challenges for what they are. Learn, so you can pass them. Literally.

If you get irritated by life's challenges, instead of learning from them, you'll stay back to repeat the lessons. The challenge will seem like it never ends. Learn from every challenge. Learn at every turn. Keep passing life's 'classes.' There's always a little fun in every class. It's not the learning that sucks, it's being irritated by the lesson that takes the fun away. Be a good student of life. Go into every challenge with the right attitude. Learn and move on! Staying back gets boring.

"That old bush just keeps on burning. Nobody seems to show they're learning."
– Earth, Wind and Fire, Burning Bush/Spirit

In the midst of every challenge life throws your way, see things in a way that makes the most sense for you and your Happiness. It's always about how you *look* at it. Always. Learn to look at challenges differently. The unwanted stuff that happens in our lives has more meaning to it than you think. What's more, these challenges poof away once you've learned all there is to learn. So, **don't get so absorbed in the frustration**

126

or sadness of the challenge that you forget to learn a lesson. Accept the challenge, then learn. You'll move past it much more quickly.

When life gives you lemons, remember that lemons are bright, natural, fragrant, beautiful and good for you in so many ways.

Get less into the nature of your trials and tribulations, and fully into **how you respond to each and every one of them. This is what marks the progress of your soul.** Times of challenge can be a fast track to wisdom if you take them head on and learn. Remember the quote from Nelson Mandela, "I never lose. I either win or learn." That's *you*, Boo.

GO FOR IT

"Ey, man, it's your m__ f__ go!
Do YOU! *Huh*!?
And don't say ya sorry,
'cause ain't *nuthin'* sorry **'bout** you!"
    – Daddy

This is your life. It's your go. **Go for it**! As you do, stay connected to your purpose in life. Use your natural desires, dreams, talents and skills as clues to your purpose. Follow them. It shouldn't be hard to know what you're supposed to be doing. All you have to do is mesh your dreams and desires with your natural talents and skills. We each have certain desires and talents for a reason. Take heed and put them in play. Be sure to consider what is needed in our world, and what patterns are already in play that fit well with *your* dreams and skills. Then, **go** for it! Do something that you love and *hope* that you can be a contribution to society by doing it. Be a tiny piece of the change we all seek, but most importantly, be a **huge piece of the change *you* seek**.

"Go steadfast in the direction of your
dreams. Live the life you imagined."
    – Thoreau

Of course you remember this Thoreau quote hanging on your bathroom wall. I put it there so it would be an unavoidable, constant, subliminal reminder to you. The one thing I can tell you about life is that it is meant to be **lived** to the fullest. What does "to the fullest" mean? It means going for your dreams and finding purposeful meaning in every little thing along the way.

As you set goals toward your dreams, remember: The *strength* of your commitment makes all the difference.

Please, don't ever be afraid to dream your biggest dreams because you think they're unattainable or unrealistic. Don't be afraid to dream big because you're worried about disappointment or that you're wrong about dreaming for certain things. Your dream is your business and no one else's. Where's the need for disappointment if you've done **all** you can to attain your dream, and it doesn't come true? Don't listen to that brain. There's no need for disappointment because **you will *surely* have gained what you were meant to gain through the process**. It just looks different than what you had in your mind. When you follow your dreams, you exert positive energy that presents results. That's just how energy rolls. There **will** be results. The results may be in a form other than what you had originally pictured. But pay closer attention to everything you learned along the way. If you are stuck on the fact that what you had in your mind didn't come true, you'll miss the gift of what you **did** materialize. I promise that you materialized something of meaning to your life. Every time you put everything you have into something towards a positive goal, whatever you do get will be the beautiful blessing that was *meant* for you. Could it be in the form of tough love? Sure it can. So what? See the blessing and learn these lessons for your soul. Be proud that you had the guts to follow your dream.

The dreams you have will draw you to something or someone important to your life. Follow your dreams without a worry in the world as to whether they come true.

The result of all the hard work toward your dream might materialize in an image or form that you never had on your radar, so pay attention and don't miss your blessing. If this doesn't make sense to you, good. Maybe we've identified a source of baggage that once released, will elevate you instantly to another level. If it doesn't make sense for you to be content with not having everything you dreamt of, you might be stuck on having everything your way. Is that it? Ok, then 'little g,' time to turn off that "Yureego" feature and bow to the big G.

The only issue, when you're worrying about being wrong or disappointed or embarrassed about not fulfilling your full dream, is that your ego can't risk that. Your ego has to stay on its high and mighty throne of being right and winning and fulfilling everything its little mind envisioned. This way, you can beam with achievement and nobody can say, "Oh. You didn't make it." Instead of taking that *risk*, you enter the state of not pursuing your dreams. You tell yourself the dreams weren't realistic anyway. What did you miss by not following your unrealistic dreams? You just missed a shortcut to your destiny. That's all. You can still get there, but now you got to walk instead of catch a ride in a limo. It's always better to travel along the route of your dreams. There are always alternate routes. Always. But following your dream would be more like a limo ride, as it holds you in a state of excitement and comfort as you travel. Walking the long road is healthy, so again, you can't lose. It's just more fun to follow your dreams to your destiny.

> **Quick Story:** When I was a kid, in the seventies, Grandma Haywood began a business venture. She designed, produced and marketed a phonics-based board game for kids that simulated Bingo, called "1,2,3,4." It was used as an easy way to teach kids to read. A decade or more later, without having sold all the games and reaching the vision of success that was in her mind, I made a trip to the Pentagon for a job I had. While sitting in the office of a Pentagon employee, I noticed the "1234" game in my peripheral. This was the eighties, so I couldn't believe my eyes. On top of the time gap, the Pentagon, is MASSIVE. MASSIVE! And his office had a lot going on. Just sayin'. I happened to sit facing the right direction and chat with him just long enough *(now, there's a shocker)* to allow me to notice the box sitting high on a shelf.
>
> His age and military rank didn't fit with learning to read, but there "1,2,3,4" was sitting on his shelf. I pointed to the game, inquiring if he happened to know Grandma. He clearly didn't. It was purchased long ago and his kids had played with it when in his office. What were the odds of me seeing Grandma's game that day? I decided to draw a lesson that despite the perception that she had not fulfilled her full dream with the game, she **had** touched lives. I knew **that** was what she dreamed to do. Who knew the significance it had to him *(to have his kids constructively occupied while he worked)* or the others who were touched by her game *(perhaps his kids learned to read this way)*? I didn't ask. I just knew, in that moment, that everything we do goes out into the world and has impact. We never lose when we follow our dreams. I knew there was more to life than what we think. The odds of me laying eyes on that game within the corridors of the massive Pentagon did not escape me. Grandma's effort with her game led to a lesson for me to follow my dreams without attachment to the outcome.

The next time a dream hits you. Sit that brain down! Follow your heart. When it comes to your dreams, all bets about being wrong or right are OFF. It's your damn dream. Dream it! Being right or wrong has some weight in school and at work. No doubt. But we're talking about you and your dreams for yourself and your life. It's not always about the destination. Sometimes it's simply about the journey. The journey towards your dreams is filled with elevating lessons for your soul. It's filled with like minds and soul mates. Your bubble is elevated just by doing it. So, **go** for it.

"The most effective way to do it, is to do it."
 – **Amelia Earheart**

FOLLOW YOUR HEART

"My heart comes down, down from the heavens,
down from above the rainbow, down into my body,
and then it soars away like an angel."
 – **Jet, age five.**

Jet asked me to spell the word "heavens." He was scribbling in his journal. Yeah, he had a journal at age five. Anyway, I have ALWAYS been vigilant about personal space and privacy, but his insistence on needing the spelling for the word "heavens" instead of "heaven" made me curious. He wrote his piece and went on to play. I eventually took a look at his journal and found the poem above, phonetically written. That was a priceless moment. There is an innate wisdom that flows through our hearts when we are children. Over time, it gets covered by the hard-wiring of all of our nifty brainwork.

I've talked a lot about your heart already. The following quote gives you a more tangible hint as to why.

"The heart is an electrical organ.
It produces, by far, the greatest force of bioelectricity in our body,
up to 40 to 60 times more than
the ***second*** most powerful source, which is the brain."
 – **Howard Martin,**
 Co-author *The Heart Mind Solution,* **Quantum Communication: Part 1**

Your heart is the center of your natural energy field. It's the center of your bubble. Today, **it is believed to carry more information and more energy than your brain.** You heard me right. The heart is believed by some top scientists, to carry **more "information" than your brain.** I am talking about the biological heart that beats within you, no less. Isn't that an astounding discovery? This fact can be used to guide your belief in ancient wisdom teachings that **the energy pouring through the area of your heart connects us, in some way, to our souls.** The heart has always been associated with love, which is clearly a soul level energy. Whatever the case may be, the heart is the smartest, wisest part of you. Take care of it by feeding it a steady diet of peace and love. Care for it as a prized body part by fueling it with heart healing, plant-based foods. Pamper, love, and trust your heart. Let all that information and the high-level energy of your heart guide your life.

"The heart, when it beats, generates a large electromagnetic field.

So that field generated by the heart radiates external to the body.

I'm not describing an aura now.

This is a literal, measurable magnetic field ...

we could literally measure my heartbeat being detected by your brain, and vice versa.

Not only can we measure it,

it (*the effect of one's heart 'field'*) can have a

physiological effect (*on another*)."

– Rollin McCraty,
Senior Researcher, Heartmath Institute, "I Am"

Science is catching up fast, but ancient wisdom had tried to get our attention to this for centuries. Your brain plays second fiddle to your heart when it comes to information storage and bioelectrical energy. According to ancient wisdom, the heart has always held the power to guide us to attain the things we truly want. Now, based on information from both sources, I'm suggesting that your heart is a power and information source that can tap into the most important guidance for your life. Unlike the brain that can only tap the knowledge (experiences and information) you have recorded, the heart can tap universal knowledge outside of you. It's like a cosmic receiver if you have it opened to receive. Your brain can't guide you the way your heart can because your brain receives the facts of our world, only. Your heart is a hotline to information from the source that created you. In the flow of what your heart has received, you can move forward with confidence that you will be in all the right places with the right people at the right times. That's good stuff.

The most successful people in the world got that way because their hearts led them to the right places, the right people, the right ideas, all at the right times. I'm not suggesting that mistakes won't be made when you're following your heart. Mistakes are relative. We make way too much out of them. Do mistakes represent life lessons tossed in for the development of our souls? Possibly, but, who knows? What I do know is that it's not that serious. Mistakes will happen and it's ok! Apparently, they're part of life. When following your heart, they'll happen infrequently. The mistakes will teach valuable lessons. Then, your heart quickly guides you back on track.

"The more we align with thought, the more removed we become from the source."

– Inner Worlds Outer Worlds Part 2, The Spiral

It's all about balance. Remember that heart/mind *yin yang* symbol. **Balance** that beautiful mind with the powers of your heart. That brain sets you apart from all other species on Earth, but so does your heart. Balance the two. Don't fail to crown your heart as ruler of your personal kingdom. The Universal wisdom that can be channeled through the human heart might flow through there for a reason. Maybe we're supposed to use it to reach increasingly higher levels of Happiness, achieve our wildest dreams and make a difference in this world? All I know is that you guys need to put that crown on the right organ. Crown, bow down to, and follow your heart … and remember this:

Ambitions of the heart hold maximum helium energy. Flow with them. Ambitions of the mind, however, must be *carefully* managed.

EAT POPCORN AND WATCH THE MOVIE 🎥🍿

When describing those who've had near death experiences, Deepak Chopra expressed how people move on with their lives in a more awakened and contented way. As I mentioned earlier, an excerpt of his description mirrors what I envision we need to do when life gets overwhelming: "They feel detached, as if witnessing how life unfolds rather than being tossed and tumbled in the chaotic stream of daily events."
– Deepak Chopra

No matter what I learn or what I experience, I come back to this philosophy. You guys have heard it a thousand times from me, but do you put it into practice? You should. It works. **When life gets overwhelming,**

"Eat popcorn and watch the movie." I'll leave you with this as the final message on lightening the weight of your mind in the face of challenges.

You've tried your best. Patience is wearing thin. It's getting overwhelming. This is when I suggest you learn to view your life as if it were simply an educational, virtual reality movie. Of course it's written, produced and directed by the best the world has ever known. You're viewing it in some high technology, virtual reality form, so it feels completely 100 percent real. Once you step into the virtual reality gear, you have no way to remember that it's a movie. You think it's real. The purpose of the movie is to learn, and it's captivating! You get so wrapped up in the movie. You're all into it, trying to make it do what you want it to do. Sometimes you want it to do exactly what it's doing. Other times, it's taking you through tragic situations and crises. At those times you're like, who wrote this thing? This is all wrong. *This sucks!* you think. You forgot it was an experience for the sake of learning. Getting distracted by disappointing moments, you missed some of the lessons. Those lessons will now be repeated through new events. You don't like the lessons anymore. You just want fun. You're thinking, *Something's wrong! Turn this shit off!* Disappointments are throwing you off your learning game. If life ever gets too intense and difficult to process, relax and observe what's going on in your life. Sit back and watch the movie for a bit.

Whenever the going gets tough, pull back.
Eat popcorn and watch the movie.

Don't allow yourself to get tossed around and beat up by the tough moments. Detach for a minute. Can I get a witness? Then, witness your life for a minute. Calm yourself and watch. Let popcorn represent the potential lessons learned. Chew and digest that popcorn extracting all the nutrients (valuable lessons) meant for you. Crunch, crunch and you will start to see that it's just another crazy scene. As you munch and watch your crazy movie scene a little closer, you'll begin to identify the lessons you can learn from the situation. Digest the lessons fully. Slow and rewind the scenes as needed. Don't miss aspects of what's going on. Chew on your feelings about the situation, without responding. Watch things play out. Pay attention to what overwhelmed you and what you can learn from it. It's extremely helpful to identify your feelings and process them into a lesson that helps you move beyond them. You absolutely must move beyond the baggage of any negative feelings the situation brings. Take the lesson learned as your nutrition, and shit out the rest! This could be an epic scene that marks an important turn in your life. Don't miss it.

Then, when you're ready, put down the popcorn and get back in! "Live" your movie. Get into every bit of the action, every single frame. Observe and learn all the while. It's **your** movie. Never get too knocked around by the tougher scenes. The tough scenes are there to help you learn. Tough scenes provide the opportunities for you to show your skills in working through and releasing baggage. Remember, baggage brings friction to your flow. Friction is a form of resistance. You release your resistance as you pull back, eat popcorn and watch your movie. Then, your energy flows much better. As you can step back and observe your life, you can easily spot developing baggage and toss it out before it becomes a part of your wardrobe. Next time you're feeling the pain, when the going gets tough, just pull back, eat popcorn and watch the movie for a bit.

"Roll wit it. Roll wit it."
– UCB, Sexy Lady.

"In moments when you feel very happy, do you also watch yourself being happy? When you happen to get angry, is some part of you totally free of anger? If you answer "'yes" to both questions, you can stop reading. You have arrived ... self-knowledge will unfold for you every day ... in time you will see yourself living in the light."
– Deepak Chopra, preface of *Metahuman*

The quote above, was in the very first paragraph of the preface of Chopra's latest book. I hadn't read Chopra for years and years, but thought it might come in handy after I saw him on TV reinforcing the perspectives I was writing in the Hookup. After reading the first paragraph of the preface, I put it down. I'm so serious. Lol. He shouldn't have said that to me because I knew it was true. I'm already eating popcorn and watching the movie. I'll probably go back and read the book, eventually. You never know what you can learn! For you guys, his words reinforced my concept of 'eat popcorn and watch the movie.'

Before we move on to Chapter Three's vital lessons on how to lift the vibrational energy of your body, I want to share some of my quick-fix methods for raising the vibrational energy of your mind. These suckers are like propellers on the top of your bubble. Put them in play, and you'll soon feel the lift.

Your Top Ten Propellers

Easy, quick-fix bubble lifts for your daily use.

intense prayer

bubble meditation

acts of kindness

inspirational music

creative expression

immersion in nature

noticing details of beauty in the present moment

full acceptance of people and situations

reflection on an unconditional love

letting shit go

CHAPTER THREE

YOUR BUBBLE IS YOUR TEMPLE

Your mind's getting light. Now, get your body right.

In case you millennials don't know, the saying goes, "Your *body* is your temple." It stems from a biblical verse from Corinthians that includes, "your body is a temple of the Holy Spirit, which is in you." Using this concept, I want you to think of your bubble as the place where your soul is housed, and the place where you and God meet. Your bubble, your temple, is divine and should be honored in the way you would an ancient, holy temple of God. Throughout this lifetime, **your body sits at the center of your personal bubble temple**. Envision your body as the altar of the temple. It is divine, as it was created by a divine energy. Treat it accordingly. Place only pure, natural, high-frequency things on that altar. Use the proper fuels to raise the energy of your altar to the highest level frequencies possible. Honor it. Don't go through life without experiencing what it feels like for your body to be nature-filled. Nature is your 'fuel mate.' When filled with your fuel mate, you reach a physical state that you can't achieve any other way. You must experience it.

Get your mind on your body, and your body on your mind. 🧘

As I've said, I've come to believe that plants, oxygen, water and sunlight are our loving, fuel partners on this planet Earth. I believe nature holds the key to our health. And as crazy as it may sound, it holds the key to our brain health and our Happiness too. Plants absorb sunlight, the air we breathe out, and one of the purest forms of water, rain. Grounded by the earth, they transform those ingredients, *with the help of a little sunlight*, into nutritious energy for us. They also set an example for coexisting in peace, as they provide us nourishment. Follow their lead for coexisting in peace, and graciously accept their life sustenance. Always keep in mind that protecting the environment keeps the plants, oxygen, and water at the healthiest peaks for our own consumption. This makes for a beautiful, healthy cycle of life for all.

Forget those propagandas filled food pyramids you've seen. Your temple needs meditation, prayer, exercise, fresh water, deep breathing, live plants and a little bit of sunlight. Anything else you put into your temple should be managed carefully. Every*body* has unique needs. You are the only one who can figure out what best fuels your body. You have to pay close, close attention to discern what your body thrives from and what it doesn't need. You're going to have to invest time and energy into figuring that out through the process of elimination diets and paying very close attention to your body. One diet that hardly gives anyone in the world a problem, is a 75 percent raw fruit/vegetable based diet. That's just a fact.

Experience, for once in your life, the healing effects of adhering to the highest quality diet for you. It takes a while for your body to release all of the substandard stuff you've put in, and adjust to functioning on pure fuels. If you actually hang in there through the process and put only the necessary things in your body, it's hard to go back to the old way of fueling yourself. The feeling of operating on pure fuels is *way* better. "Pure fuels," feels is as good as it sounds. Try it.

The Fuel Pyramid

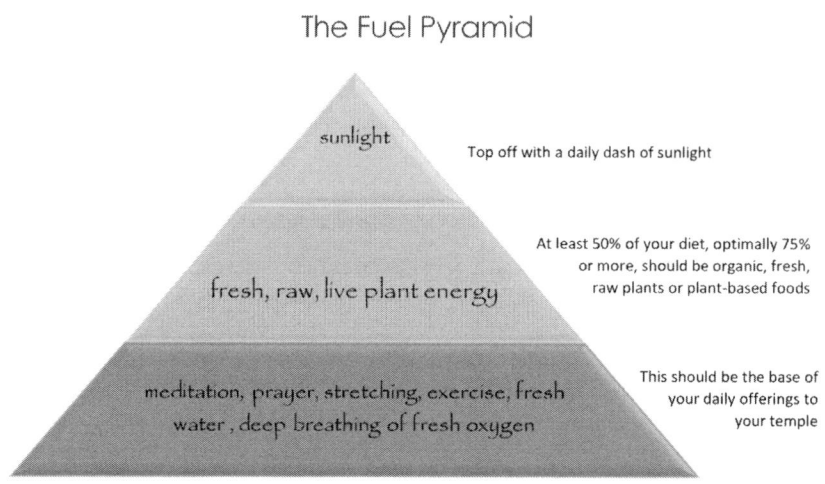

sunlight — Top off with a daily dash of sunlight

fresh, raw, live plant energy — At least 50% of your diet, optimally 75% or more, should be organic, fresh, raw plants or plant-based foods

meditation, prayer, stretching, exercise, fresh water, deep breathing of fresh oxygen — This should be the base of your daily offerings to your temple

Fuel, here, refers to everything you subject your body to, including thoughts, beliefs, posture, exercise, foods, etc. Each moment of our lives, our "fuel" choices determine whether our body makes anti-aging, sex hormones or rapid aging, stress hormones. Anti-aging or rapid aging? Sex or stress? Which hormones would be your choice? Keep eating that bullshit and gulp in all the ingredients for aging hormones, while health freaks consume up all the youthful, sex hormone producing foods. Can you hear me now?

Your health is an expression of your power to care for and heal yourself. It's important to be in a state of health that allows you to heal quickly from life's bumps and bruises. If the proper things are fed into your body, you automatically begin to heal physically, mentally and spiritually. How cool is that?

You are what you consume yourself with. Whether it's thoughts
or food. There's no way around it. It's simple science.

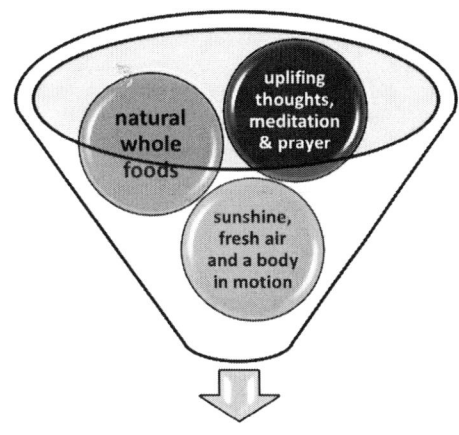

A Healthy, Happy Person

Everything that you expose your bubble to will affect your altar. Everything counts, including your thoughts and attitude. Even atheist doctors acknowledge the unexplained power of the human mind and will on the body's ability to live and heal. It's just a fact.

Your body benefits from circulation and motion. I won't harp on exercise because you KNOW its power to miraculously heal. You already know that exercise is literally MEDICINE to your mind and body. You already know. So, keep that body in motion for your entire lifetime, please. **Motion helps the body to regenerate cells. Regeneration is creation. Think of your body's motion as god-like, as it stimulates creation inside you.** Creation of new cells means healing. View all motion of your body as healing.

And love your body because your body hears you! It hears your innermost thoughts. There's a method to my madness. That's why I told you that loving yourself was so very, very important. Those **messages of acceptance and love for yourself have tremendous power of healing for your body.** You have to love your body, guys. I mean LOVE. Say your name, say your name!

"I admit that thoughts influence the body."
– Albert Einstein

We've all heard, "drink water," "get proper sleep," "eat breakfast," "sugar is bad for you," "take your vitamins," "watch your posture," yada, yada, yada. Turns out, there are some amazing reasons for each of these. Not taking them seriously will have an effect on you at some point. I wish I had known all of the reasons why each of these suggestions was so important when I was a kid. I would have taken them a little more seriously. I want to point out some reasons why each is so important for you. Before I do, please promise me you'll do these two *extremely* important things EVERYDAY for your Temple:

FLUSH and RECYCLE!!

Flush means drink water. Recycle means deep breathe.

Drink water to flush the "pot," so to speak. It takes about two liters a day to fully flush. Think of that strong swoosh sound of a strong, powerful, full flush. Any less than two liters, and you should imagine a partial flush where 'particles' float back and settle in your temple.  If you don't fully flush with **two *full* liters every day**, don't act all surprised about your health situation. Fully flush. Everyday.

Deep breathe every day. Deeply inhale fresh air every chance you get. Exhale all the carbon dioxide (CO_2) out of your body. CO_2 is what you breathe out when you exhale. The deeper you breathe, the more CO_2 you release from your body. **Excessive CO_2 levels cause the oceans to be acidic, destroying coral reefs and softening the shells of crabs and other shellfish. Breathe all of that shit out!** It not only heals you to release it, but plants will breathe it in. Hook them up! It's exactly what plants need to survive. In turn, they produce the fresh oxygen *you* need. I can't say it enough, **deep breathe every day**.

INHALE

HOLD

EXHALE

REPEAT

Next up, are my top ten, "**That's all they had to say in the first place!**" advice points. Perhaps knowing at least one reason **why** you need to do these things can help you to remember to actually **do them**.

Top 10 "That's All They Had to Say in The First Place!"

"drink plenty of water"

- Water takes your blood from thick and sluggish to flowing freely within 10 minutes; without ample fresh water, all the nutrients and oxygen you put in your body can't travel to all of your cells, that includes brain cells. Your body is literally starving without water. You're electric and water conducts electricity, never heard that referred to but it hit my mind as I typed. Now, I'm thinking water may increase your ability to generate power within you? Anyway, 2 liters per day are needed for optimal health.

"eat your vegetables"

- Vegetables reduce risk of cancer, stroke and diabetes, and that's according to the medical profession; vegetables, fruits, and other fresh, raw plants like herbs, nuts and seeds, provide live enzymes which significantly speed up the rate of virtually all the chemical reactions that take place in your cells.

"get some exercise"

- They had me on exercise 'makes you look good,' but nobody said that each day, failure to move a particular joint or muscle causes brain cells for that particular joint or muscle to shrink from loss of protein, resulting in a tiny loss of ability to move that joint or muscle. that's when use or lose gets real; add that getting exercise each day improves memory and prevents and heals disease.

"eat breakfast"

- Skipping breakfast reduces cognitive function, leads to hair loss. Let's stop there.

"deep breathe"

- Deep breathing literally helps shut off the flow of damaging adrenaline. It flushes out old toxic air for new fresh air, and that's only if you're '**deep**' breathing, btw. It increases the capacity of your lungs and speeds the regeneration of your body's cells.

"sugar's not good for you"

- Sugar makes wrinkled, saggy skin. Oh, hell naw. That's all anybody had to say, but add some chronic disease to those wrinkles.

"keep your chin up"

- That head weighs a ton, when your chin is down it tips your balance out of alignment, draining your energy. Studies show that a chin held up increases your sense of well being. Your outlook on life literally can improve when your chin is up. Just not too far up!

"early to bed, early to rise"

- Proper sleep maintains your brain health, when you don't get it the daily processes that restore your body and mind won't take place; staying up past 10pm puts you off your Circadian rhthym causing cortisol imbalance, aiding things like the infection of your mucus membranes, rapid aging and autoimmune disease; lack of energy might be just a sign of the damage occuring; Circadian rhythm runs on a schedule. It's up to you to follow it, but if you don't follow it, you pay.

"take your vitamins"

- ONE missing nutrient can cause disease!

"watch your posture"

- Poor posture limits oxygen to your brain, and all the other organs of your body.

😐 **PS- ¼ Teaspoon of Baking Soda in a Glass of Water?** Grandma swore by this one. Now, I know why. It alkalizes the body. Make sure your body maintains a healthy pH! Most disease, illness *(including cancer)*, and bad bacteria thrive in an acidic environment. When your body is acidic, it borrows minerals from organs, bones and tissue to neutralize the acid and remove it from the body. You need your minerals! Trust me on this. Over acidity weakens *all* bodily systems. *Read up on it* and balance your body's pH with a raw, organic vegetable and fruit diet, two liters of water and daily deep breathing. Yeah, deep breathing helps lower your body acidity too.

You've heard the words of advice from the chart before. My hope is that now, you'll realize that not heeding the advice is not just costly to your health, but your Happiness too. We've talked only about your mind up until now, and that was for a very good reason. Without the framework for managing your thoughts, you'll never do what it takes to raise the vibrational frequency of your body. But, now that your thoughts are elevating, you're about to enter into a whole new world as you honor your body as the beautiful temple of your soul that it is. Elevated thought patterns, combined with a body filled with the high frequencies of nature, will change your life. I'm trying to tell you! Your body holds a great deal of energy that also needs to be helium-level.

> The things you eat and the ways you treat and care for your body are the offerings you set before the altar of your temple. Place only the most beautiful things there. Bless your food. Bless all the water you drink. Keep everything pure, natural and full of uplifting love energy.

YOU'RE ALL THE WAY LIVE

TAKE "CHARGE" OF THAT ELECTRIC BUBBLE TEMPLE OF YOURS

You have a life force energy flowing through you. It has long been acknowledged by the ancient cultures of the world. The Chinese call it *chi* or *qi*. Indians call it *prana*. The Japanese call it *Ki*. Some Native Americans call it *ni*, and some call it *manitou*. Some Egyptians call it *Sekhem*. Today, Russian researchers call it bio-plasmic energy. For purposes of wrapping your mind around the concept, let's call this energy your **power flow**.

Your power flow has to course freely through your body for optimal mental and physical health. The Chinese tell us that when your power flow is blocked, physical and mental disease is the result. Having a strong flow of power within you is believed by all of the ancient cultures to elevate your bubble. Or in their way of putting it, elevate your states of consciousness. No matter which way you put it, you need to focus on bringing your body to the highest states of power flow possible for you.

You are in "charge" of your power flow. You literally manage whether it's positive or negative. The amount of power flowing through your body is something you **can** control. Until now, you have probably felt that outside forces have played a part in the amount of energy that you have, but I want you to understand, right now before we move forward, that YOU are THE ONLY ONE in "charge" of your energy. Your flow of power has nothing to do with anything but you. If you don't have a good flow of power, don't blame anyone but yourself. YOU control every decision that determines how much, and what kind of power flow you have. You can make every change necessary in your thinking and way of life to bring higher flows of power to your body and mind. Let me say this one more time, **your personal power flow has nothing to do with what is going on *outside* of you**. You have to take responsibility. You are in "charge."

Your power flow, life force, chi, whatever you prefer to call it, is a reflection of you. Make it a beautiful, beaming reflection of your light energy. Let that light fill your temple. Imagine your power flow having such a force that excess energy flows out of your body and out of the top of your head. That's a halo, actually. Redefine a halo in your mind. Before now, you probably associated it with otherworldly spirits and/or those who have superhuman capabilities of love and compassion. Now understand that the halo was always an indication of a power flow at the highest states, achievable by anyone, and everyone. Higher states of power will bring you the kind of feelings, peace of mind and quality of life that you associate with angels. It's not just for angels, though. It's your birthright. This level of flow is exactly what I want for you.

How do you increase your power flow? Everything in this book is designed to increase your power flow. All you have to do is read and take action on the things you read here and you're good to go. What's most important now is that you accept the fact that you're filled with a live energy flow that could be increased much, *much* more.

FUEL UP WITH LIVE PLANT ENERGY

A *super,* natural body is within your grasp with raw, organic plants ... your ***best*** soul food.

You know mom goes to work on collard greens and **all** traditional soul foods. So, **my old hard-wiring hurts when I say that raw, plants are the *best* soul food**. But, alas, I must keep it real guys. The raw, whole, fresh and 'full of life' energy of plants is the perfect food for our bodies and souls. Plants, somehow, have everything we need for health. They give us oxygen; their peace and natural beauty calms us; they provide all the nourishment we need. Be thankful that live plant energy is available to you! Take more advantage of all the blessings that plants provide.

No one can do it *for* you. It's up to you to change your perspectives on what's good for you. That's another re-wiring exercise. Food is more than an earthly pleasure, it's how we fuel our vehicles for our life journey. Place a great deal of self-respect and balance into your fuel choices. I'm all about earthly pleasures, when they are good for you. My best advice and personal trick of the health trade is to figure out how to associate earthly pleasures with the healthiest foods and concoctions. You'll **have** to rewire, though. It's not just that your life depends on it, which it does, but the quality of your life depends on it. Your quality of life depends completely on whether you have the energy you need. The things that your taste buds have been wired to love, most of them, hold very little energy for you. Most of what we have come to eat on a regular basis actually holds the power to *drain* our energy. Unfortunately, you'll have to rewire your taste buds and your mind. Every day that you continue to consume things that drain or provide inadequate energy, you're actively damaging yourself. If that seems fun to you, at least know that it's not free. You'll be paying for it later. For your own self-preservation and ultimate Happiness, you'll have to step up your plant fuel game.

Who's checking to make sure you've had the proper nutrients in the proper amounts? Who makes sure you're not missing anything, making sure you have the energy needed at the proper times for optimal health and performance? I admit, it's a job. It is a *job*. There's no way around it. So, welcome to life. Do what you have to do. Handle the most important business of your life. Step the hell up, soldier. You got work to do.

"Sometimes it seems like I'm neglecting you ...
I gotta make it for you, gotta make it for me ... I got work to do."
– Isley Brothers, Work to Do

No work is more important than fueling yourself. It's not a real option. You MUST make 100 percent sure that you're ALWAYS doing your best job to properly fuel and nourish yourself. Every**body**'s looking for a hero. YOU are the hero for your **body.** Don't disrespect the miraculous vehicle that has been granted to you. You have to step up.

Your taste buds need not freak out. Calm down. Your taste buds are hard-wired just like your thoughts. You can train your taste buds to like anything you want them to like. The process starts by telling your taste buds to go sit down, the same way that you have to control your brain's thought patterns. Don't let taste buds pull your health down! What the hell? Toughen up. Rewire your taste buds by first feeling the rush of gratification from knowing that you have installed live, healing, uplifting energy into your body. Feel the rush of placing high frequency energy onto your altar. Changing your taste buds starts with a mentality. The satisfaction doesn't usually come from the taste buds at the beginning. True. But if you find satisfaction mentally, if good feelings course through your mind as it relates to fueling your body properly, you can change your preferences. Tell your taste buds to talk to the hand while you cater to something much more important. YOU. With repeated acts of placing live plant energy in your body, things will start to change in ways that you can literally **feel**. All you have to do is get yourself to the point where you start to "feel" the difference. Your taste buds, immediately, begin to rewire and start preferring the good stuff! It is **amazing** to experience. Hang in there long enough to witness this. It's takes about a month. It's easy from there.

There are so many amazing things about plants that we didn't know. I've come to accept that the incredible live energy of plants is something that elevates us both *mentally and physically*. It is now believed that plants can reprogram our DNA. I am not shitting you! There's an intelligence in nature that we're just discovering in the last couple of years. Personally, life's too short. Ain't nobody got time for science to catch up and teach us all the juicy details. Use common sense. Common sense should tell you that nature holds what we truly need. Think about it. Please feed yourself a constant diet of plants, guys. You can research more on it while you do.

Organic means not just, "nothing artificial," but that it "contains no fake killing agents." The financial savings of buying conventional produce are a drop in the bucket to the medical costs you'll face later. Pesticides kill the biological cells of insects, but we got biological cells too, y'all! I don't like knowing that I'm eating something that contains cell-killing properties. If I can eat the exact same thing without the killer ingredients, I'm on it. Don't discount yourself. The pennies saved now won't offset the cost of disease later.

The Prevention. The Cure.

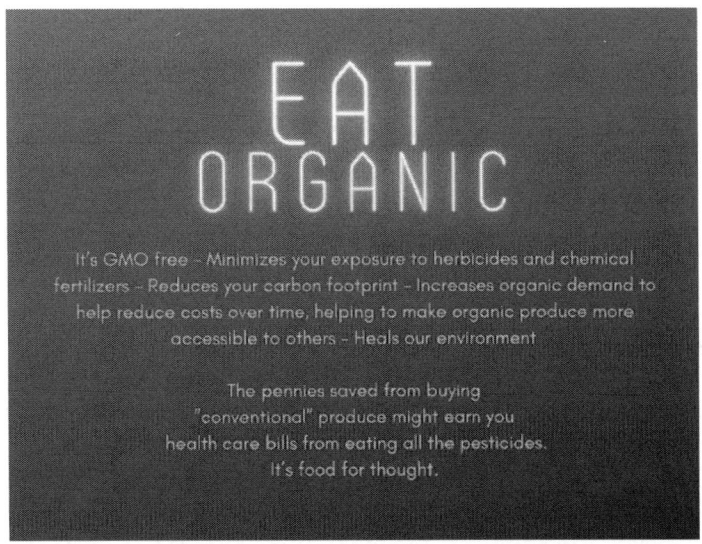

Eat lots of fresh, raw, whole, organic, plant-based foods.

Changing your diet with a focus on organic, whole plant foods changes who you are, your health, and your vitality. It heightens your life experiences because great health feels amazing. **On TOP of that, it simultaneously reduces demand for the processed foods that deplete our rainforests. It helps preserve ecosystems of our planet. It reduces your carbon footprint and increases demand for organic fruit and vegetable farming. Ultimately, you help to employ organic farmers, make healthy eating more accessible to others, and save the environment. Eating organic is a win-win.**

You, literally, are what you eat.

Every day, the first thing to have is water. Always keep a bottle beside your bed, so it's there when you wake up. **Don't forget to silently bless all the water you drink.** For breakfast, eat ample amounts of fruits, nuts and seeds. Think much more along the line of salads when it comes to lunch and dinner *(I, personally, like to eat salad for breakfast too when I can. Traditional American breakfast food is unhealthy for countless reasons).* You can put any and everything over a bed of dark, fresh leafy greens. Use lettuces like organic spinach, arugula and baby kale. Start there. As a supplement to your nutrition and a high-energy infusion for your body, juice vegetables and fruits, when you can. Take vitamins derived from whole foods to make sure you're getting *some* of every basic nutrient each day.

The plant world is bountiful and packed with the nutrition and energy to provide everything you need. There's even a sea plant or seaweed as we call it, that's packed with nutritious energy for you, kelp (try seaweed snacks or seaweed salad for dense nutrition). You've heard all of the reasons why vegetables are good for you. I encourage you to Google each one for its benefits. You will be **surprised**, I'm telling you. While I'm counting on you to investigate the powers of plant-based foods I'll share one reason to eat vegetables that sticks out in my mind. **Vegetables and kelp provide the collagen and elastin necessary for your connective tissues to be strong and flexible. This is very cool because your connective tissues not only surround and connect *everything* in your *entire* body including your brain, but connective tissue also conducts energy throughout your body. Be sure to feed your connective tissues with fresh, raw vegetables** and be sure to give your connective tissues good energy, and good emotions. Otherwise, you're going to wreak havoc throughout your body. Your connective tissues are starved for the live energy of plant-based foods. Every bit of food you consume is flowing throughout your system, either healing or harming. You've been warned.

"Trees are releasing chemicals that are ingested by us through our lungs and through our nervous system, that actually affect cortisol levels, which then lowers the risk of heart disease, cancers, and other stressful kinds of events that happen to the human body."

- Paul Allison,
Horticultural Therapist | Ageless Gardens,
Season 1, Episode 2 /Prime Videos.

I pray that you understand that plants are our partners on this planet! Just being amongst them is healing to us, but consuming them in their most live and energetic state is a power surge. Do the math on your own and make your own decisions. Whatever you do, it won't be because you weren't aware. Your decisions are markers for who you are. Be you, 100 percent. I just want you to be hip to what's going on with plants. I'm not against eating other things, I just think other foods need to be considered in the same way that we eat candy. Occasionally and in moderation. There is a threshold for each of us, for how much bullshit ingredients our bodies can take and still function optimally. Walk that line carefully. Personally, I'm on the 'seefood diet.' When I see something I **want** to eat, I'm eating it. Period *(this is a blessing for which I have immense gratitude as hunger grips so many)*. It's just that the way I **want** to eat has shifted more towards the things that I know will bring a good feeling to my body, and lightness to my bubble. I tend to prefer the things that will elevate my health. I absolutely do treat my taste buds to comfort foods regularly. I just watch that threshold of what my body can and should easily be able to handle and try to never cross it. I never anticipated this, but I find myself avoiding grains now. A former brown rice fanatic, I tested the elimination of grains from my diet and surprisingly found that I like the feeling and I don't want to lose it. I had never noticed it before, but I feel more bloated when I eat grains, especially wheat. That's just me. You guys should test it and see. Grains have been linked to chronic disease for some. Finding what works best for **you** makes a lot of sense, right?

Read up and watch documentaries on different foods and their effects on your body. There are lots of documentaries that will bring you up to speed very quickly. Find out more about food additives. For me, avoiding food additives feels natural, because **they're NOT** *(natural)*. I strongly urge you to stick with natural foods. Keep your fuels as natural as possible. I'm not even going to ask you not to eat meat. Do what your instincts tell you to do, but on that note, I'll share a poem I wrote back when you guys were little. *I was vegan then*.

And The Beef Goes On

The meeting's called to order by some leaders in the west.

They're tired of living to be killed.

They're planning to protest;

They know us well,

So worried that their cries will catch deaf ears.

They cleverly devised a strategy that would take years.

Before their beef with us is settled,

We will have gone through

Attacks, cancers

Strokes, deaths

The loss of loves we knew;

They think survivors of this war

Will live as one, in peace.

But they're just cows and pigs,

And don't know

We will never cease!

YOUR NAV SYSTEM

YOUR GUT IS YOUR 3RD BRAIN *AND* YOUR IMMUNE SYSTEM

Apparently, your gut is "all that." Your gut is your navigation system. It guides you like a third brain (1. Heart, 2. Brain, 3. Gut, in that order). Plus, it's your immune system! A guide and protection all in one. It's like Waze. It can guide you to where you need to be while protecting you from the things lurking to catch you. Before we delve into why you should follow your gut, let's look a little more closely at that gut of yours.

"The enteric nervous system, sometimes referred to as the "gut brain" is capable of maintaining a complex matrix of connections similar to the brain, with its own neurons and neurotransmitter. It can act autonomously, that is, with its own intelligence.

You can say that the gut brain is a fractal version of the head brain, or perhaps the head brain is a fractal version of the gut brain."
— **Inner Worlds Outer Worlds Part 2, The Spiral**

Some scientists now think that your gut is your original brain. We've long imagined that our gut was connected to our intuition and instincts. Perhaps there's no coincidence that the center of your body, your gut, your solar plexus, is the area where your umbilical cord originally infused life into you. Isn't it amazing that scientists are recognizing your gut as a form of brain at all?

Your body is a whole lot more **miraculous**

than you give it credit for.

Feeding it trash is a flat out sin.

Apparently, this "core," which holds your immune system and your vital complex of nerves, is far more significant than we knew. **Your gut is the seat of billions of microbes that govern your health** *(it's believed by many that* **you have more microbial cells in your body than human body cells, by the way… I know, right!?**), and it may sound wild, but scientists think these microbes may also affect the way that you behave. Why the way you behave? Because the microbes have **needs** and drive you to fulfill them by way of cravings. If you have a beautiful balance of healthy microbes, you'll feed your good microbes (your good bacteria) with the healthy things they crave. If, on the other hand, you have a huge batch of bad microbes, you **"will"** feed them the sugar and processed foods that they require to survive … or else! You're actually eating it up, all because the bad microbes said so? Without realizing that's why? That's too creepy for this kid. I'll starve those suckers!

You want a healthy, good microbial environment in your gut. To achieve that, the main thing you have to do is eat the healthy foods that allow good microbes to flourish in your body. If you guessed that raw, plant-based foods, fresh water and oxygen were exactly what it needs, you were right. There are some favorite things that most guts love, like Kombucha, fresh pineapple, green tea, Echinacea, and apples. As you enter the world of raw, plant-based foods, you will be amazed at the variety of options and how completely satisfying they are. Eat fermented foods like miso and kombucha, and raw, plant-based diets as much as possible. Healthy foods assist the health of good microbes, while causing the bad, sugar and acid loving microbes to slowly fade out of your body. The bad ones starve to death when they don't get sugar and acid. Let those bad news, disease causing microbes GO (*How ya like me now, suckaz?"*).

Allow your good microbes to thrive. Keep your immune system and your overall health flourishing. You actually need them.

If you insist on eating junk foods, high in sugar and low in nutrients, you'll increase the membership of what I want to call "gangster" microbes in your body. Like little thugs, they "***make*** you feed them sugar" and all of the other bad stuff they like, just *so they can thrive off of YOU*. If you keep feeding sugar and other junk foods to your bad microbes because it, 'tastes good,' or is 'comfort food,' those microbes exponentially multiply inside of you *(invading your connective tissues and causing inflammation)*. Your body becomes a 'trap house' for billions of gangster microbes. Let 'em keep on using you until they use you up, if you want. Hanging with gangster microbes usually ends one way. Instead of colored bandanas, your membership with this gang is identified by compromised immunity and life-threatening disease. I know it's hard to leave, but it's your life.

So, now that you're starting to understand what to do to keep your gut healthy, let's talk about what's meant by trusting it. We've all heard of a "gut instinct." It made sense somehow. That's because we've all experienced having a "gut instinct." You know what it is, even if they hardly ever happen. By definition, a gut instinct is "an instinctive feeling, as opposed to an opinion or idea based on facts." We talked about this on the topic of knowing the difference between a thought and a "sense" about something. Somehow, perhaps because of the proximity of the heart and the gut in the center of your body and bubble, both the heart and the gut seem to carry the ability to sense. You have probably had the feeling that instinct hits you in both these areas. Most people have had that sensation at some time in their lives. How do we tell the difference? Which is which? I have no idea how you tell the difference, or if there truly is any difference between the senses received through your heart or gut. The good thing is, it doesn't matter. Just recognize that there exists the potential for your gut to channel intuition as well.

As I suggested with your heart, learn to identify when you are having a "sense," or gut instinct, and whether your instinct turned out to be right. It takes practice, over time, to discern the difference between a thought and a gut instinct. Once you get used to identifying your gut instincts, you'll probably notice that your gut is right **every time**. Just like your heart. They both provide some *valuable intel* for your life. You may not always have a gut instinct on something. It can be difficult to decipher between what's a gut instinct and what you "think" or "want" to occur. With practice, I promise you'll begin to tell the difference. I wish I could tell you exactly what's going on. I wish I could help you to distinguish what comes from the gut, what comes from the heart, and what the difference between the two truly is. All I know is that the heart/gut/instinct/intuition/sense comes from something more intelligent and informed than our brains. I do know that. So, work on developing the skill of knowing the difference. The more attention you give to it, the more this wisdom source will show up for you. Once you develop the ability to tell when you're having a gut instinct, by all means follow your gut.

Do not ask me how, but your gut will know things that it's impossible for you to know. It will direct you to where you are supposed to be. It will help you to avoid pitfalls and dangers. It will keep you away from toxic people and environments. Your gut is like a best friend with connections of the highest kind. If you get good at connecting with and following your gut instincts, the benefits to your life will be immeasurable.

As the ultimate navigation system, your gut doesn't just help you navigate through life, it helps you navigate to good health. As your immune system, it's keeping you safe from threats that enter your body. You should absolutely LOVE your gut! What an amazing part of your body! Treat it like your new BFF.

FAST FOR 12-HOURS DAILY

All you have to do, here, is not eat during the four hours before you go to sleep. The other eight hours, we're counting on you being asleep. You CAN rise to this challenge.

Our bodies are on a Circadian rhythm. The Circadian rhythm is a natural thing. It's our body's natural clock. Yes, our bodies have natural clocks. We're natural creatures. Night and day, the seasons, and the tides all flow on rhythms. Our sleep cycle is on a rhythm, not unlike the rhythm of a menstrual cycle in that it is automatic and put in place by nature. When you go against your natural body rhythm, you can end up paying for it in the form of compromised health. Our bodies perform at their best when rolling on nature's rhythm. Fasting supports this rhythm.

Nature is in charge. Tell yourself whatever you want, nature is on my side on this one. When possible, going to bed at a reasonable hour and getting as close to eight hours of sleep as you can, is a really good thing. Sleeping while it's dark and awakening with the sunrise, puts you in synch with nature. There are soooo many reasons why this is good. Look it up. I can't go into all of them here. I *will* say that **in the evening, our bodies are busy working on hormone repair and preparation, as well as other repair and prep cycles. When you add a little extra work to the equation with your late dinners and snacks, your body tries to handle the overload of work. It really does try its best, but it's overworked and eventually your entire system is affected by this**. You can help your body out in a big way if you just stop eating about four hours before bed, every night. That alone will make a huge difference to your overall health. Read up on it.

WATER IS AMAAAZING! DRINK THAT LIQUID LIFE

If you adopt only one thing from this whole book, choose to drink two liters of fresh water every

day. Each morning, as soon as you awaken, drink a glass of water before you do anything else.

Nature's most miraculous elixir is more amazing than you think. Water is not only absolutely necessary to sustain your life, but it's miraculous in other ways. The fact that we can't make it, even though it's a very simple formula, always held a clue that there was something unique and special about it. The incredible fact that we **can't** make it, however, is just the tip of the iceberg.

Did you know that all things are vibrational energy? Lol. I figured you did. Well, water can receive and hold onto vibrational information. Seriously. I was floored by this too. Water responds to wave energy. Vibrating water makes up the majority of mass in plants. Vibrating water makes up the majority of mass in YOU. You should look up, on the Internet, how water responds to vibrations of sound when cornstarch is added to it for form. It shows how water responds to vibrations in a very physical, see it with your own eyes, way. It's interesting.

Water's deeper than you think ;-). Many scientific studies at top universities around the world have confirmed that water molecules have **consciousness** and that positive and negative energy affect the structure of water. Water has been demonstrated to have memory in numerous studies. Studies have shown that our thoughts and feelings can be recorded by water. Our emotions effect water. Google it! I am NOT making this up. (Look for pictures of water before and after prayer over the water. Then, Google "Chi of Love Water Experiments," and check that out.) You already know that we are 90 percent water, so if you don't think water is amazing, what does that say about you? You are 90 percent water and water is affected by vibrational energy, including thought and emotional energy. So, you are likely affected by vibrational, thought and emotional energy too. Deep, right?

Remember the proven effects of thoughts and emotions on water when you reflect on the power of your own thought energy.

On top of all of this amazing news about water, know that within ten minutes, water can add buoyancy to your blood cells allowing them to move freely and carry more oxygen to your brain and organs. Water helps to alkalize and oxygenate the body. Water is naturally, slightly alkaline. Alkaline is the opposite of acidic. Acid is free of electrons, while anything alkaline is packed with them. The more electrons you have swirling, the more oxygen that can be absorbed by your body. This means the more hydrated you are, the more oxygenated you *can* be. The positive effects of water on your body just go on and on and on. So, drink water! Lots of it. As a matter of fact, you technically don't need to drink anything else, so be cautious about what you drink as a replacement. I **love** lots of other beverages, but I see every sip I take as a choice between water or fun. Be conscious of the importance and need for water in your body. Try not to waste opportunities to hydrate your body with fresh drinking water. Drink responsibly, please.

Our bodies are fields of electrical energy and water happens to be an *excellent* conductor of electricity. On top of that, as we goal for helium level energy, there's only one element known to man that's lighter than helium, and that's hydrogen. Guess what's packed with hydrogen? Yep, water. That's all water IS, hydrogen with a dash of oxygen. What better way to nourish and lift?

Drink lots of water every day to cleanse and hydrate yourself. Sip it slowly throughout the day. You need enough water to create a full, swooshing flush for your system, but drink it little by little throughout the day. If you can't drink two full liters, a partial flush is better than no flush at all, but it a*in't nothing to brag about*. Don't report that you're drinking water if you're not drinking two full liters a day. 😑

FILL UP WITH NATURE'S BUBBLE FUEL: OXYGEN

Not only do our lives depend on what plants breathe out, but what we breathe out is what plants require for *their* survival. More proof that we're, literally, partners for life. Fill your body with the breath of nature, released just for you. Oxygen is fuel to our bodies, even more vital for our survival than food or water. It is a blessing to be able to breathe it in. Don't take it for granted. **Fill up** at every chance!

How much oxygen do you need? Your body needs all it can get! Breathe it in as deeply as you can. Fill your lungs completely, to distribute as much as possible to every nook and cranny of your body. I know it sounds silly to tell you to breathe. You may be thinking, "I think I'll be ok, I've been breathing for over twenty years." Right, ok. Did you know that regular breathing keeps you alive, but deep breathing detoxifies your body? Did you know that regular breathing allows for many pockets of old oxygen to stay stagnant within your lungs and body? Did you know that by deep breathing, you can clear out the stagnant pockets and restore your body to optimal health? If that doesn't get your attention, did you know that it increases your cardiovascular capacity? Deep breathing can reduce your blood pressure. It promotes core muscle stability. It helps you tolerate intense exercise. Deep breathing helps to regulate your weight. Deep breathing prevents the lungs from losing their elasticity. I could go on and on, but I'll stop by saying that deep breathing also calms the body and the mind, slowing the flow of damage-causing adrenaline, while filling your body with nature and elevating your bubble.

SLEEP TIGHT

When you sleep, your body recharges, and I think your soul may be free to roam for a little bit, unbound by the body. That ain't proven y'all, just something I like to believe. Imagine with me, that being free from our bodies is like getting out of jail for our souls. So, free your soul for eight measly hours a day! Your Circadian rhythm is already on that program. All you have to do is roll with nature. There's no word for the value that sleep brings. Here's a clue to its immense power: **You literally *cannot* live without it**. Do your body, mind and soul a favor and get your proper amount *and quality* of sleep. Ritualize it. Invest in soft, silky sleep stuff. Keep an amazing pillow. Use sleep masks. Listen to binaural beats or relaxing music before bed. Whatever makes you feel calm and pampered at bedtime, do it. Create your own special ritual to put yourself in the most relaxed mood. Do it every night just before bed, during the hour before you sleep. And make sure that you are fully hydrated a full hour before you go to sleep.

If you want optimum health, make it a goal in your life to experience the highest quality sleep. Quality sleep will physically invigorate you. It'll enhance your energy. Most *healing* occurs as you sleep. Sleep increases your ability to elevate your mind. The relaxation and rejuvenation gained from sleep has a clear psychological effect. You've felt it yourself. It's a refreshing mental and physical experience that I don't have to sell you on because you already know. You can read up on all the scientifically proven benefits of optimal sleep, but whether you do or not, accept that sleep has immense power beyond what **any** of us know. So, goal for a great night's sleep, each and *every night.* Consider it daily fuel for a buoyant, healthy and happy bubble.

7 TIPS FOR OPTIMAL SLEEP

1. Exert yourself *physically* during the hours of the workday, *if at all possible.*

2. Sleep eight hours *during* your natural Circadian rhythm cycle:

Early to bed, early to rise energizes you. I know you're laughing, thinking this sounds like old people stuff. This goes for babies, old people and every age in between. Try the 11:00 p.m. to 7:00 a.m. as the latest window for most nights. It puts your body on its most natural energetic cycle. It has a noticeable rejuvenation effect. Try it as much as possible, but especially when you want a physical and emotional boost in your life.

"Early to bed, early to rise, makes a man healthy, wealthy and wise."
– Ben Franklin
(as usual, Ben was onto something here)

3. Be well hydrated one hour before you go to sleep.

4. Don't watch TV or eat for *at least* an hour before you sleep.

5. Invest in good mattresses, pillows, sheets and blankets throughout your life.

6. Deep breathe for a few minutes before you go to sleep.

7. Say prayers of gratitude before you sleep.

DEVELOP YOUR SLEEP ROUTINE

Whether you go to sleep or not, as the evening enters into the 10:00 p.m. hour, your body enters into a sleep *cycle*. Light and action disrupt your Circadian rhythm with negative effects on your metabolism. Today's lifestyles make this sound **ludicrous**, and impossible to adhere to. I agree with you on that one. No matter what we think, our natural rhythm is put at a disadvantage when we're not 'early to bed.' We truly suffer when we break the Circadian rhythm. If you're trying to heal, don't mess around with this one. Follow your Circadian rhythm to gain high quality sleep. You will be rewarded with health, slowed aging and an overall refreshment of mind and body. It doesn't get **easier than that.**

POSTURE FOR ENERGY FLOW

Streeeetch that charger cord that we call our spine. Good posture is but one more thing that enhances your natural energy flow. **A straighter, more elongated spine channels more energy throughout your body.** You'll increase your chances for a more buoyant bubble. So, keep that spine as elongated as you possibly can.

Straighten it out and open up as much space as you can between each vertebrae. Give some breathing room to those organs. Your organs are masses of swirling electrons and love to breathe, just like you. An elongated spine allows for increased circulation inside your body. It will not only increase your energy flow, but you'll boost the health of your bones, muscles, back, and ligaments while increasing your lung capacity and circulation. There are many more health benefits from good posture, look 'em all up, but remember that our number one focus here is maximum energy flow. Stretch out that charger cord! On top of all the health benefits, you'll look twice as good, I promise, when you rock good posture. Who's mad about that?

PHYSICAL MOTION & PRODUCTIVITY: THE WIND BENEATH YOUR BUBBLE

DO WHATEVER MOTION COMES NATURALLY

Every day that you don't move one of your muscles or joints, as you may remember from one of the charts, the brain cells that control that muscle or joint lose protein and shrink. The cells shrink every day that you don't move because they have not received stimulus from the spinal cord. Eventually, the shrinkage of the brain cells means your muscles and joints slowly lose their ability to function 😲. Send stimuli from your spinal cord every day! Engage in some form of motion to retain your precious ability to MOVE.

Do **whatever** you love to do. I don't think God designed us with the expectation that we required a gym membership to be fit. Fitness and physical health should come naturally. And it **will** if you commit to staying in motion as much as possible. It's great to have natural forms of exertion to stay fit. I naturally love to stretch and walk. Between the two of you, you like pushups, general ripping and running of every kind, free weights, household chores and occasional gym time. You both had multiple sports that you loved. Consider them again! It doesn't matter what you do, just stay in motion. Find natural ways of staying in good shape that fit comfortably with your life.

As I said, I love *serious* stretching. That's just what I love. Once, someone told me *that* wasn't worth anything without running or some kind of aerobics. I let that get in my head and believed it, *like a dummy*. Running wasn't my thing. I started planning to do **something** but never got to it. Buying into that led to a decline in the stretching I love, as I had broken my daily habit. The amazing tone and flexibility, combined with my natural **need** to stretch and workout "my way," wasn't enough to convince me that I was doing the right thing for me. Tough life lesson, but a great one. Now I know better. Always, always do YOU. Now, I do "**my chi**"... whatever the heck I want! It's a combination of stretching, some motions that resemble tai chi, official yoga poses and poses that *resemble* yoga, and dancing to my music playlist whenever and however I feel like it. "My chi." Find **your** chi. Whatever form of body motion/exercise you LOVE to do, do it!

SUNSHINE BRIGHTENS YOUR LIFE *AND THE CORNERS OF YOUR MIND* ☀

"A beautiful sky, clouds go by, and make my heart happy."
  – Jet, **age five, scribbled in his journal.**

Let's try to get some sunshine, every day that it's available, for say, five minutes a day. We all know that sunshine provides vitamin D, but its energy is also necessary fuel for your brain and body. Use sunblock and UV shades. Don't get **too much** sun because we're messing up the atmosphere that protects us from sun damage. Still, make sure to get a *little bit of sunshine*.

"Exposure to sunlight stimulates serotonin synthesis and better dopamine release, which recharges your brain and helps to raise neurotransmitter levels" (Source: honorsociety.com).

The accepted benefits of sunshine include lifting your spirits; fighting stress; building strong bones; cancer prevention, and healing skin conditions. Research suggests sunlight as a potential treatment for rheumatoid arthritis, Lupus, inflammatory bowel syndrome, and thyroiditis. *Seriously*. Vitamin D from the sun literally strengthens your immune cells. Go, get yourself sun ;-).

"Sunshine, you brighten my life. And you brighten up the corners of my mind."
  - **Babyface**

DON'T SUGARCOAT WHEN YOU *KNOW* THAT IT'S TOXIC

"It's getting late to give you up.
I took a sip from my devil's cup.
Slowly, it's taking over me."
  – **Britney Spears**, Toxic

Medications, illicit drugs, alcohol, processed sugar are not only toxic, but some find these toxins addictive. Actually, many do. So, they don't just take your bubble down for a minute, they can **keep** you down. Toxins mess you up, then take hold of your brain so you feel you **need** them. Whatever that's about, I don't like it. Completely aware of their toxic nature, I've indulged each with enthusiasm at **least** once. Ok, twice, w*hatever!* So, I get it. I totally do. I'm just asking that you **ALWAYS** *recognize the depth of danger of toxic substances, so you can control your level of attraction and usage*. Don't sugarcoat. Know the dangers well.

MEDICATIONS:

I would flow with medications to sustain life and limb in an emergency. Otherwise, I'll **always** explore natural options, first and *thoroughly*. When it's not a first aid/ER type of situation, fueling your body naturally is the answer to most healing. When it comes to chronic illness and disease, you're either getting something your body doesn't like or not enough of something your body needs. Work through the process of eliminating things from your diet while taking in all the live enzymes, nutrients, minerals and vitamins that you know you need. The healing derived from this process can eliminate need for medications. We already know that it's proven that 30 percent of people who take placebos heal from their ailment without medication or any other changes in their lives, simply because they *believed* in the proposed medication. There are so many possibilities for natural healing. I'm going to try my best to prevent illness and cure myself WAY before I put medicine in my body. It's worth your best efforts. Practice prevention above all else. Do your best to heal with the power of nature combined with personal determination. Avoid medications as the end-all answer. Emergencies are ***always*** the exception.

ILLICIT DRUGS:

I'm glad we're past the, "It's a plant, Mom!" days. I'll admit, *now*, that's true. It's a plant, consumed straight out of the ground. It's still criminalized here and there, *which is silly*. How on earth alcohol was legalized before weed is beyond me. As for all other illicit drugs, the awful statistics speak for themselves. If you enjoy altered states, be smart, safe and creative and stick to legal weed, beer and wine. The rest are simply too toxic to your body and mind. Illicit drugs, in particular, always stand firmly in the way of true Happiness. They're low, toxic energy.

ALCOHOL:

Alcohol earned its toxic title early in my life. When I was twelve, my best buddy in the world, my beloved Poppop Davis, at the young age of sixty-three, suddenly died from an alcoholic liver. At that time Poppop was the love of my life, my everything. Then, he was suddenly gone. That didn't stop me from getting drunk on multiple occasions ten years later. I, totally, get the hype on cocktails, but now, I'm conscious of the fact that I'm toxifying my body and mind when I drink. When you drink, drink responsibly. Turn up. Enjoy, but don't fool yourself. Your liver ain't happy 'bout it. You're likely lowering your vibrational frequency and limiting the float of your bubble.

SUGAR:

Processed sugar is **toxic**. I want to call processed sugar **poison**. On the other hand, fruit, honey, maple syrup, a stick of sugar cane and any other purely natural, whole sources of sugar are cool. They're actually healthy in moderation. Processed white sugar and high fructose corn syrup, found in everything on the shelves in grocery stores, are flat out **toxic**. The ways in which these sugars are toxic to your body are

mind boggling. I don't want to give energy to talking about it. Google the dangers of processed sugar or high fructose corn syrup. Find a documentary. It's disgusting.

If you're very serious and vigilant about your health, you *could* enjoy just a spoonful of sugar here and there with no adverse effect. As I mentioned before, there's a threshold that you can stay within and still have great health. A couple of teaspoons of sugar a day might be ok. That, however, is **impossible** to do on a standard American diet. Staying away from this particular toxin ain't easy. Start by recognizing sugar as highly toxic. It's so hard to avoid sugar that I encourage you to watch a documentary on the many issues with processed sugar. That might help you to commit to centering your diet around fresh produce and limit your intake of processed foods from boxes and cans altogether. Start there to chart your path away from toxins in your body.

I'll close where we started on this one. Your bubble is your temple and your body is divine. Place only pure, natural, high-frequency things in your body. Stay away from toxins. Use natural fuels to raise the energy of your body to the highest levels possible. **Do not go through life without experiencing what it feels like to have a nature filled body. Don't knock it 'til you tried it for ninety days.** Now, you're more in tune with what your body needs, and experiencing some lightness of mind. This is a good time to delve into more understanding of our *reality* in Chapter Four. The more you understand about the nature of our world, the easier it can be to achieve a buoyant frame of mind. When you understand nature, it's easier to flow with it.

The Environment for Your Temple

The more loving energy and wisdom that courses through you, the more you will come to respect *all* of God's creations. Plants are not just our partners in life to be used by us. Plants should be recognized, as should every natural aspect of our environment, as wondrous creations of God that deserve our love. If you're not taking steps to protect our environment, how connected can you be to our shared creative force? Reduce your carbon footprint. Take this seriously. Start by planting and nurturing something. Perhaps a little herb garden in your kitchen window or a tree somewhere. Don't stop there. Help fight Climate Change in *any* way that you can. It's the buoyant move.

CHAPTER FOUR

FULLY ACCEPT AND EMBRACE YOUR SOUL JOURNEY

(and everyone else's)

"God, grant me the serenity to *accept*
the things I cannot change."
– Reinhold Niebuhr

By now, your mind and body are much more primed to take off on a meaningful soul journey. Your mind is more open, free and properly focused. Your body is more flowing with life. You recognize that life is school for the soul and you're ready to be a great student. To do well in this "life school," you really have to be skilled at **acceptance**. This is key. Absolutely dream, and push to fulfill those dreams, but **accept your life as a uniquely designed learning experience**. Fully **embrace the good with the bad. Learn at every turn**, accepting everything along your journey. Like it or not. When you can accept things as they are, you're ready to truly live.

In this chapter, I want to share concepts that can enhance your understanding of the forces of nature in our universe. It'll help you to accept things as they come in your life. As you understand more about the forces of nature, the understanding helps you to let your life flow with these same forces. We'll also cover some perspectives that I call 'soul basics.' Each of these areas are for the purpose of broadening your consciousness. The more expanded your consciousness about the nature of our world, the more enriching and rewarding your soul journey. An expanded consciousness and understanding of nature allows you to see so much more. You can understand more and feel more connected. You can broaden your perspectives. Most importantly, your expanded consciousness can help you to feel content with **whatever** happens along your life path. It helps you to see that forces beyond your control are in play.

"The world is his, who can see through its pretension ...
See it to be a lie, and you have already dealt it its mortal blow."
    – **Ralph Waldo Emerson**

GOD IS

LIFE'S A G THANG. GOD IS THE G.

To readers other than my kids: Heads up. My beliefs differ from most. I urge you to deactivate your auto-defense system, in advance, as my beliefs differ from what's already hard-wired for you. It's hard to hear conflicting beliefs when your belief system is already hard-wired. Keep in mind that avoiding judgment brings helium to your bubble. Your belief system is not being challenged because mine is different. All I can tell you is that love, unity and the existence of a higher power are the chosen fundamentals of my faith. I accept all prayers for my salvation.

God is. This is in no way a definition, it's just me sharing my instinctive feelings. I know you will come to your own understanding, but here's my guidance. Somehow, figure it out, but know that I am begging you to accept that God exists. My belief is that everything in this Universe and all existing universes, everything in existence, collectively, exists as one 'organism.' The collective, creative, energetic, loving consciousness of the full organism is what I call God. I refer to both the organism (everything in existence) and the force that brought it into creation, as God. I don't see it as necessarily religious. God just IS. For me, the combination of science and instinct make the **existence** of God indisputable. The **definition** of God **can**, however, be disputed. Although, not here. I believe disputes over the nature of God to be the most wasted energy in existence. Follow your heart for your definition. I've followed mine and this is what my heart tells me. God's unending, conscious energy field runs through all things seen and unseen. It goes through you and everyone else, and every*thing* else. We, each are a tiny particle of it, which makes us all connected. We're each part of the same Universal energy field (sort of like being part of a soup). Our separateness is an illusion; we're literally connected. The creative consciousness of this force, God, is the root of all the world's great religions. The American Indians aptly named God, "The Great Mystery." It's not important to try to wrap your AI brains around God. It's totally ok for God to remain a mystery. Tap your instincts. That's all that's needed. *[Look at the ant, sluggard ;-)]* It's not necessary to define God or try to read God's mind to know what God thinks or what God wants. Just wrap your heart around the heart of the force we call God. Feel your connection to your Creator's loving force. Know that you are part of something much, much, **MUCH** bigger than yourself. This force is a powerful energy that courses through your life whether you connect strongly to it or not. To experience the *heights* of Happiness, however, I highly recommend that you deliberately and continuously connect to this love-filled conscious force to fuel, empower and guide you.

"You see, the sea is only drops of water that have come together."
– Bishop Desmond Tutu; featured in "I Am"

I have called it 'God Energy' or 'that Universal force' or 'God' to keep it simple enough for everyone to understand. You can call it Mother Nature. It doesn't matter what you call it. All that matters is that you feel the creative, loving, all-powerful force of your Creator. Acknowledge it, appreciate it, and connect to the force in your way. Conscious connection is powerful to your life experience, but some people are naturally connected without effort. Some live and breathe with divine energy coursing through them. There are no religious precursors required to get you there. Access is a natural reality of life. All you have to do is open your bubble to it, to let that loving God energy pour throughout.

As far as understanding God is concerned, I don't believe our minds have the capacity to absorb the full concept and knowledge of God *(understatement)*. I'm actually wary of folks who **know** the mind of God, "his" personality and "her" needs, with certainty. Anything is possible, but that's too much for the kid! I believe our souls have the capacity to know all that we *need* to know about God, intuitively. **To understand God and your connection to God's loving force, do so only with your heart, your gut and your feelings.** These are the wisest, most spiritually connected parts of you anyway. These are the only parts of you that can come close to true understanding of God.

It's possible for a person who has never been exposed to the concept or teachings of God to be closer to God than some religious leaders and our best biblical scholars. All that's needed is to be open and receiving of God's loving energy. Allow it to course through you, fill you up and guide you. It's that simple.

Feel God through things that can't be explained. Feel God in nature. Feel God in your happiest moments. When you feel love, feel God. God, to **varying** degrees, is in everything and everyone. Recognize this and connect to God's intelligent, loving force throughout your life. It's the most important concept. The other philosophies lose potency if you don't feel this powerful, unifying, loving force within you. This is what connects us all. This is the concept that humbles and infuses us with endless love. Tap it.

JUST BETWEEN YOU AND GOD:

You'll never truly realize your power until you humbly acknowledge that you're a part of something bigger, and fill yourself *completely* with the love energy of our creative force, God. No matter how much you believe you're already filled, there's always room for more. Test the limits. There are higher heights. Attempt to fill yourself completely. Wait 'til you experience the transformations and buoyancy that take place within you.

"Everyone thinks of changing the world, but nobody thinks of changing him or herself."

-Leo Tolstoy

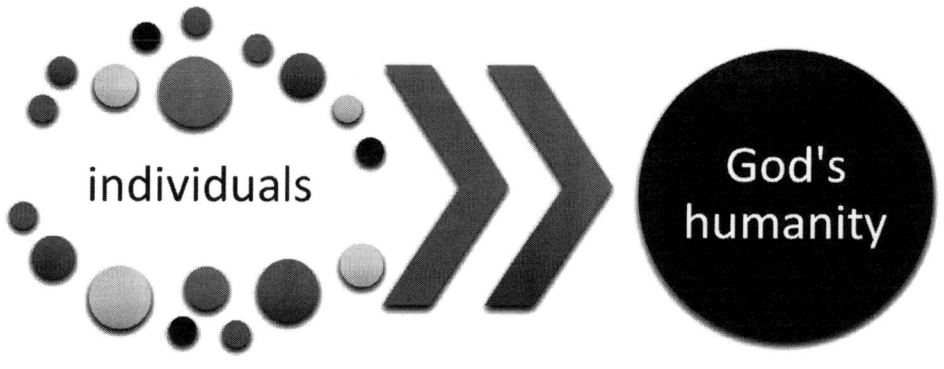

As each one of us evolves individually, we contribute to the evolution of those around us, and the advancement of the whole of humanity. Your personal progress is a big deal.

You are part of God's humanity. Each one of us is. Live out your role. The lessons you learn along your soul journey feed into the whole of human consciousness.

"We are one. And that's the way it is."
– **Frankie Beverly**

THE HIGHEST OF GOD'S ENERGIES IS LOVE.

As you fully awaken to your nature as part of something much, much bigger, a heavenly feeling comes over you. The feeling is magnified as you allow the highest energy of this divine, all-encompassing force, **love**, to course fully through you. The full effect of this experience reaches a peak as you release the dense energy of baggage. Swap all baggage for love energy from the source. Heaven is what we call not having to deal with all of our thought energy anymore and being enveloped in divine love. While we expect to reach a constant state of heavenly existence when we shed our bodies from our bubbles, we don't have to wait for that. Right now, we each have access to Cloud Nine. That's where Universal Love fills and charges us while we're still rocking our beautiful bodies. Our challenge is to maintain a full charge of this love energy as we work our way through the struggles of life.

That's the whole point of this book, guys. I promise that you **can** feel absolutely immersed in Happiness while living your soul journey. Just do what it takes to get to The Happiness Zone.

It's comforting to anticipate a heavenly existence when we leave our bodies. This gives us something "ultimate" to look forward to. That sure works for me. I hope it works for you. Let's all goal for Happiness here, and heaven later. While we're on the whole heaven thing, let me address the concept of hell. Hell has been misinterpreted as something that awaits you on the other side. BAHHHMP! *(sound of a 'wrong' buzzer)* Wrong. Hell is experienced right here on Earth when you're not connected to the source. Hell is what you experience on Earth when your leash is long. Hell is reliance on Yureego to guide your life instead of using your heart. Hell is carrying excessive baggage. The Vile Station, *that's* Hell. And there are stations lower than the Vile Station. That's hell right there! Hell is having to live out the negative karma that you've generated. Hell is not a ***place*** where you will go after you leave your body. Hell is "lived," **with** a body. Hell does not exist on the higher frequencies that you enter after your body exits your bubble. *That's straight from the heart, not brain*. God would never let us endure the harsh realities of life, allowing us to fail our life challenges in negativity and misery, ***then*** allow us to burn in hell for eternity. Only a human AI would think of such a course. Only humans could subject someone to THAT. You do, however, have the choice to live in hell on Earth or rise to the Happiness Zone.

ACCEPT THAT A CREATIVE FORCE EXISTS AND FILL YOURSELF WITH THE LOVE OF THAT CREATIVE FORCE

"All matter originates and exists only by virtue of a force.

We must assume behind this force is the existence of a conscious and intelligent mind.

The mind is the matrix of all matter."

> **– Max Planck,**
> **Considered the father of quantum physics (1858-1947).**

IT'S OVER YOUR HEAD, 'CAUSE REALITY'S *DEEEEP*

I want you both to have, at least, **some** understanding of our Universe. Everyone should have some conceptual knowledge of what modern science has determined as our reality. This includes an understanding, *to some tiny degree*, of things like space/time, dark matter, the God particle, and the universal forces. It sounds like science fiction or some comic book type stuff, but it's realer than real. You should at least know *SOMETHING* about our reality. Knowing **something** about it, opens your mind to the world of possibilities you have before you. As I write this for you, we face **serious** challenges as a collective humanity. The more awakened each of us is, the more able we are, not only to achieve personal Happiness, but to save each other and our world.

"Humanity is going to require a substantially new way of thinking if it is to survive."

> **– Albert Einstein**

"If we're still here in 200 years, we will be thinking in new ways."

> **– Daniel Quinn, author of** *Ishmael*

Let's start with a few facts about our reality:

1. Nothing is what is appears to be.

We perceive each other, objects and so on as solid things and yet nothing could be farther from the truth. In fact, everything that we can perceive is preeeeety close to being entirely empty space.

Let's put this into perspective. All matter is composed of atoms and atoms are composed of protons, neutrons and electrons. These particles, in turn, are composed of yet smaller sub-atomic particles. Each of these levels of structure is inconceivably small, and inconceivably empty. Inconceivably small and empty, meaning that shit is, like, not there! As an example, hydrogen that is the most abundant element in the Universe is nearly 99.99999999999 empty space *(Speaking of hydrogen being so empty, remember that every molecule of water holds two hydrogen atoms and one oxygen. Water **should** be invisible! Water is amaaaazing! Drink it, guys!).*

Nothing is solid. Now let's look at this from a much larger perspective. You've heard of The Big Bang Theory, right? I pray so. The Big Bang Theory is the most commonly accepted theory held among physicists to explain the origin of the Universe. This theory holds that our entire universe was once compressed to a point the size of a grain of sand. **Think about it**. Our top scientists of this world are telling us this. So, I'm thinking, if our entire universe (and that's a lot of planets, moons, stars, asteroids, galaxies, black holes and some more) spanning billions of light years in diameter could be compressed to a single point, then **anything** is possible. Solid matter could be merely the *illusion* some top physicists think it is. Read *The Holographic Universe* if you want to delve into this more deeply.

2. Empty space is not empty.

I know, right? Crazy! But, there's a branch of science called 'quantum thermodynamics,' which has produced evidence that empty space ain't empty at all. We already know that everything, including empty space, is energy in the form of electrons. Einstein proved it mathematically a long time ago. Until we have pictures of what exists in empty space, and everyone in the world accepts it, realize that empty space is **not** empty. Recognize that modern science holds that empty space is "something." So should you.

Think of it like this. When a fan is on, if it's going fast enough, you can look straight through it as if nothing is there. Empty space is kinda like that. It is believed that empty space is a web of particle activity with connections weaving through it. Those connections weave through empty space and everything else. This may help you with the concept that we are all connected. There's no gap between us. There truly isn't.

3. We may be living in a hologram.

I know. I know. But the absurdity in your mind exists because of lack of knowledge. Keep reading.

When I was in high school, back in ancient 1982 times, a physicist named Alain Aspect performed an experiment at the University of Paris, which proved that paired electrons could communicate with each other **instantly** regardless of the distance between them. This phenomenon is known as 'quantum entanglement.' The Standard Model in physics (describes known forces/classifies elementary particles) accepts that nothing can travel faster than the speed of light (if I might add here that the discovery of the 'God Particle' recently filled in a missing link to our Standard Model. We keep learning more! It is believed by top physicists that much more will be discovered to expand our current Standard Model. We're still finding particles, and who knows, maybe a new force of nature! Look it up if you're interested). Ok. So, nothing can travel faster than light, but the interaction between entangled particles is *instantaneous* even when the particles are on opposite sides of the world *(which means electrons, including those within your bubble, can defy the current laws of physics when observed).* Based on this research, a *very* famous physicist, David Bohm, suggested that objective reality does not exist 🜨 and that our massive universe may be a very sophisticated hologram. Objective reality doesn't exist? Life is but a dream? This idea has been growing in popularity in the theoretical physics community. The 'Einsteins' of our day are very seriously looking at the possibility that our entire universe could be a "projected image from a yet higher level of reality" (Book reference: The Holographic Universe).

The heading says it's deep, so don't act shocked. We're just getting started. If you have to ask yourself if the science I'm talking about is real, who's in the present moment, me or you? Why wouldn't you already know all of this? It's mostly old, with *some* current news. You've certainly heard of Einstein, the God Particle and parallel universes, right? You've heard it. You just let it bounce off and away like a buoyant bubble. It's all good. I was keeping up for you. There's more.

THE GOD PARTICLE

Several years ago, scientists were looking for, and found, the God Particle. It's really called the Higgs Boson (God Particle is a nickname, long story) and is believed to enable energy to form into matter. They've identified the particle, but I'm not sure that it's still believed to actually be what allows energy to form into matter. I've wondered, since consciousness is realized by scientists to be a basic, fundamental force of nature, are scientists *truly* looking for the particle responsible for consciousness? Maybe I'm just rationalizing a cause worth spending billions to build a seventeen-mile wide machine that sits over a hundred feet below the Earth's surface. They say the purpose of the machine (Large Hadron Collider) is to help physicists decode the Universe. I know that's true, but wonder if part of that decoding could be finding clues to the origins of consciousness? Finding that in a particle would surely be reason to call it the God Particle, huh? I haven't heard much new information since the thing was discovered, except that it helped to complete The Standard Model of Physics. So we're learning more and that's cool. Of course, as with all scientific revelations, it opens up the door to new mysteries. The one thing we know as a result of the search for the Higgs Boson or God Particle is that **empty space is indeed an invisible energy field**.

ENERGY

"The field is the sole governing agency of the particle."
– Albert Einstein

(Translation: The field of conscious energy *that I refer to, collectively, as God*, is guiding the movement and form of every particle. Says Einstein. So, any laughter at my insistence that there is a conscious force governing the Universe can be directed to Albert.)

Energy is always there. Even when not presented in object form, like empty space. Einstein was the first scientist to figure out that empty space holds vast amounts of energy. We still have a lot to learn about the possibilities that exist as empty space, matter and energy are manipulated.

"The day science begins to study non-physical phenomena, it will make more progress in one decade than in all the previous centuries of its existence."
– Nikola Tesla

You've heard of a Tesla. They're nice, right? The car company, owned by Elon Musk, carries the name of the renowned scientist Nikola Tesla. Tesla was a physicist referred to as "the man who invented the twentieth century," because of his discovery of **alternating current electricity** and many other deep discoveries that led to inventions that we now take for granted. Tesla, like many great scientists, did not ignore the mysteries of the world. He *(correctly)* believed that a field extended through all things. He referred to it as Akasha. Akasha, in ancient teachings, is considered empty space, but also includes the space filled with matter. Tesla believed, as do I, that space, as presented by ancient teachings, is filled with vibrational energy. Tesla believed this and used this knowledge to make his amazing discoveries.

Mass and energy comprise **everything**. They are both generated from the same creative source. Mass (particles) can be converted to energy and energy can be converted to mass. It's all relative ;-). This is a play on Einstein's observations, in case you didn't catch it, (Theory of Relativity) that E=MC2. This famous equation points out that energy (E) is equal to mass (M) times the speed of light squared (C2). The bottom line for us right now is that mass and energy are the same thing. Mass is energy (a literal "form" of energy = everything that doesn't appear to be empty space). Energy (invisible, although we feel its effects) comprises everything, including the form of mass. Even if you don't get it, just know that everything is energy and it's all relative.

Everything in the Universe is energy. Every last thing. Thoughts, emotions, rocks, bubbles, love, it's all energy. You MUST see the world this way! This viewpoint is the rock of the Happiness Hookup. It may be that negative energy is in the process of evolution toward the positive. A girl can dream, right? My dream is that you flow in the right direction with *your* energy.

DARK MATTER & SPACE/TIME

Regarding dark matter, at least know this about it:

> "The visible Universe including Earth, the sun, the other stars and galaxies, is made of protons, neutrons, and electrons bundled together into atoms. Perhaps one of the most surprising discoveries of the 20th century was that this matter makes up less than 5% of the mass of the Universe. The rest of the Universe appears to be made of a mysterious, invisible substance called dark matter (25%) and a force that repels gravity known as dark energy (70%)"
>
> **– National Geographic, Dark Matter and Dark Energy, Science and Innovation.**

NOW, ON THAT THING CALLED SPACE/TIME:

Turns out, guys, that space and time have an inseparable relationship. They're married, you could say. Or let's say space and time are like conjoined twins, when one is affected, the other is affected in some way. The two are combined. We now refer to this combination as *"the fabric of space/time."* Our perception, the way we see space, is as a three-dimensional thing. We're limited in our ability to perceive what's going on here. We perceive time as something that is linear, going in one direction (one dimensional). That's how we've always seen it, but **like I keep trying to point out, nothing is how it seems.** The fabric of space/time is woven and inseparable. To really get your brain going, try to understand that space/time can be bent by forces such as gravity. Have fun with that, but don't get brain freeze trying to process it all.

If you're interested, look into it. There's probably a "Space/Time for Dummies" or something that makes it easier to grasp. Don't hesitate to explore it. Einstein's E=mc2 helped explain the relation between space and time and that space and time could be manipulated by the force of gravity. This mathematical, scientific fact is accepted by ALL top scientists. It mathematically proves that time can be manipulated. And, get this, it proves that time travel is *possible*. Brings new mystery to the question, "Where on earth is the time going?" Reality is deep, y'all. That's all I got to say.

UNIVERSAL FORCES (STRONG, GRAVITATIONAL, ELECTROMAGNETIC, OH, MY!)

THE STRONG FORCE

The strong force is like a cosmic glue. This force holds your atoms together. It holds the nucleus of the atom together, keeping your neutrons and protons from flying apart. The most basic components of the Universe, the electrons that I've been talking about, are governed by the strong force that holds these particles together like glue.

GRAVITATIONAL FORCE

You're very familiar with this one. We call it gravity. Gravity is what keeps you from being the real bubble you are and floating off into space. We call it an attractive force because we see it as pulling things together *(although it is now believed that the gravity of space is actually pushing us to keep us from floating away, rather than the Earth's gravity pulling us. Who knows! Still, even as our knowledge of science evolves, gravity will always be a fundamental Universal force)*. We are surrounded by gravity. Gravitational force, with its push and pull on all forms of mass, is what holds everything in place in space. The moon's gravity causes the waves in our oceans. The Earth's gravitational force is different from that of other planets. Here on Earth, gravitational force causes your weight. It causes our earthly objects to move in the ways that they do. Consider the weaker gravitational pull of the moon and how astronauts seem to have much less weight there. That's an example of the difference between our Earth and the moon's gravitational force. Gravity affects both mass and energy. Remember that mass is energy and that all things are energy. So, gravity affects, well, *everything*.

ELECTROMAGNETIC FORCE

Electromagnetic force is the force that allows for light (and the electricity that allowed me to use my computer to type this). Electromagnetic force occurs when electrons physically exchange photons between themselves, causing the electrons to be attracted or repelled from each other. When an electron absorbs a photon, it can get enough energy to jump to a higher energy station or level *(you may or may not remember the rings, or levels within atoms and how electrons can jump from one level to another ... that jumping is a result of electromagnetic force).* When an electron wants to go to a lower energy level it releases a photon to jump back down to a lower energy level. *Kinda like you, when you decide to manage your thoughts and elevate up, or let your bubble drift down. Electromagnetic force is what governs the up and down flow of an atoms' electrons. Self-control governs the ups and downs of your bubble. You* **could** *imagine your self-control over your thoughts and feelings to be a 'force,' like electromagnetic force.*

THE WEAK FORCE

This force is responsible for the nuclear decay that atoms, sometimes, undergo *(despite the name, gravity, the force you're most familiar with, is the weakest of the four forces, just heads up).*

STRING THEORY

It is believed, by top physicists of today, that there is a theory that somehow escaped Einstein. This relatively new theory, String Theory, accounts for the endless discoveries of sub-atomic particles that continues to occur. *Here's one more reason why we shouldn't get too wrapped up into the sense of "knowing" exactly what is going on with our reality ...* **we keep learning**. *Our awareness continues to increase, so always be open and expect that there may be more to your thoughts and beliefs than what you have hard-wired as fact.*

String Theory helps to explain why when we smash atoms, we get such an endless array of new sub-atomic particles like holons, leptons, quarks, neutrinos, Higgs Bosons and on and on. There are thousands of subatomic particles. String Theory is a master theory that explains that all of these subatomic particles are part of a tiny, invisible, vibrating, rubber-band like, string. The string contains **all** *particles. The particles reveal themselves based on how the string is stimulated. Much like notes are revealed based on how you strum a guitar.*

"This is incredible...these (subatomic) particles are nothing but musical notes on a vibrating string. What is physics? Physics is nothing but the harmonies on these strings. What is chemistry? Melodies. What is the Universe? The Universe is a symphony of these strings."
– Michio Kaku, Theoretical Physicist

THE MANDELBROT SET

REFERRED TO AS THE THUMBPRINT OF GOD

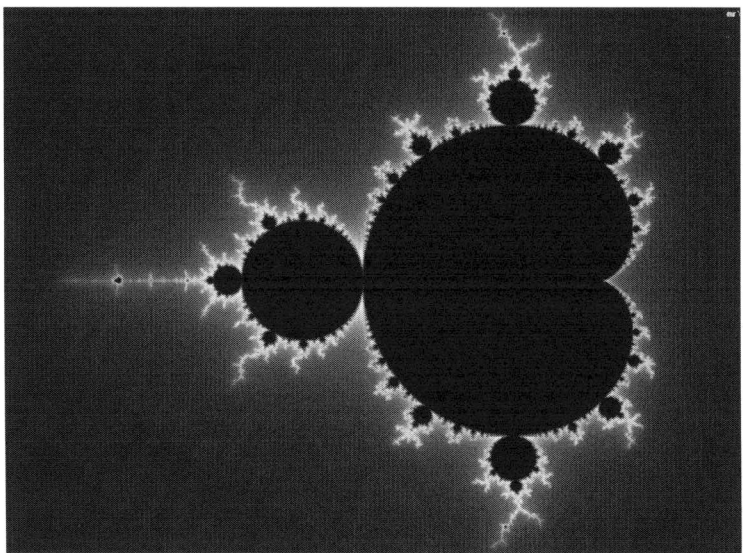

I actually love this one. "The Mandelbrot Set" is a math equation, a set of complex numbers founded by one mathematician who named it in honor of another, Beniot Mandelbrot. The Mandelbrot Set was first used in 1978 to draw a fractal image. The set led to the creation of the seemingly simple math equation, $z=z2 +c$, that when expressed by a computer, reveals an amazing fractal graphic (above). The resulting graphic was not created by man. It's a computer interpretation of the math equation. When you observe and zoom into the details of the fractal image, as you can when you watch a Mandelbrot Zoom, you see a breathtaking display of interconnected images. What's so striking, as you observe, is that the infinite, constantly changing images are not the artwork of man. It's chaotic on one hand, but there's a distinct order as it flows. What you are watching, as you witness a Mandelbrot Zoom, is **nature** being translated by a computer. Realize, as you watch one, that you are witnessing a design of nature, *not man*. It's a visually expressed math formula that's infinite change can be recognized to reveal aspects of our nature. Math, as I have pointed out to you before, is the language of the Universe. Accept the Mandelbrot Zoom as a visual message from nature. Very interesting and revealing.

"Look deep into nature, and then you will understand everything better."
– **Albert Einstein**

What I Learned from a Mandelbrot Zoom

It's *crazy* hypnotic and even calming to watch, but what's most interesting is the aspects of nature that this visually displayed math equation reveals. It's more than just a bunch of fractals. You get to peek into some of the aspects of how nature flows.

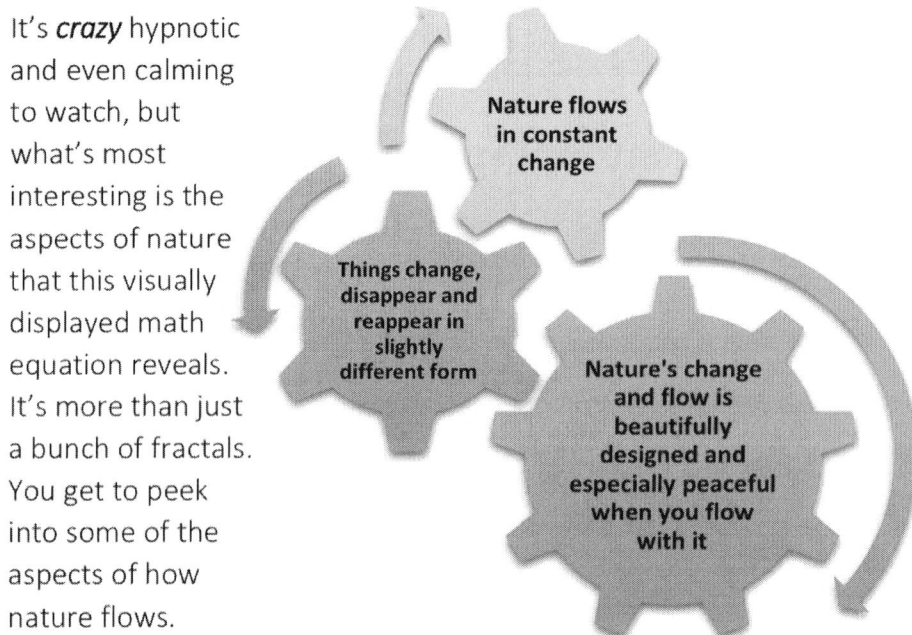

The thing that's interesting is that, as I pointed out about energy, the Zoom doesn't end. Like energy, it flows out in all directions, and everything in the Zoom connects to and has an effect on everything else. The Zoom never dies, it just changes form. I like to use this as a visual analogy for life. Imagine yourself as one of the tiny images. As you watch a Mandelbrot Zoom, see the connectedness, change, patterns, flow and rebirth of the images into something brand new, yet kinda the same. The Mandelbrot Zoom exhibits these facts of nature. It actually IS a fact of nature. Connect this to the nature that you see play out in your life. See the connectedness, change, patterns, flow and rebirth in your own life. They're all natural aspects of the flow of life.

CYMATICS

Squeeze in a quick peek at Cymatics, after you've looked at a Mandelbrot Zoom YouTube video. See how sound waves create form in matter. It's amazing. Connect that with the concept that there is an ever changing wave of vibrational energy that permeates everything, even empty space. That vibrational wave of energy can create form, the same way that vibrational sound creates the forms you witness when viewing Cymatics. Connect the dots. It's not such a stretch anymore. Your thoughts and beliefs are vibrational energies that *can* materialize your dreams.

Your thoughts are vibrations, just like music.
Your thoughts can materialize things.

QUANTUM ENTANGLEMENT

All explanations of quantum entanglement are mind boggling. Still, the fact that it proves that there are innate connections at the most fundamental parts of our existence makes quantum entanglement one of my favorite scientific discoveries.

"Quantum entanglement occurs when two particles become inextricably linked, and whatever happens to one immediately affects the other, regardless of how far apart they are" (Fiona Macdonald, Sciencealert. com, 7/13/2019). Einstein called it, "spooky action at a distance," partly because quantum entanglement apparently defies our known laws of physics *(how crazy is that? science confirms something that defies all known laws of physics?)* The connection and actions of the entangled particles occur simultaneously, faster than the speed of light, when the particles are separated by vast distances. Nothing's supposed to move at speeds faster than light, so that's amazing. What strikes me is the fact that if particles can be connected in these ways, and we're made of particles, then maybe there's your answer for a lot of connections that we couldn't otherwise answer? Connections exist. They exist at the most fundamental levels of nature. Quantum entanglement scientifically proves that unexplained connections exist. It's not just a belief anymore.

We're all made of atoms, which are swirling electrical particles. Now I want to stray away from proven science for a minute. Think about it. Given what we have learned about quantum entanglement, who's to say that some of the particles that exist inside your bubble aren't connected *(entangled)* to other particles in the Universe? Science has proven that some particles are entangled. There's absolutely no proof that this could be the case for particles of ourselves and others, but why wouldn't it? Let's just imagine that some of your particles, from birth, are "entangled" with particles of another person. Now let's imagine that the other person has just found out the most joyful news ever, and in real time, you experience an uplifting thought or even better a wave of euphoria out of the blue. With entangled particles, when something happens to one of the particles there's an effect on the other particle. It's also simultaneous with absolutely no gap in time. Particles separated by distance are flowing as if one. Science didn't believe that was possible, until it was proven. Even Einstein was freaked by it. The possibilities for connections between all things in life are endless. Today, everything scientifically proven about quantum entanglement is presented in math and laboratory experiments. It's super boring, but this "spooky action at a distance" stuff is interesting, in theory, and very, very real.

What's intriguing to me is that this may offer *one more* reason for our connectedness to other people and other things. Perhaps, the reason I called you at the exact moment you were thinking about calling **me**, was driven by quantum entanglement? Who knows! But we have one more reason to believe that anything is possible and we are all connected. That's a good thing.

10 DIMENSIONS? PARALLEL UNIVERSES/THE MULTIVERSE?

"The Milky Way (our galaxy) is just one of a hundred billion galaxies. It's been estimated that there are more stars in the Universe than there are grains of sand on all the beaches in all the world. Just think about that for a moment."
— **Everything and Nothing: The Amazing Science of Empty Space**

With the infinite vastness of space in mind, let's look more closely at our reality. According to String Theory, a leading physics model for today, the Universe operates with ten dimensions. As stated on Smithsonian-mag.com *(you can read it yourself)*, some of the dimensions "include all possible futures and all possible pasts, including realities with a totally different physics than those in our universe." I. Am. Not. Shitting. You. This is modern day science. Then, you have parallel universes. That's on TOP of the ten dimensions, guys. The New Oxford American Dictionary describes the concept of a parallel universe as "a universe theorized as existing alongside our own, although undetectable." *Scientific American* published an article, "The Case for Parallel Universes: Why the Multiverse, crazy as it sounds, is a solid scientific idea." Parallel universes are now referred to as the Multiverse, same thing different name. It's a prediction of the theories of quantum mechanics that multiverses exist. So far, other predictions have been correct. Apparently, **anything** is possible in this world.

I'm not even remotely interested in trying to explain either of these, nor am I able! The point of all these deep scientific realities is that we live in a world of amazing, **mind-blowing** realities, and the bubble concept I'm delivering is **NOT** one of the mind-blowing varieties. You enhance your soul journey with knowledge and acceptance of the truths of nature, especially your nature. Be aware of what science has revealed. Expand your consciousness. Do your own research and let science guide you to these facts:

- SCIENCE HAS DROPPED ITS BELIEF IN A PHYSICAL WORLD. MAYBE YOU SHOULD DO THE SAME.
- ENERGY CREATES REALITY. AND, YOUR ENERGY CREATES YOUR REALITY.
- YOU ARE PART OF AN ONGOING, NATURAL CYCLE OF EVOLUTION.

- AN AMAZING FORCE OF NATURE BROUGHT YOU INTO EXISTENCE. ACT LIKE YOU KNOW.

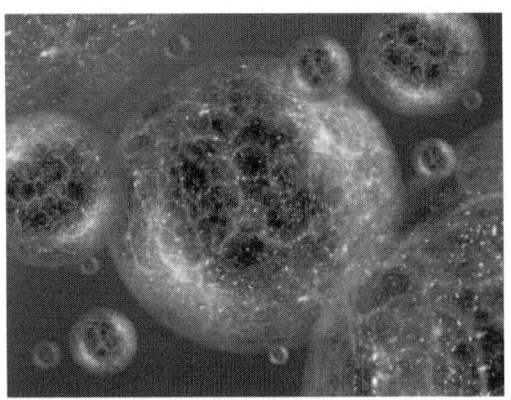

Note: This image was used in a 2016 Smithsonian magazine article entitled, "Can Physicists Ever Prove the Multiverse is Real?" I had no idea the multiverse had a theoretical likeness to bubbles! Apparently, it's *all* **about bubbles**. My "Bubbleology" may not be as funny as I originally thought?

SOUL BASICS

LOVE

Of everything in the world, love is the most significant and powerful energy. Having love to give is like having a magic wand. Love is a creative force. With a wave of it, you can create what otherwise could take years of blood, sweat and tears to accomplish. It has a transformative quality that all are receptive to, *to varying degrees*. Throughout your soul journey, use love energy to bring your dreams to fruition. It can heal. It can enlighten. It is the most powerful energy you can ever have. Use it wisely and often.

THE LOVE OF FAMILY AND FRIENDS

I'm 3. Grandma's 48.

Grandma's 99. I'm 54.
(and we're loving the
invention of filters! ☝️🤍)

"Bonds of love
are bigger than images or words or actions, or even life itself.
They are divine and eternal. Just feel them." - M

Family relationships are obvious spiritual connections. Don't miss the opportunity to nourish your soul by relishing, building and strengthening those relationships. These relationships are right in our faces, designated by the force that created us. These relationships offer opportunity for our souls to grow as we develop them. There's lots of valuable soul journey lessons hidden within our families. These lessons usually come in the form of challenges and exist in all families. It's part of life. No family is immune. There's always something to be gained from it in the way of a lesson learned.

Sometimes we're meant to learn something from our relatives. Sometimes we're meant to teach something. Sometimes we have to heal or forgive or broaden our understanding of others. But most of all, we are meant to love. Embrace the value of *every* relative. Accept and respect your relatives for the part they play in your life. Value the connections of everyone 'connected' to you. Don't take the journey of family members personally. Learn and benefit from the lessons they teach. Fit each relative into a peaceful and loving space in your own heart. That puts first things first in your life.

Friends are not designated by birth. They are very special spiritual ties of your choice *(we think that it's a choice, but it may be more divine than that.)* There are souls to which you are attracted for a wide range of reasons, and *choose* to insert into your life. The philosophy behind the connection is the same. Each friend is in your life for a reason. You are to learn something or teach something or share something. **Pay closest attention to the friends with whom you have a natural, mutually giving relationship.** Always be there for your friends when they need you, and even when they don't. Avoid building new friendships with 'needy' prospects. You can't fill other people's needs. You can only support, inspire and guide. No friend can fill your needs, so don't look for that. *You got your own needs under control, right?* Look for mutually giving, uplifting relationships. Those are the healthiest and most beneficial friendships. Always take an opportunity to show love and appreciation for your friends. Be loyal. If you are at odds with an old or new friend, heal that relationship. Heal every one of them if you can, even if only in your own heart and mind. As they say, "friends are the family you choose." That makes your friends 'family.' Family is family. And family first, right? Have friendships that carry bonds that remain very strong even when you have not communicated with each other. Friendships hold important bonds of love. Bonds of love are bigger than words, or actions or even life itself. They are divine and eternal. Just feel them. When you do feel strong bonds of love that last over distances and time. Hold tight and nurture it.

On the other hand, don't feel like you *have* to hold on if you've clearly outgrown a friend relationship. It's ok. Everything changes, and it's natural for relationships to change. It will be obvious when it is time to move on. Sometimes you have changed. Sometimes the friend has changed. Sometimes the change is for the worse. It happens and it's ok. Life holds stories! Flow with it, and don't be down if a groove is gone or a friendship change is in your best interest. "God wants you to look out for you!" No hard feelings. Recognize and adjust when it's just time for you to move in new directions. When you do release friend relationships, never do it with anything but love for the old friend. If they taught you lessons, appreciate them for it. Move forward positively with your new knowledge. Every time one door closes, another opens. *Believe and embrace that.* When you *must* move on, another door *always* awaits.

ROMANTIC LOVE

"I'll give you my heart, my soul, my time, my love is a fountain ...
All that I've got is yours. I'll give you everything.
I love you more than you could know and that's for sure."
   – After 7, Ready or Not

Always remember how love flows. Look back at that if you need to. Self-love HAS to fill you *completely* **before you even** *think* **about having powerful romantic relationships!**

When you're truly in love with someone, they love you too. Trust me on this fact of nature. Like the laws of physics, there are laws of love, and one law of love insists that true love is mutual. It's always, always mutual when it's true love. Never be confused about that. This understanding can end a lot of unnecessary pain before it begins. So, once again ... True love is **always** mutual. I believe there's an 'entanglement' when love is true. It's a vibration that's impossible to miss or top. Appreciate it as a divine energy.

For your Happiness, it's important to understand the difference between true love and all the other feelings and urges that simulate romantic love. Some originate from Yureego, so beware. Your feelings can trick you if you're not paying attention. If you find that the love you thought was real isn't mutual, don't fret. You've probably mistaken the excitement of meeting a personal need *(generated by Yureego)* with true love. That happens, and it's easy to fix.

First, take responsibility. Recognize that it's *your bad (even if you feel you've been misled ... claim no foul!)*, you were not in touch, enough, with yourself and your heart. Immediately drop two tears in a bucket and pivot to a focus on **yourself**. It's important that you don't blame **anyone**. Don't beat yourself up. You never lose, you **learn**. The rush of feelings you confused with heart-based love, came from Yureego's identification that some **'needs'** could be filled by the object of your affection. The mere thought of a 'need' being filled is usually quite a rush to the ego. There are lots of potential benefits to our egos that can be gained from love interests including a heightened self-image, money, social status and/or sexual benefits, just to name a few. The rush of receiving these benefits can easily be confused with the rush of love. It happens all the time. While the feeling of filling that need can be intense, it isn't to be confused with true, heart-based love. True love is a whole different experience. True love is not based on any so-called needs. True love is pure nature at work. A connection of soul energies, as if magnetized.

You've learned, now, to connect with your heart, not your brain or the needs of your ego when it comes to love. That's a win. You will avoid this kind of heartbreak in the future and be well on your way to true love. All you have to do is remember that true love is mutual. **Never look to fill a 'need' from others or**

180

for others. The best romantic relationship comes from the union of two 'complete' people. Always be poised for change if you get on the wrong track. Love up on yourself! You will magnetize true love to yourself, and be more than ready for what comes.

When it comes to true love, just because it's not *apparently* mutual, doesn't mean that it isn't. Some people can be in love and not show it exactly the way you wanted it to be expressed (romantic gestures, accommodating behaviors, etc.). This can happen for a million reasons, including personality and past experiences. For your own Happiness, I suggest you don't guess about **why** it's happening. If you're filled with confidence about the love you share, then the way the love is displayed doesn't truly matter. You know they love you. Don't try to measure love. That's a big mistake. Yureego's at it again.

Never try to measure love.

**It can't be measured. So don't ever look for measures of someone's love.
Let that go. Just feel it. Know it. Absorb it. Then, lovingly return it.**

If you know in your heart the love is real, trying to measure it is busy brainwork. That's your AI, always generating "need" in the effort to feel secure. Your **heart** doesn't "need" any of that. Love is a heart based experience. It can't be measured. Relinquish the need for proof or displays of love. Love is pure just as it is. Look into the different "languages of love," and make doubly sure you aren't being needy. People show their love in a myriad of ways. Appreciate the love from others in its natural form. Let them be them. Try not to place expectations on the way the love is expressed, or make demands from them in the name of love. Why spend time worrying about small stuff like that when you've been blessed with love in the first place? Fill your own needs and bask in all the love you receive. When you love up on yourself **enough**, you won't have the need or time to wonder why the love from another is not reflected the way you want it to be. You'll be too full of love to think about it! The bottom line is true love is mutual and a blessing beyond blessings. When you have a love bond, just trust in it and enjoy the feeling. The feeling of loving another, in itself, is an amazing feeling and a precious source of energy in your life. If you insist on measurements of love to be safe and secure in your love, you are also insisting on undermining the love. Be prepared for whatever happens. All you ever need is YOU to take care of YOU. Don't forget it. If there's something you want so bad, get it. Let romantic love be a pure space to share the excess love you each have, without need.

A keen intuition and a healthy ego make true love impossible to miss. Relish in your loves without drama. Only passion. Don't be a victim of Yureego and need and want the love of another because you "think" that would be perfect for you. It's ok to indulge in infatuations, just know the difference from the start and be cool with that. I just don't want you to **ever** be *confused* about love. That's a real Happiness buster, right there.

Without a Romantic Love? Stay tuned to the thought processes and attitude that keep your energy buoyant. Tune to the station where you and your future love will meet. Get completely **filled** with self-love. Overflow with your light. Appreciate the "you" time you have now. Make the most of it! Immerse yourself in things that elevate you. **If you're truly interested, someone *perfect* awaits**. You don't have to search. All you have to do is stay-tuned, in loving appreciation of your Boo before Boo arrives. Claim them, sight unseen. Let go of any expectations, except for a wonderful soul connection. "Virtual text" love notes to your future soul mate. Bubble to bubble. Put it out there, but you don't have to search. Elevated self-love and genuine intent to find a true love someday, will magnetize them to you. Be patient, but be ready.

True love is some potently powerful energy. Enjoy and have full appreciation for any and all love that comes your way. ***Just never NEED it, please***. I cannot emphasize this enough. You're supposed to understand how love flows by now. You should always be so filled with love from the source and for yourself that true, heart-based, romantic love is just icing on the cake. When you do make that connection, remember this:

Two people, overflowing with self-love, yet *completely unselfish*, make for the happiest and most rewarding relationships.

MANY LIVES

"I'm so darn glad that he let me try it again,
'cause my last time on Earth I lived a whole world of sin.
I'm so glad that I know more than I knew then.
Gonna keep on tryin' til I reach my highest ground."
  – Stevie Wonder, Lyrics from Higher Ground.

Guys, I'd love for you to give some **serious** consideration to the concept of living many lives. It releases your mind from the lead-energy "senseless, cruel world" perspective.

> *Let's imagine that you live many lives. Imagine that your bubble becomes more radiant, bigger and higher in frequency as it evolves from each lifetime. Your body, and the circumstances of your life change with each life. The bubbles to which you are connected or entangled, whether living on the other side of the Universe, world or on the other side of life, are still very connected to you. Even when you're alone.*
>
> *On each trip, you get a brand new computer brain. Virtually all memories from your old brain are erased (with some exceptions of residual memory). The heart-based memories are stored in your bubble, available to your heart, but not readily available to your new brain. You slowly learn to identify with the new vehicle and the new mind. You receive a name for the new vehicle and that becomes the identity you will project and aggressively protect. You strongly identify with your new vehicle, totally unaware of your bubble. You move forward in life, again, blind to who you **truly** are. Back in the game, you slowly sense your way to your whole self, over the course of time.*

HOW'S IT ANY MORE OUTRAGEOUS TO BE BORN MULTIPLE TIMES, THAN IT IS TO BE BORN ONCE?

This life is just a *part* of your soul journey. It's likely not your first rodeo and probably not your last. There **is** such a thing as reincarnation. Perhaps in your lifetime, more light will be shed on why this widely held belief has credibility. Someday we may have irrefutable proof *(proof exists now, but folks are hardwired to other perspectives)*. We know that we are fields of energy, and that energy does not end, it transforms. We just haven't transferred this fact-based knowledge into proof that our souls live on after we make our exits, or that our soul energy can get another go at physical life. For now, just consider the possibility.

Most of the great religions of the world embrace that the spirit lives on. It's also a widely held spiritual belief of cultures around the world that our souls reincarnate. It may not be the **popular** belief of the American or Christian culture at this time, but cultures have changed beliefs over time, when faced with mounting evidence. Today, a **quarter** of Americans, Christian Americans, believe in reincarnation (according to data released by the Pew Forum on Religion and Public Life in 2009). Beliefs change, particularly as we learn more about our reality. According to Wikipedia, the percentage of people who believe in reincarnation ranges from 14 percent to 44 percent, depending on the country surveyed. Proof exists, but people don't believe what they're seeing and hearing. For me, it makes all the sense in the world, both spiritually and scientifically. It lightens my mind with hope and possibilities. I want this feeling for you. So, my message to you guys is this: **We live many lives, and what goes around comes around whether in this lifetime or another. Consider it, and live accordingly on your soul journey.**

This life is one tiny slice of the full picture of who you are. Imagine that every life you see reveals merely a slice of the full person. That's why it's ridiculous to judge people, you don't know their story in this life or any other. The homeless man may become a king, the slave may have been a queen. This life does not paint the whole picture of you or anyone else. Don't try to be everything in this life. Just **be yourself**, the way you were born to be in this lifetime. Make this life count by fulfilling your current destiny in the here and now. If you're not true to the self you were born to be in this life, you may hold up progress for your soul. Get into it and live out the full slice of *this* life.

Since what goes around comes around, it's a good idea to plant a lot of good seeds through heart felt deeds. Don't you think? It makes sense to increase the odds that whatever comes around to you is good stuff, right? Whether in this life or the next, you're the one who'll have to live with it.

Belief in the concept of reincarnation, many lives, can relieve you of many burdens in life. First, it helps you to accept the fact that you are not in control. There's a bigger picture that is playing out. Accept it. While it is difficult to feel at peace with a lot of the things that you see in life, it is virtually impossible to rationalize anything with the 'one life to live' theory. It flat out makes no sense to the *heart or mind*. Sorrow, confusion and frustration are often the result of the **one life** story. It's hard to accept the senselessness of some people's life experiences. It's senseless if it's that soul's only chance for life experiences. These same senseless experiences might make sense when considering the span of many lives. **Tough life situations are lessons** for each of us. Lessons elevate our souls. Especially tough ones. **Karmic experiences are not for reward or punishment, they simply allow lessons to play out that contribute to the growth of one's soul.** Physical pain and suffering is a soul thing. Seeing it that way helps to release some of the pain. Pain is part of the process that develops the soul. Helping to relieve one's pain is another soul thing. The act of suffering presents an opportunity for soul growth on multiple levels. While the individual experiencing tough life situations may not be processing the situation in the best way, it's still a process for the growth of their soul. The experience of suffering is not the end of our stories. Death is not even the end of our stories. Soul stories go on and on. Bad things are relative experiences. That which we consider "bad," may involve suffering, but suffering is just another experience. We are not responsible for ending the suffering that life delves out. This isn't heaven. This is life. If we perceive the experiences without resistance, they might not be as bad as we originally thought. These tough lessons become easier to process *positively* when we let go, accept where we are in our life journey, and take the 'learn' to heart. If we tap into the energy of the creative force, and that energy wells up inside us, *any of us*, we're charged for whatever our journeys hold. **Make this life count for all it's worth, so you can grow spiritually. Keep on trying 'til you reach your highest ground.**

Fate
Be not depressed by suffering,

Nor should you envy bliss.

I feel I've known that depth and height,

And thus can offer this ...

Each one of us has his own path,

Or her own life to lead.

And all the joy and pain we see,

Are meant to fill a need.

For our souls are developing through

Our life here on Earth.

Each soul has learned from everything

Experienced from birth.

And each of us is but one part of

What makes this world whole.

Our lessons **must** be different

We're each a different soul.

Evolving from the lessons learned,

From our experience.

And so the lack of equity we see,

Makes perfect sense.

To worry of his suffering,

To envy all her bliss,

Could take your mind off lessons,

Meant for your soul not to miss.

Respect and understand

The different paths we have to take.

Consume yourself with peace and love

And please believe in fate.
- Mom

KARMA HAS MAD PATIENCE

BELIEVE WITHOUT SEEING KARMA'S FULL CYCLE.

Karma generates from our thoughts, feelings and the actions we take. I see karma as basic science. Karma is energy first *generated,* then *received* by the source that generated it. Envision it as a boomerang of sorts. Except the karma boomerang moves in an ellipse motion, like the movement of planets in our solar system. It eventually returns, full circle, back to us. Just as the ellipses of the planets vary in size and duration, so too do karmic returns. Karmic energy returns in a different form, but with the same vibration of energy. The energy each of us puts out, eventually returns to us in a different form at a different time. It doesn't necessarily return in the same lifetime, by the way. Karmic ellipses vary in duration. But, good or bad, that karma's coming.

Energy follows universal laws. Karma's just one example. Since karma can span many lifetimes, who could possibly know the answer to the question "why" something is happening to a person? The answer may lie in a past lifetime. Acceptance of the laws of karma enable you to be at peace in the midst of chaos in the world. Accept karma as a scientific law of our energy. Generate good karma with good thoughts and actions.

Don't get frustrated trying to understand injustices in life. Life is a process of growth and adjustment. Why do some people suffer? We don't know! I do believe love, in the form of action, is the *only* answer to our deep concerns for others. We've wondered why bad things happen to good people. We've been concerned about unfairness. These concerns can sometimes present emotional burdens that we're not meant to carry. Always take comfort that karma is in force. Accept the unpleasant realities of life. There's duality in life. Opposite, competing and complimentary forces and realities operate in the lives of each of us. Don't get swept away in too much thought about it! **Put that heart in *action* instead**. See opportunities for your own soul growth in **how you respond** to the situations you see. Push good karma out into the world. Remember that your job in life is to follow your feelings and dreams. If that includes putting a coat on the back of someone who needs one, then take that action. Feed the poor if that calls to you, but don't burden yourself with trying to understand why bad things happen. Nor do you burden yourself with the feeling that you should solve life's challenges for others. I've had trouble with this one myself, but I've learned. Not one of us can solve the world's ills and that's *probably* by design. Each of us must accept life as presented and keep pushing toward our dreams. We each have our hands full with our own lives. And that's ok! We can't adjust the life plight of other souls. Life's too complex and many factors are at play.

We CAN have enough love energy pouring from us to share with others. **Do what it takes to be so filled with love and good karma that you're effortlessly showin' love for those in need.**

KARMIC RELATIONSHIPS

See anyone who comes into your life as being there for a reason. The world is filled with billions of people with whom you will never meet or cross paths. The people you DO meet have significance in your life for reasons that may forever remain unknown. One thing to remember is that people in your life may represent karmic relationships that have presented themselves to you as an opportunity for your soul to grow. This viewpoint gives value to everyone in your life. Value **all** relationships, however important or insignificant they may seem. Try to have impact on the lives of others in a positive way. Resolve conflicts. Forgive in order to heal. Teach if given the opportunity. Listen and learn if you are blessed with information or wisdom to come to you from those you know.

KARMIC DEBTS

The concept of karmic debts should be self-explanatory. We call it a debt, but it's really just a way of learning. Once you generate negative karma, it's like you placed an order for a pop test as to why you should've gone positive in the first place. That pop test is coming. But it's not about punishment, it's about *learning* something that elevates your soul. Once you learn, you've resolved the karmic debt. The lessons are hands on, every time. Whatever you don't learn in this lifetime, you will eventually learn through an experience in another. If you don't like pop tests, don't place orders for them ;-).

In a lifetime, a lot of knuckleheads are going to build up negative karma. You don't actually get away with murder. Nor do you get away with being mean and nasty to people. In fact, nobody gets away with anything. Sadly, many people do not believe this. Many lie and cheat and steal and deceive and harm others in a variety of ways, believing all the while that if they are not "caught," they get away with not taking responsibility for their actions. The problem for them is karma. Negative actions, seen or unseen by others, incur a karmic debt that someday will be paid through a pop test experience. *Some are looking at mid-terms and finals combined, for their pop test experience*. The debt may be repaid in this lifetime or the next, *or the next*, but the pop test WILL come and the karmic debt will be paid. It's Universal Law. Those who persecute, will be persecuted. Those who humiliate, will be humiliated. There is no better way to learn why those things should not be done than by the experience of living through them.

We always want to know why? Why did this have to happen? Why do bad things happen to good people? Well, good people are here to learn lessons too. No one is immune to life's plight. No one. Things happen because they do. It is what it is. Karma's in play so that lessons are distributed *exactly* where they need to be. Real world, real life experience is an amazing teacher. Living life through challenge is easier when you accept and flow. Once you generate good karma consistently and accept your karmic lessons, you'll find that the karma thing isn't so bad after all.

Since we'll never know what karmic debts a person, including ourselves, has to pay, have an open heart and mind that everything happens for a reason. Have acceptance of your soul journey and that of others. An attitude of full acceptance, with no judgment about your life or the lives of others, makes a world of difference to your shot at Happiness.

KARMIC ENERGY OF THOUGHTS AND WORDS

Your thoughts and words are pure energy. They hold the power to affect your life. They also can affect others, so take your thoughts and words seriously. It's your karma we're talking about. Don't place orders for pop tests! Pass 'em in advance! Be honest and true to your word. Especially don't waste time making negative comments or false promises. Say what you mean and mean what you say. Make every thought and word reflect your character. The karmic effect of doing so will catapult you in the direction of Happiness.

"Ey, man. She ain't sellin' no wolf tickets."

– Daddy (referring to someone always true to their word).

Speaking of wolves

FEED YOUR GOOD WOLF

There is an old Native American parable that goes like this:

A grandfather is talking with his grandson and he says,

"Grandson, there are two wolves inside each of us. The wolves are always in battle. One is the good wolf, which represents things like kindness, bravery, and love. The other is the bad wolf, which represents things like greed, hatred, and fear."

The grandson stops and thinks about it for a second, then he looks up at his grandfather and says, "Grandfather, which one wins?"

The grandfather quietly replies, "The one you feed."

Every thought you have, every emotion, every action you take, feeds one of your wolves. *Of course, I want you to feed your good wolf.* Doing so will create so much good karma for you.

DON'T BURN BRIDGES – IT'S A SOUL JOURNEY THING

I believe everything that happens in life is for a reason. Who the heck knows why some people are introduced to your life? What you DO know is that it was written into your story, your soul journey. You sometimes regret that certain people were written in, true, but there's a lesson in every connection. When you find that you don't see the value in some of your life connections, don't burn the bridge down as a sign of moving on. Especially don't burn it for fear you will cross it again. And don't burn it in anger. Let's leave **virtual arson** out of the equation, please.

There's a lot of thought out there to the contrary. Some feel it is a release and an assurance that you won't go back and will actually move on. *I get it.* I believe in taking an attitude that everything and everyone in your life can hold a valuable lesson that benefits you, and learning not to focus on the pain is a skill that needs to be honed until perfected.

Recognizing that there are no accidents in life; seeing clearly that life was meant to be filled with challenges; and not being mad about it is a *much* lighter energy. You don't have to ever plan to travel that road again. Once you have a strong constitution and self-control, you can KNOW that you won't. If the bridge sucks, then be determined not to travel it again. Have no worries about it because you're moving on.

The more positive, bubble lifting thing to do is to acknowledge that those bridges were part of your soul journey. Acknowledge the lessons learned and the growth that occurred from them. Respect that transition in your life. These are the paths you traveled to get where you are. Respect and appreciate the lessons. By not burning the bridge, you show respect for God's plan, and reveal your own strength and growth. Forgive, forget and attribute enough value to God's plan that you can let the bridge exist in peace. Then, move on with a lightness. If you thought of letting it burn, chances are you're right to never, ever go back. Life is complex. Leaving bridges intact can be a fearless, no-baggage, show of respect for every step of your path. These bridges can be seen as symbols of forgiveness and progress, and the strength of your humility and tolerance. Bridges, left intact, can be powerful symbols of strength as you progress on your soul journey.

You never know where life's journey leads and whether God presented you a means for travel completely contrary to what you expected. Burning the bridges that brought you where you are today would be arson directed to your own soul journey. Arson's bad karma! Even figuratively, it's a lead level energy. Just throw peace at the situation and continue on your soul journey.

YOU GOTTA STAY IN YOUR LANE

This perspective can help you to appreciate everyone for who they are while staying focused on maxing out **your** life. Consider that each of us was designated a "lane" at birth. We're each born on a soul journey path. Collectively, we're on the highway to human evolution. There are many "lanes" on this highway. Each individual "lane" represents different aspects of human life and society. Not one of us can be all things. We each represent just one particle of society.

We each travel through life on a particular path that effects both our lives and the whole of humanity. That general path is our personal "lane." Represent your path.

We don't **pick** whichever "lane" looks most attractive. I think that's where some of us get confused. We're born to our lane and responsible for knocking our lives out of the park from that vantage point. Each of us is on an assignment, so to speak, to live out OUR individual soul journeys. The sky is the limit for **every** lane. No lane is better than the other, no matter how green the grass looks along the side of that road. Each road is equal in the most important of ways. There's a bigger picture than what's in your brain.

How do we identify our lane? It's actually very easy. We use the clues given to us at birth. Take your cognitive skills, natural physical strengths and abilities, natural talents, inclinations, personality, parental experience, birthplace, race, sex, appearance, etc. Then, combine those with the skills and natural interests that you've developed since birth. With that combination, and some forward momentum, go in the direction of what's naturally attractive to your heart. You'll *automatically* be in your lane.

I caution you, again, not to try to pick whichever life lane Yureego identifies as most "protective" or the lane that caters to Yureego. If you try to use Yureego to calculate the most impressive lanes for your soul journey, you will just complicate your life. This is a common trap that lures people onto life paths, relationships and careers that leave them feeling unfulfilled, inadequate or out of place. Even when you're lucky enough to be cool with a randomly chosen path that doesn't truly suit you, you're still missing amazing soul treasures that had awaited you.

The lane designed for you is always more beautiful for your soul than ANY of the others. It's a soul thing, at the end of the day, guys. Yureego is not a feature that's connected to your soul, Yureego's purpose is to keep your physical existence secure. Don't let it confuse you. Use your intuition. Find your lane based on what nature has given you. I promise that if you follow your interests, skills, talents, abilities and other clues provided by nature, you will connect with your lane. Just, PLEASE, don't idolize the lanes of others and get lost in that. Recognize that your natural lane holds the most reward for **you**. Don't doubt it. Go for it and find out, firsthand.

Respect everyone who's identified and taken their place in **their** lane. See the lanes of others with an eye of appreciation, no matter what that lane looks like or how it fits into your worldview. Keep in mind that there's a space in this world for everyone. Everyone has a lane. Every person fits in somewhere. See everyone as fulfilling a unique role by design of our Creator. Each of us is working and learning along the way. No matter how far away someone is from the heart of God; no matter how important their role appears; no matter how positive and productive, destructive or negative; each of us exists for a reason. See this. Appreciate each soul journey. While each lane may not be divine in the eyes of Yureego, each soul is absolutely divine. Chalking people up to good or bad, valuable or worthless reflects an unenlightened perspective. *We don't get into that.* Each individual is important to the masterpiece of human evolution. There's a bigger plan in play.

Don't allow yourself to believe that you got a bad or disadvantaged lane designated to you. Stay away from labels and LIVE! If you can't see your lane as interesting, perfectly challenging and divine, accept it as the lane you got this go round. Play your hand. Push forward, true to your circumstances and your nature. Anything that lures you to negate your nature and interests is bad news. Don't fall for it. Your lane is perfect! Live it out with the attitude that **"It's my lane, and I'm cruisin' it all the way through."** That attitude takes you where you were meant to be.

When everyone stays in their lane, life's more in sync. Everyone's doing their thing. Humanity is on target to become a masterpiece of evolution. As long as you're alive in that body, life experiences await that hold treasure for you. There are people, places and things for you to see along your soul path. Keep pushing. Pay attention. Don't miss them. Some of the experiences will be delightful, some will be tough. That's life! Enjoy the journey either way. Just stay in that lane.

We don't receive wisdom; we must discover it for ourselves
after a journey that no one can take for us or spare us.
 – Marcel Proust

RELIGION: CULTURAL INTERPRETATIONS OF A UNIVERSAL TRUTH

Understand and respect religion, completely unbound and free in your own faith. When it comes to all the great religions, all roads lead home.

Each of the great religions of our world has the same message at heart:

1. *There is an all-powerful, creative, conscious force that exists in the Universe.*
2. *Everything and each of us is part of that force.*
3. *Flow with the love from the heart of that force, and pay it forward.*

Religions and spiritual beliefs are like languages. Don't let the fact that you speak a different language be a barrier to recognizing what is shared at heart. Chosen beliefs don't matter. If a person's heart is on a road that leads "home," what else counts? Interpret languages. Connect with hearts.

You may laugh *(you're **always** encouraged to laugh out loud!)* as I tell you that all the world's great religions and *many if not most* atheists believe pretty much the same thing. Go ahead, laugh out loud … but whether *practiced* or not, most of the people of this world share **belief** that…

Love is good;

Actions that show love reveal goodness;

Unity of all people is inherent and powerful;

Grandeur of the individual is innate and presents potential for each light to shine;

Humility to the powerful force of nature that brought each of us and the world into creation makes sense (i.e. God, Jehovah, Allah, Jah, Yahweh, the Great Creator, Mother Nature, Nature, the Universe, the Creative Force, the Universal Life Force, Jesus, the Man upstairs or **whichever term** one prefers to use to reference this energy, there are at *least* 100 of them).

The common thread of belief that connects us is as universal as laughter. Details, cultural and language differences and perspectives don't matter, only love does. Most of the world is on the same page at the root of it all. Respect how everyone "LAUGH"s.

"And we should call every truth false,
which was not accompanied by at least one
laugh … Even the gods love jokes."
- **Friedrich Nietzsche**

There are many paths to God for a reason. Believing that there is only one route to God is a potent seed for intolerance and separation. It achieves little in the way of fostering oneness for humanity. Spiritual evolution lends itself to unconditional brother and sisterhood. It's cool to connect with like minds. That's a beautiful thing. What's **not** cool is the exclusion of and blindness to the beauty of other paths. There's nothing positive that comes from that. History proves it.

Christians *(Catholics and all Protestant religions)*, Muslims, Jews, Hindus, Buddhists, nearly every religion under the sun *(and don't be ignorant to that fact that many if not most of those who don't believe in a deity, do believe in a universal creative force of nature)* holds the same **core** beliefs. The differences are cultural and insignificant in achieving connection to our shared Creative Force, that we call God. Always keep your focus on the heart of the religions and the core beauty of all the world's religious practices.

Many get hard-wired to a 'one path to God' mentality. And you can't blame them because they were trained to take that view, usually during childhood. The problem is that an often subliminal but very separatist energy channels through a mindset that holds fast to a one path is right theory. All it indicates is that a brain is at the controls of the faith. **While the heart can easily process 'many paths' to God, the brain, already hard-wired to a 'one path' theory cannot.** Theology is awesome. But brains need to sit down on the topic of our relationships with our Creator. It's basic science that we were created by an unbelievably powerful, conscious "force." How one finds connection to that force is the domain of the heart, not brain. **The heart holds the ability to see that we're all brothers and sisters of the same great Creator with equal, unconditional access to that loving force.** Whatever religion or belief system a person follows, always recognize that we're **all** truly on the same page, even if on uniquely different paths.

Religion, by definition, is the belief in and worship of a superhuman controlling power (God). It is also defined as a system of faith and worship. Religions inspire cultural interpretations of core Universal truths. **Each religion originated from a time period in history and a culture of people with core beliefs in our innate goodness. Each religion already accepts that we were all created by the same force.** Religions evolve just like everything else. **No matter one's religion, honor others as equal creations of God, not for their shared belief system with YOU.** Imagine, at the very least, that each religion and belief system leads "home." Meet people in the space where you LAUGH together ;-). Appreciate the connections to God that you *feel* from people of every religion. Witness their true godliness through their *actions, not their religious practices*. The moment your ego mind delves into judgment of someone's religion, recognize **that** as a moment for self-reflection and self-improvement. Get your mind back on the things we all share.

Religions are practiced by people. Again, people are subject to baggage and issues, so it's no wonder that things get messy. Don't be distracted by those who've, because of their own baggage and faulty AI/Yureego, strayed from the teachings of their religions. Don't judge religions by the actions of those who've twisted and used the power of the religion to express their baggage. Olympic-level baggage handlers and the world's *top* clowns join religions too. Every religion experiences negative practices of people who propose to follow it. In this case, don't hate the game, the players are the culprits. Don't focus on the actions of *some* of the people practicing religions and label the religion. Behind the negative actions of some, are thousands, millions of people who use the religion for love and connection to God. **At the heart of each religion *(and most of those not following any religion at all)* there is pure love and goodness.**

What a negative moment in time for you to judge or put down anyone's preferred practice of faith. We never allow our minds to *ever* go there. Most of the people practicing a religion are using the religion as a guiding tool to become closer to the loving force of our Creator. This is always the case with the great religions of our world. Accept, understand and respect that. Also understand and respect that your spirituality doesn't have to fit nicely into a brand, a name or a particular religion to be real, effective, and absolutely beautiful. You have a direct connection to God anytime you want. Everyone gets to choose what works for them. If everyone felt this way, we'd be **that** much closer to world peace.

"Love is my religion."
– Bob Marley

All I want is for you to connect with a higher force in your preferred way, and respect the chosen connections of others. You were born to an *immediate* family to which love is the preferred religion. You have an ancestry that overflows with religious leaders and spiritual people who've actively practiced love, service and respect for their fellow man. **I pray that what you inherit is a genuine belief in religious freedom, open mindedness and full acceptance of the belief systems of others.**

Whatever you believe, recognize that all evidence (scientific and otherwise) points to a Universal creative force. **How you understand, appreciate, relate to, connect to, communicate with, honor and love that force is completely up to you.** That's part of your personal soul journey. Do it your way, but do it. There are many beautiful, organized forms of worship. Don't underestimate, look for them if you want to share a communal religious experience. At the same time, know that your **private connections** are equally valuable. I want you wired with a belief that God is love and that **God is accessible to all**. Recognize hearts and souls not beliefs. Understand the necessity of differing beliefs, because of the vast diversity of humans and human culture. Accept them **all** without ever a thought about a religion being right or wrong, good or bad.

Our family's role is to strive towards goodness and love, therefore you need only to follow the instincts of your beautiful soul. You both have goodness and love at your core. Always live with humility and love for that force we call God. Recognize that every person and everything is a particle of God. Honor the God within yourself and others. Remember Namaste? ;-) That's what Namaste is all about, recognizing and honoring the light within yourself and others. Accept everyone else's belief system as precious. Never, ever engage in judgment of the practices of other religions. Let everyone do their thing! Be your absolute best self and by all means, share your gifts to serve the world. That's it. Have faith. Worship your way. Fully respect anyone who practices love toward humanity. What else matters?

TO KEEP YOUR CONNECTION AT 5 BARS
YOU *MUST* DO DAILY MEDITATION & PRAYER!

We know that empty space is believed by the top scientific minds to be a web work of electrical channels through which signals travel. That's based on evidence. It makes a lot of sense when you think about it. It helps to answer so many things like, "How the heck can I *think* of something to materialize it?"

Thoughts are electrical signals. We receive and transmit thought energy as if they're super high-tech, biologically generated text messages. We don't think twice about FaceTime with a friend on the other side of the world, but we **can't imagine** that the force that created humans could've produced a natural, biological equivalent to that process. Try to imagine it, though. It's no more far-fetched than FaceTime. Imagine that your thoughts go out like virtual texts. Imagine that we also receive information via virtual texts sent by way of thought energy from others. While our brains may not be able to read the *virtual text messages*, our hearts **can**. Our hearts are like virtual text message readers by nature.

It's all about the strength of your reception. Let's imagine that you can materialize your thoughts and receive the answers you seek, messages from God, we might say, based on the strength of your connection to the creative force. The stronger your connection, the more chance of messages getting through accurately. A stronger connection can be achieved through meditation and prayer. Time spent doing both will increase your ability to materialize your dreams and desires. You'll also increase your ability to receive future guidance from your Creator. Meditation and prayer, when practiced regularly, will exponentially increase the power of your connection. The more you meditate and pray, the stronger your connection becomes.

Meditate daily. This means sit quietly and spend some time having NO THOUGHTS at all. Do this to connect and fill yourself with the energy of the creative force. Ancient wisdom has always known what I'm trying to tell you. You have to sit that brain down in order to connect. The more you quieten your mind and meditate, the higher your "reception" will be to the force that lifts your bubble. Think of your cell phone reception for example. Imagine that those who fail to meditate are fluctuating from absolutely no reception to one bar of reception. On the other hand, those who meditate *daily* have five bars strong. With a stronger connection to the signals of the highest level of energy and guidance (God), you'll have a better chance of receiving the guidance that leads you in all the right directions. You have the best chance of elevating to exactly where you need and want to be. You have the best chance of sending virtual texts that materialize your dreams. Of course, I have recommendations for your meditation practices. You knew that, right? So, let's see what I got. We have what I call **dream meditation**, then we have **chakra meditation**, and my new favorite … **bubble meditation!** We'll start with my new favorite.

BUBBLE MEDITATION
(Use the bubbles I gave you with this book or get some. Imaginary bubble blowing works too)

The purpose of bubble meditation is to release the baggage you hold within. The truth is, we ALL hold *some* baggage from unpleasant life experiences. Sometimes, we've even held onto baggage from *perceived issues* that weren't real issues at all. That's just life. You're about to let it all go. Through bubble meditation, you'll have the chance to release any sticky baggage that you may not even know was there. Remnants of old wounds that prevent you from sustained Happiness have sometimes been a part of you for so long, you think they're part of you. Even recent baggage can sink in and stick. This is a clearance for you. All baggage is outta there! You will be baggage-free, lighter in spirit and flowing with a stronger power force in no time.

Sit comfortably with your back straight, so your electrical cord has a clear, smooth channel for all that energy to pour through you. Whip out your bottle of bubbles. Take the 'magic wand' out and as you hold it, recognize the incredible power it has to release all negative energy within you. Here's your opportunity to release all known and hidden baggage that you hold within. Reflect on an area of your past from which you *know* you still carry some disappointment and/or pain. You are about to finally release that energy! Reflect on the situation for a moment. Admit to yourself any "feelings" that you had about it. Announce to yourself that the situation is **past** and you forgot to fully digest and release, but you're **ready now**. Find *something* beneficial that you learned from it. Something empowering. Hold that. Repeat the lesson learned to yourself and imagine, for a minute, how you will benefit from that lesson throughout your life. Feel blessed to have found a way to elevate from it. **Deep breathe to blow each bubble**. Blow to release all negative energy that was tucked away inside of you. Free yourself of the baggage energy that stuck around from the situation. Forgive. Ask for forgiveness. Say, "I love you," to yourself. Say, "I forgive you," to any perceived offender. Blow bubbles to release and be cleansed of the energy of that old situation, once and for all. Imagine as you blow into them, that any and all worry, frustration, sadness or toxicity of any kind, was pulled from you. It's released, finally, into those bubbles. All of that hidden, but draining energy is floating far away to regenerate into beautiful energy again. You are detoxified. You've released the denser energy that was trapped inside. Watch it float away. Feel your bubble lightening, becoming more buoyant. You're elevating. The release, the relaxation, and the increased power flow that now channels through you should feel pretty darn good.

CHAKRA MEDITATION

True story. I used to see stuff on chakras and felt it was a little too "crystal bally" for me. Just being honest. But, the more I started to learn about our body's energy, the more I started to connect with the notion of chakras. Once I found out that the heart chakra had been discovered and proven by medical science as an energy center, I took the concept more seriously. The ancients were apparently tapping into some serious wisdom, *somehow*. I'm not waiting on any more science on this one. It's all about energy! Chakra meditation is all about **your personal energy**. That's good stuff.

WELCOME TO YOUR NEW METHOD TO MANAGE AND MAXIMIZE YOUR ENERGY!

Chakra meditation is a priceless tool for your journey to health and Happiness. Don't short-change chakra meditation by viewing it as

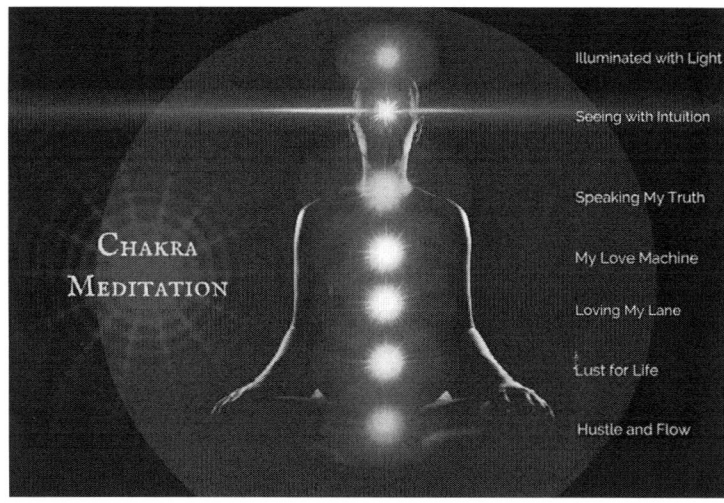

"crystal bally," like I did. And don't imagine it to be connected to any particular belief system. **See chakra meditation for what it is, a genius way to control your internal energy flow**. It's priceless in its effect on your overall wellbeing. It will increase your ability to heal, both emotionally and physically. It opens your heart and mind as it allows you to increase your connectivity to that Universal force.

We've well established that you're an energy field. Chakras are simply the individual energy centers that run along the spine of your energy field. Each chakra meditation helps to balance and align these centers to increase your internal energy flow. The higher and smoother the flow of energy within you, the better your life. This is why chakra meditation is so valuable.

We each have seven chakra energy centers that correspond, coincidentally, to internal organs along the spine. Imagine that each chakra churns out energy similar to what has been already identified by medical science for your heart area. Each is an area that holds not just an organ but a high concentration of electrical energy. In addition, each of the chakras is held by ancient wisdom, to correspond to physical, mental and spiritual aspects of our lives. Since the heart chakra has already been confirmed by medical science as the powerful electrical energy center the ancients claimed it was, I'm inclined to accept the existence of the others in good faith.

Each of the seven chakra centers flows with energy. Except, of course, when they don't. Turns out, baggage will weaken, slow or even stop the flow of these energy centers. Here's just one more reason to let shit go, and meditate, right? It's been proven, by some super high-tech bio-electrography, that the energy of your chakras balances and strengthens the more you do chakra meditation. **Meditation increases your flow of energy and connectedness to your life force**. Who can't use that? The beauty of it is that all you really have to do is *want* to balance and increase your energy. Then, just take the time to focus on your energy to improve it. Your focus on the meditation, alone, will bring all the power you need. That's been proven with the super, high-tech bio-electrography, by the way. I, personally, think that's an amazing fact,

197

and a blessing. All you have to do is **do it**. You'll, then, flow forward, more empowered to surf through the waves of life's challenges. More empowered for health and Happiness too ;-).

SHOW YOURSELF SOME LOVE WITH A QUICKIE 5-MINUTE MEDITATION

The ultimate show of love to yourself is to take, at least, five minutes a day to connect and allow the flow of life force to fill you. All you have to do is sit comfortably with your back straight, to lengthen the power cord (spine). Deep breathe to infuse your body with oxygen and calm your spirit. Then envision each of the chakras, one by one, starting with the red root chakra. Imagine filling each with the power of love energy from the Source. Visualize the color of each chakra glowing more richly and more brilliantly. Spend thirty seconds, or so, envisioning pure natural energy pour through each chakra, lighting it up. Imagine the physical, mental and spiritual strength that you are receiving as the energy from the source increases within you. Five minutes of this a day is powerful, but the sky's the limit. Try thirty minutes when you can.

GET YOUR SWIRL ON

Each chakra is believed to swirl in a spiral of energy, much like the swirl of the galaxies, or hurricanes viewed from above. Envision the swirl of each of your chakras with your spine through the "eye" of each swirl. When a chakra is not energized properly, the rotation of the swirl is very slow and not much power is being generated. Without a good power source to the regions of yourself that are supported by that chakra (your organs), you are at a disadvantage. Get your swirl on! Power up! (*This reminds me of when Jet was about three. He would get soooo excited when Power Rangers came on TV. He'd jump up high, land in a wide-legged stance, put his fist straight in the air and shout "POWJERS!" Lol. That's what I want you to think when you are envisioning each chakra power up and swirl with a force that spills over to the next chakra, and the next. Think, POWJERS!* ✊🏽)

In learning about chakras, I found that each of the chakras touched on a different aspect of our character and overall wellbeing. After practicing with a focus on each chakra for just a couple minutes, I felt more energized. I literally did! Seriously! Maybe it's me, but please, please try it. If nothing else, just by focusing on each of these areas every day, you have **got** to be better off. **The conscious focus on each area of your body and life is invaluable.** There's no way you won't elevate. On top of that, each chakra corresponds to centers of your body that deserve a little healing concentration on a daily basis. You can't lose. By focusing in this way, you increase your connection to that conscious, loving, omnipotent universal force we call God.

MEET YOUR CHAKRAS

It's like a family reunion where you're meeting relatives that are closely related to you for the first time! Except these seven chakra friends have been with you every day from birth. It's time to get acquainted. Let's meet your chakras starting with the red one. You can peek back at that image of the chakras lined up in the body (a few pages back). The red "Root Chakra" sits at the base of your spine (electrical cord). This is your 1st chakra. It is believed to connect you to your earthly existence. It represents your *powers of survival.*

1st
The Red Root Chakra

Hustle and Flow

Above your Root Chakra, is your 2nd "Sacral Chakra" that sits just under your belly button. This orange "Sacral Chakra" is responsible for generating abundant energy that fills you with so much love and appreciation for yourself and your personal life that you have no problem seizing the day and enjoying life's *earthly pleasures* (healthily and balanced, of course).

2nd
The Orange Sacral Chakra

Lust for Life

Now, meet your 3rd chakra. This yellow energy center located right above your belly button is called your "Solar Plexus Chakra." It powers your self-esteem, allowing you to be *emotionally grounded and confident.* The colors, by the way, are caused by the frequency of the energy of the chakra. Just as frequency of light creates the colors of the rainbow, each chakra vibrates at different frequencies that create the colors of your chakras. A rainbow runs through you, make it shine ;-).

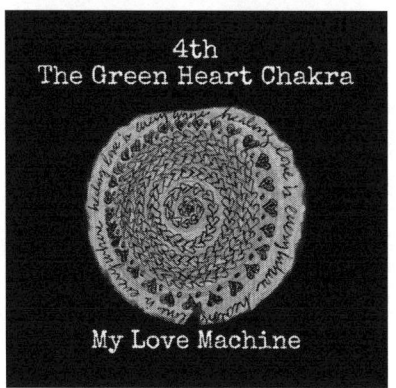

3rd
The Yellow Solar Plexus Chakra

Loving My Lane

The 4th, green energy center represents your "Heart Chakra." This is a friend that you already knew. It's the power center located in the area of your heart. When balanced, you'll feel *love for yourself and for everyone.* When your Heart Chakra is balanced and full of energy, your love will come from such a place of strength, you are never hurt from outpours of love to the world.

4th
The Green Heart Chakra

My Love Machine

The 5th lighter blue chakra is the "Throat Chakra." The Throat Chakra is located right in the pit between your collar bones. It sits near the thyroid gland. When balanced, it enables you to naturally and effortlessly *speak your truths with love* (*This releases a power force that enables you to handle life's toughest experiences*).

The sixth, and darker blue chakra is the "Third Eye Chakra." The "Third Eye" is located right between your brows and enables you to *see both the physical and spiritual worlds with clarity and understanding*. It sits in the same space as your powerful pineal gland. **This chakra has the *most* to do with attaining Happiness.** You will want all of your chakras lined up strong to get this one balanced and brimming with energy.

The seventh "Crown Chakra" sits just above the tippy top of your skull. This is the chakra that *connects you to that REAL reality, that spirit from which we all originated*, where all things being connected is common knowledge.

Now that you're all acquainted with your chakras, who's ready for some chakra meditation?

You've seen the lotus flower symbol before. Now, you'll know what it means ;-)
Even when its roots are in the dirtiest, scummiest, murkiest of waters, the lotus flower
blossoms with the most beautiful flower. It's a symbol of enlightenment, purity and rebirth. It
represents our innate nature to triumph, beautifully, over life's toughest battles.

Now, that you've been introduced to each chakra, let's do a quick, practice, meditation. **Sit comfortably** with your back straight. **Deep breathe**, slowly, three times. **Envision each chakra wheel swirling** with balanced power as you read the significance of the chakra. **Meditate on each chakra**, one by one as you read what I've summarized for you here. **Close your eyes** once you've read each one. And just for a few moments, imagine you can **feel the swirling energy** as it powers up, balances and illuminates within you.

The Red Root Chakra = Hustle and Flow

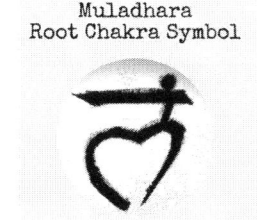

Muladhara
Root Chakra Symbol

You've got strength and confidence in the abilities of your earthly survival skills. **Think**: I'm grounded in this earthly existence. I hustle, but I know how to flow.

My animal instincts are strong and I use them to handle my business *while I flow in balance with life.* [I doodled each chakra symbol for you, so you'll know what these symbols represent ;-)].

The Orange Sacral Chakra = Lust for Life

Svadhisthana
Sacral Chakra Symbol

The overwhelming love of yourself and your life is so strong and fulfilling that you indulge in, and enjoy, life's pleasures.

Think: I love and understand my human journey, and my power to create. Knowing how to flow makes me immune to negativity and not worried 'bout a thing! I'm wide open to enjoying life's pleasures ... *the ones that are good for me (and I promise anything else is in moderation).*

The Yellow Sacral Chakra = Loving My Lane

You have a powerful strength of will and self-confidence that keeps your emotions controlled and wonderful.

Manipura
Solar Plexus Chakra Symbol

Think: I love me some **me**, and I'm proud to be a warrior of life! I understand my lane, love it, and stay in it to stay on the track of my destiny. Because I **know and love** my personal lane, I'm so emotionally powerful and secure.

The Green Heart Chakra = My Love Machine

Your heart is a biological machine that **cannot be broken**. You know to manage a mind that tells you otherwise. Your heart is naturally strengthened by peace, love and understanding. You magically self-heal and heal others.

Anahata
Heart Chakra Symbol

Think: I love and I can feel that I'm loved. My heart is my center because I am a being of love. My heart is **the** central most powerful energy I have. I'm feelin' my beautiful, powerful 'love machine' core.

The Blue Throat Chakra = Speaking My Truth

You voice your personal truths naturally and with love.

Vishuddha
Throat Chakra Symbol

Think: I always speak my truth with honesty and love. I can listen with love to the truths felt by others. I easily accept. I do not require agreement from others.

The Indigo Third Eye Chakra = Seeing with Intuition

You are equally in tune with the physical and spiritual world. Your intuition is strong and it's the guiding force in your life.

Ajna
Third Eye Chakra Symbol

Think: I see both the physical and spiritual worlds very clearly. I am balanced between the two. My intuition is strong and crystal clear.

The Purple Crown Chakra = Illuminated with Light

Sahasrara
Crown Chakra Symbol

Your Crown Chakra connects you to the force we call God. It connects your awareness to realities beyond your brain and physical existence. This chakra facilitates your understanding of the connectedness and divinity of all things. You'll have to work, work, work to get all the way up to that, though. For now, just envision that purplish wheel of light energy churning.

Think: I am very connected to all that is. I am Divine. All is Divine.

Do NOT sleep on meditation. Meditation is like sex for your brain.

Get it in. Meditation's like a sexy natural high for the mind and spirit. Don't be that person that's not gettin' any. Be a meditation freak. Get in all you can. You will be stimulated by this meditation when you take it seriously and drift into some **real, deep** meditation. Experience the fueling and release of doing it properly. Then, keep getting some meditation in, every day that you can. Common sense tells you that there's a possibility that all that meditation could have a positive effect, **but science has already *proved* that you stand a *very high chance* of improving your overall health and Happiness**.

INCREASE YOUR POWER UP WITH SOME "POWJUICE!"

I **love** this idea of chakra juice, which I'm immediately nicknaming Powjuice 👊. That's what I'm calling fresh-made, organic juice that matches the color of the chakra I'd like to balance and energize. When you drink the juice, imagine it "fueling" your chakras. Visualization has scientifically proven power! So, visualize the increase in the power of the chakra swirl as you drink. Make it a ritual, of sorts, to get fresh, organic ingredients (or you can find ready-made fresh juices at juice bars and natural grocery stores, but making them at home is a beautiful, hands-on show of love to yourself). The fresh, live-enzyme, plant energy of the chakra juice will nourish you AND get your swirl full ON.

Mom's Secret Powjuice Recipes *(on the off chance that you'll actually juice)*

These juices will lift your energy and nourish you! Use anything you like, in any amounts that suit you. Be creative. Fresh, organic juices are a delicious chakra body boost for your mind, body and soul.

RED AND READY

Strawberries, raspberries, 1 beet, 1 apple and some watermelon if it's in season.

THE RED ROOT CHAKRA IS IN THE AREA OF YOUR GONADS, AKA SEX ORGANS. THE ROOT CHAKRA'S ROLE IS TO CONNECT ALL OF YOUR ENERGY WITH THE EARTH (KEEPING YOU GROUNDED). ITS POWER LEVEL IS BELIEVED TO HAVE AN EFFECT ON YOUR **SENSE OF SECURITY AND PROSPERITY**. BOOST YOUR SURVIVAL STRENGTH.

THE LUST FOR LIFE ALREADY BEGAN

6 carrots, 1 organic orange and a small slice of fresh ginger

THE ORANGE SACRAL CHAKRA IS IN THE UPPER GROIN AREA. THIS CHAKRA'S ROLE IS TO CONNECT YOU WITH YOUR INDIVIDUAL SELF. ITS POWER LEVEL IS BELIEVED TO HAVE AN EFFECT ON YOUR **CREATIVITY, SEXUALITY, PLEASURE AND LUST FOR LIFE.** WHAT'S NOT TO LIKE, HUH? TAKE GOOD CARE OF IT. IF THIS ONE'S OUT OF BALANCE, ADDICTION AND/OR HORMONE IMBALANCE CAN BE THE RESULT. NOTE: USING ORGANIC CITRUS FOR JUICING IS PARTICULARLY IMPORTANT, BECAUSE THE SKINS OF CONVENTIONAL CITRUS FRUITS CAN HOLD LOTS OF PESTICIDES, HERBICIDES, ETC.

LIQUID SUNSHINE

Half a fresh pineapple, 2 yellow beets, and an organic lemon

THE YELLOW SOLAR PLEXUS CHAKRA IS IN THE AREA OF YOUR PANCREAS AND ADRENAL GLANDS. THE SOLAR PLEXUS IS YOUR ENERGETIC "GUT." ITS POWER LEVEL IS BELIEVED TO HAVE AN EFFECT ON YOUR **WISDOM, DECISIVENESS AND POWER OVER YOUR LIFE.**

I'M JUST A LOVE MACHINE

6 celery stalks, 1 cucumber, quarter slice of lime, an apple and a sprig of fresh mint

I find it to be just one more clue that plants are our life partners, in that green is the associated color for both plant life, and the heart center of our bubble. I think plants and trees are the heart of the earth.

THE GREEN HEART CHAKRA IS IN THE AREA OF YOUR THYMUS GLAND. THE HEART CHAKRA IS THE SEAT OF YOUR KINDNESS, LOVE AND EMPATHY. ITS POWER LEVEL IS BELIEVED TO HAVE AN EFFECT ON YOUR ABILITY TO FEEL EQUALLY ABUNDANT **LOVE FOR YOURSELF AND OTHERS**. (MINE FELL OUT OF BALANCE. IT WAS **OVERACTIVE**. THAT'S ACTU-ALLY SELF-DESTRUCTIVE AND COUNTER-PRODUCTIVE. ANOTHER EXAMPLE OF HOW VITAL IT IS TO HAVE ALL OF YOUR ENERGY IN **BALANCE**. *BALANCE IS ABSOLUTELY CRITICAL TO A HEALTHY, HAPPY LIFE!*)

PURE AND TRUE BLUE

A pint of fresh blueberries, 6 celery stalks, 1 apple

THE BLUE THROAT CHAKRA IS IN THE AREA OF YOUR THYROID GLAND. ITS POWER LEVEL IS BELIEVED TO HAVE AN EFFECT ON YOUR ABILITY TO **SPEAK YOUR MIND WITH CONFIDENCE, TRUTH AND LOVE**.

MY KEEN INTUITION

A pint of fresh blueberries, a few blackberries, 6 celery stalks and a cucumber

THE INDIGO THIRD EYE CHAKRA IS IN THE AREA OF YOUR PITUITARY GLAND. THIS "THIRD EYE" IS SUPPOSED TO GIVE YOU ACCESS TO INFORMATION BEYOND YOUR BRAIN AND THE WORLD AROUND YOU. ITS POWER LEVEL IS BELIEVED TO HAVE AN EFFECT ON YOUR **INTUITION**.

PURPLE REIGN

A pint of fresh blackberries or *blueberries and strawberries*, dark red or purple grapes, a few celery stalks, a half cup of red cabbage, half a fresh lemon and an apple

THE VIOLET CROWN CHAKRA IS IN THE AREA OF YOUR PINEAL GLAND. YOUR CROWN CHAKRA REPRESENTS PURE COSMIC CONSCIOUSNESS. ITS POWER LEVEL IS BELIEVED TO HAVE AN EFFECT ON **YOUR CONNECTEDNESS TO UNIVERSAL CONSCIOUSNESS, CLOUD NINE, AND OF COURSE, HAPPINESS.** THIS IS THE CHAKRA THAT CONNECTS YOU STRAIGHT TO THE SOURCE. WHEN THIS ONE IS BEAMING, ALL OF YOUR CHAKRAS ARE BEAMING STRONG AND IN BALANCE. WHEN THE BEAM OF ENERGY FROM YOUR CROWN CHAKRA IS VERY STRONG, YOU HAVE ARRIVED. YOU BECOME A BEAMING SOURCE OF ENERGY TO THE WORLD.

PRETTY PLEASE, TRY CHAKRA MEDITATION AND POWJUICE. 🙏

DREAM MEDITATION

Dream meditation lightens your vibration in a unique way. Your brain is at work with this kind of meditation, but in a way that brings a beautiful, balanced interplay of heart and mind.

First, identify a dream that you have for yourself and your life. Pick something that makes you feel happy and fulfilled. As always, dream big. When I say 'dream big,' I mean for you to envision exactly what you want whether it seems or *is* improbable or even impossible. Once you have identified your dream for this meditation, set a backdrop sound on your cell phone, like the sound of the ocean, for example. Deep breathe a couple of times, then close your eyes and begin to dream until you see it, clearly, in your mind. Each 'dream meditation' has to be the most vivid and focused daydream you can possibly have. It should feel as if you have drifted away into a wonderful space just for you. Visualize everything, every detail about your dream. Visualize and 'feel' the excitement, pleasure, and contentment that comes from truly experiencing your dream. See the details you love most. See colors. Hear sounds. Feel that you are favored, loved and protected by the beautiful sunlight or moonlight that fills your dream. Feel the joy that comes from having the things you dream of. Take note of that feeling. Relish in it for the whole five minutes. Then, open your eyes. If your dream was vivid and strong, you just tuned into the Happiness Zone for a *hit*. The more you stay tuned to the feelings you had during the dream meditation, the higher your chances for Happiness and *everything else* you want.

"I see it ... Yeah ... I *SEE* it."

– Carl Weathers in that scene with Bill Dukes when he saw the 'Predator.'

DAILY PRAYER

"Call me when you get some free time. Love you."

Pretend that a similar message is coming to you, every day. Your message is from the Creator. Find the free time to make the return call in the form of prayer. Connect to that empowering conscious force that's ready and waiting to course through you. Receive all that helium energy until you're full. Offer gratitude for both current blessings *and those to come.*

According to the New Oxford American Dictionary, prayer is a solemn request for help or expression of thanks addressed to God or an object of worship. The act of prayer and the connection to the source is powerful and beautiful even if all you do is ask for stuff. So, don't be discouraged to put in some asks. You are here to create, so push toward your dreams and ask for the energetic force to flow through you to help you to materialize them. Grandma Haywood always asks God to put it in her head what should be done to help God's work move forward. That's a great daily prayer to do in honor of her beautiful bubble while she's here, and even more when we have only her bubble. Whatever you do, don't forget to use the time for expressing gratitude. **Pray every single, solitary day. No exceptions.** As often as you can get on your knees and pray **aloud**, please do it. Just silence your mind and connect to God, however you do it. There are no rules whatsoever, just quality time with the Big G. Just ten minutes out of the twenty-four hours of your day spent praying will generate pure helium for your bubble. Keep a strong connection and nature will take its course, guiding you on your soul journey.

CHAPTER FIVE

DON'T LOOK, HAPPINESS IS EYEING YOUR BUBBLE

YOU'RE ALL HOOKED UP

"Don't you worry 'bout a thing."
— **Stevie Wonder**, Innervisions.

The tippy top of your bubble is 'bout to break through the entrance of The Happiness Zone! As I predicted, Happiness already has eyes on you. You've already noticed that you're feeling a lightness of mind that you hadn't had. You're feeling more energy already too, and you're just getting started! You're much more confident about your life and your future, and you haven't even finished the book yet. This is a sign of great things to come for you. Happiness aside, just hanging out within the heightened vibrations of The Happiness Zone will naturally increase your creativity, intuition and luck. This is the zone where dreams come true. Love and peace is ever-present, and that's on an average day. You are no longer swept up into life's twists and turns the way you used to be. Dense bubbles look straight through you as if you aren't there. This is the perfect backdrop for your life. Keep doing what you did to gain entry. Watch yourself! At this rookie stage, you can slip back out of The Zone in a heartbeat, if you don't stay on your game. It's like balancing on a skateboard. It takes practice. After you get used to staying on the Happy Station for long enough, you have options for ascending higher. I'm so HAPPY! You have everything you need to live your life in true, continuous Happiness.

GO ALL THE WAY UP

"Nothing can stop me, I'm all the way up...
And if you ask anybody where I live, they'll point...and say,
go all the way up."
  – **Fat Joe**

Now that you know all that you know, what's the bottom line? The bottom line is that **you have to be focused on going up.** Keep your goals on positivity, higher frequencies, higher elevations, and the highest of heights. Goal for Cloud Nine. That's where I'm trying to go! Shoot for *all the way up* and you'll land solidly in The Happiness Zone for life. My dream is for us all to meet there, while we still have these awesome bodies in our bubbles. It is so possible, I can feel it. I'm going, whether you decide to join or not! Lol. But, wow, to have you guys there with me would totally take this lifetime to the next level. Totally.

Be conscious of whether you are drifting up or down. Do the things that take you up, then ...

"Hit it, *again*."
  – **Hans Gruber, Die Hard**

PUT 5 ON IT

To give you something that you can take with you after you've finished the book, I've isolated 5 focus areas that I think will elevate you most. Recite them to remind yourself. Count them on one hand. Then, thumbs up when you finish reciting them all. Use those fingers to remind yourself of each of these mindsets. Thumbs up when life gives you lemons. Thumbs up each day to remind yourself that you got this thing called life. If it's possible to *"put some respeck on my name,"* then it's possible to **put these 5 principles on your life.** Follow these life principles as your new "rule of thumb." 👍 Put 5 on it.

> **Love Deeply** - Love yourself until enough love pours over to fill others.
>
> **Stay Tuned** – Tune your thoughts to the vibration of love and dream fulfillment.
>
> **All You** - Be unapologetically you and fully in your lane.
>
> **Stop, Drop & Roll** *(play it off, it's a 3 for 1)* Have no time for nonsense. Offer peace and acceptance of others and life. Then roll with what elevates YOU.
>
> **Dream Hard** - You're a mini creator. Dream!! Then, live out your dreams or die trying.

"Now, you doin' things."
– **Chris Canales, "Showin' Love" rap song**

LAST BUT NOT LEAST

Remember that I suggested that each of our lives were stories written by the greatest writer the world has ever known? Well, now yours is a major motion picture. You're the lead role. You are the STAR of your story, no matter what your story is. Live your life in a way that makes every scene worth reading, worth watching. Get into *every moment*. Not just the wonderful moments. Get into **every moment**. Live them through. Every movie is simply a collection of still images. Each still frame of your movie should be an image worth framing. Learn lessons that would entertain and resonate with anyone who'd watch your movie. Notice and appreciate the perfection and imperfections written into your set. See the so-called imperfections as adorable details that mark *that* time in your history. Don't overlook all the things that your costume represents in every scene. See the natural art of life woven into every moment. Notice the lighting of every moment. Notice the nuances of every character. Savor the soundtrack, the dialogue, the comedy **and the tragedy**. Especially pay attention to the relationships. Don't miss that each relationship, each encounter was written in for a reason. This is your amazing soul journey called life. It's showing for a limited time. Try to live every day with the appreciation of a final scene.

You, now, realize that all you have to do is let shit go to maintain a *lightness within yourself* and have Happiness throughout life. You finally understand what's meant by the phrase "Happiness is within" *(that phrase can be so irritating when not explained)*. It's said that Happiness is 'within' because it's generated ONLY from you. Your light has to shine brightly, first. No one in the world can make it shine, except you. You know that you'll have to practice wiring new tracks for new trains of thought. Once an expert at letting go and picking battles; once you have well-established positive thinking habits hard-wired, Happiness will be all over you like Diva on a steak burrito left on the coffee table for **one** minute *(still sorry about that one, Jet)*. The lightness of your mind, body and soul will have your bubble floating and beaming with peace, love and positivity. You'll become en*light*ened. On your new path toward Happiness, be reminded to avoid the most common pitfalls that I call 'Happiness repellants.' They're like "Off," but instead of keeping mosquitoes away, they keep Happiness at bay. Be on the lookout.

BOLO: Spot Dangerous Happiness Repellants

Each of these is like spraying **mace** in the face of your Happiness. Don't be that bubble. While there are many other Happiness repellants, these are known to be the *most* effective.

- **AI/Yureego's off the leash, running the show like a boss.** Let your heart step up, gain balance with your mind, but let your heart be the boss of your life.
- **Disconnection from the power source.** You don't have enough 'juice' flowing through you to balance yourself. Meditate and pray every day.
- **Malnourishment.** Get oxygenated, hydrated, exercised, and infused with a variety of live plant energy nutrients ... *and don't forget the dash of sunlight.*
- **Overexposure to toxins.** Here, we're calling everything that compromises your body, mind or soul, 'toxins.' Toxins take countless forms, so pay attention. Depending on the individual, toxins could include wheat gluten, lectins, sugar, dairy, dust, certain environments and people, alcohol, medications, illicit drugs, food additives, pesticides, chemical fertilizers, household chemicals ... the list is endless and everyone is so unique. All you have to do is want to get to the bottom of what's healthy for you and what is not. You'll begin to eliminate toxins from your life. If your instincts are good, and your heart is running the show, you will identify and remove **all** culprits, very naturally, from your life. You will introduce the things that bring you buoyancy, health and joy. Take this seriously. Don't **mace** Happiness!

While on your soul journey, fueled by love for yourself and others, simply **Dream. Drive. Accept. Learn. Repeat.** You can't lose. If something isn't good, let that shit go. If it's good, appreciate every moment until it's gone. Flow and float to higher heights of Happiness. You help this world simply by achieving those heights of Happiness for yourself.

Living in "Flow" doesn't mean that everything is perfect. That would be Heaven. You're here on Earth to grow. Challenge is a part of growth. As long as you live, challenges **will** continue to confront you. As the challenges of life present themselves, see them as "bitchin' waves," and you'll be better able to surf them. You'll feel your growth in the midst of the challenges. Life *is* challenging. I am NOT lying. But it's also damn good.

We are each born with a package, a gift, I like to call it. The combination of talents and abilities, life circumstances, and challenges that make us who we are, that's our package. The sooner you recognize what your package is, the sooner you can connect with your path, your lane, and what you were born to do in this lifetime. During the course of your life, I hope you'll develop talents and abilities that you've had all along, but weren't using to your potential. The talents you were born with are like a bread crumb trail of clues, used to bring you closer to your purpose in life. The more you utilize what you were given at birth, the more you fulfill your life purpose. The more you fulfill your life purpose, the happier you become and the more you bless the lives of others with your unique gifts.

"Live everyday as if you deliberately came back to that one day to enjoy it as if it was the full final extraordinary day of your life."
- About Time

Every moment has to be lived as **THE** moment of your life.

As a final metaphor, I want to point out something. We recognize Yureego as our security system, right? Now that you're well on your way to having that thing under control, I want you to realize that it's a security system, similar to a guard dog. Let's say Yureego's a 100 pound pit bull. It's a loyal, trusted companion that means no harm to anyone. Just doing its job to protect you.

Keep that pit bull leashed, watched, well-loved and cared for. Feed it a steady, virtual diet of your own self-love. Train it to *only* respond to real, physical threats, and that little buddy will serve you well. Yureego's a good dog when healthy and well-managed. It must be balanced in how you use it in your life. Your heart and instincts have to walk that dog. If you let it run wild and lead the way without a leash, however, as most do, you contribute to the dog eat dog world we live in. Don't contribute to that. Have that little buddy healthy and by your side. We all know that this game of life ain't no joke. That's, in large part, because most have their pit bulls running wild, creating a "dog eat dog," "wild, wild, west" atmosphere. We're not blind to that. We see what's going on. We're just trying to navigate through to realize our dreams, experiencing as much Happiness as we can regardless of what is going on around us.

With your trusty pit pull by your side, healthy, controlled and ready, you have an advantage. You have a much better chance of securing everything you want out of life. Your power and view of the world is stronger and clearer than all those fighting dogs. You walk right through the dog fights. Straight to what you want out of life, unbit and unscathed by the other dogs. With Yureego in control and your heart at the helm, you're one of the badder sons of bitches in the valley.

"Yea thou I walk through the valley of the shadow of death, I fear no evil. For I'm the baddest son of a bitch in the valley."
– Poppop Haywood's basement wall plaque.

It's a trait of the truly happy, to fear no evil. Stare life, without reservation, right in the eyes as you move through it to your dreams. If you want to know the honest truth, nothing is a threat to you when you believe that it isn't.

Contrary to popular belief, you WILL get out of this life alive and well *(your body won't, but YOU will)*. Make life count for what it does to expand your soul. **That**, you **can** take with you.

211

There are few things I want more, than for your life to be filled with Happiness. It is the purpose of this book to help you get there. Each time you touch this handbook, feel the love that was placed here for you. Not that you are reliant on that love to feel loved, of course, but this love is part of your own karma. Feel it, thoroughly. Never forget that I created this as a gift of love *(and that goes for whoever is reading this. There are no accidents, if you are reading this, it was written for you, too).* This book was meant to be scribbled in and highlighted. You're supposed to fold pages and tuck in pieces of inspirational information. It's a handbook, a manual, for you to use as a guide. It's supposed to expand into something that is very personal to you and your way of thinking. Keep it accessible for whenever you need a lift.

The secret of mind over matter is old news. It's time for more people to realize that the power to achieve health and Happiness is squarely in our hands. It always was. Share this information, verbally, with your friends, throughout your lives. My prayer is that the state of mind required to enter The Happiness Zone will be widespread, held by people **everywhere**. I pray that this widespread state of mind creates a natural harmony that will heal, improve the quality of our lives and elevate our planet. A girl can dream, right?

I've always told you that life is like climbing a mountain. You have to climb to get to the top. As you climb, you feel the challenge. Then, you get to a spot where you can stop for a bit and enjoy the view. As beautiful as the view may be at your first stop, you have to climb more. You know the view will be more spectacular farther up the mountain. So you climb and endure more challenge. At the next landing, as expected, you reach a new and more beautiful level. The view becomes more breathtaking. You see more of the world. You realize that the more challenge you endure, the better the rewards. You may find one level so beautiful that you are willing to stop there, wanting never to have to climb again. But your mountain is your life, you can't stop until you get to the pinnacle of your journey. You have to hustle before you can flow. As you realize this, you begin to savor the challenge of the climb and appreciate what it means to your life. The challenges are part of moving up, evolving, learning life's lessons, but they give way to more and more spectacular achievements. Challenge will always be a part of the process until, of course, you reach the very top of the mountain. That is your pinnacle. In each of our lives, that pinnacle is what we call heaven ... reached when we are in that "better space." Learn to enjoy the climb of life while you're here.

I want to close with these words that Grandma Haywood, at age 99 3/4, said to me out of the blue as we were wrapping up on a long phone conversation, "I have *ALWAYS* loved you." And I'm adding to that, "and I *ALWAYS* will."

Finally, I wrote this poem when you guys were little. I scribbled it immediately after an experience that I later realized might be referred to as a self, or spiritual "realization" *(the moment when you sense the true connectedness of all things, and perhaps that you're a bubble?).* This poem, because it ties to that beautiful experience, happens to be one of my favorites. It was an amazing moment. I swear I felt like a bubble the evening that I wrote it, but the bubble concept came decades later. I hope that someday you too will experience that feeling of realization, and be reminded of your experience, as am I, each time you read The Fog.

The Fog

The fog that night was dense enough to carry me in flight,

I rose above the crest of trees to bask in full moonlight.

While under that angelic and illuminating light,

I felt that I absorbed, at once, enlightening insight.

The fog connected everything,

Eliminating space,

Concealing all identity behind a cosmic face,

And yet I **was** that fog with all its peacefulness and grace.

I thought I'd stay that fog,

And lift from there without a trace.

Yet, I began a slow descent from that enlightening height,

To marvel at how clearly

I saw through the fog that night.

Guess what, you beautiful bubbles? You're all hooked up. Go be the bad-ass, high floating bubbles full of Happiness you were born to be. And never stop lightening your vibration.

The Beginning